Biblical Meditations
for Ordinary Time
Weeks 1–9

by
Carroll Stuhlmueller, C.P.

D0121843

PAULIST PRESS
New York/Ramsey

Library of Congress
Catalog Card Number: 84-60390

ISBN: 0-8091-2644-3

Published by Paulist Press
545 Island Road, Ramsey, N.J. 07446

Printed and bound in the
United States of America

Contents

PART THREE—Feasts and Solemnities of Ordinary Time
(Weeks 1-9)

Dedicated
to
Emma Stuhlmueller
Albert H. Stuhlmueller
Ferd and Patty Stuhlmueller

Seasonal Table of Principal Celebrations of the Liturgical Year

Year	Sunday Cycle	Weekday Cycle	Ash Wednesday	Easter	Ascension	Pentecost	Weeks of Ordinary Time before Lent		Weeks of Ordinary Time after Easter season		First Sunday of Advent
							ending	In week no.	beginning	In week no.	
1981	A	I	4 March	19 April	28 May	7 June	3 March	8	8 June	10	29 Nov.
1982	B	II	24 Feb.	11 April	20 May	30 May	23 Feb.	7	31 May	9	28 Nov.
1983	C	I	16 Feb.	3 April	12 May	22 May	15 Feb.	6	23 May	8	27 Nov.
1984	A	II	7 March	23 April	31 May	10 June	6 March	9	11 June	10	2 Dec.
1985	B	I	20 Feb.	7 April	16 May	26 May	19 Feb.	6	27 May	8	1 Dec.
1986	C	II	12 Feb.	30 March	8 May	18 May	11 Feb.	5	19 May	7	30 Nov.
1987	A	I	4 March	19 April	28 May	7 June	3 March	8	8 June	10	29 Nov.
1988	B	II	17 Feb.	3 April	12 May	22 May	16 Feb.	6	23 May	8	27 Nov.
1989	C	I	8 Feb.	26 March	4 May	14 May	7 Feb.	5	15 May	6	3 Dec.
1990	A	II	28 Feb.	15 April	24 May	3 June	27 Feb.	8	4 June	9	2 Dec.
1991	B	I	13 Feb.	31 March	9 May	19 May	12 Feb.	5	20 May	7	1 Dec.
1992	C	II	4 March	19 April	28 May	7 June	3 March	8	8 June	10	29 Nov.
1993	A	I	24 Feb.	11 April	20 May	30 May	23 Feb.	7	31 May	9	28 Nov.
1994	B	II	16 Feb.	3 April	12 May	22 May	15 Feb.	6	23 May	8	27 Nov.
1995	C	I	1 March	16 April	25 May	4 June	28 Feb.	8	5 June	9	3 Dec.
1996	A	II	21 Feb.	7 April	16 May	26 May	20 Feb.	7	27 May	8	1 Dec.
1997	B	I	12 Feb.	30 March	8 May	18 May	11 Feb.	5	19 May	7	30 Nov.
1998	C	II	25 Feb.	12 April	21 May	31 May	24 Feb.	7	1 June	9	29 Nov.
1999	A	I	17 Feb.	4 April	13 May	23 May	16 Feb.	6	24 May	8	28 Nov.
2000	B	II	8 March	23 April	1 June	11 June	7 March	9	12 June	10	3 Dec.

a) The First Sunday of Advent indicates the beginning of the new liturgical year and belongs to the preceding civil year: i.e., the liturgical year of 1985 begins on 1 December 1984.

b) A few feasts of the Lord and solemnities of the saints take precedence over the ordinary Sunday mass. Please consult the parish calendar or bulletin for these changes.

Foreword

The story of these meditations seems as long and tortuous as the journey of Abraham and Sarah from Ur of the Chaldees to the Promised Land.

This book owes its origin to a suggestion several years ago from Robert Heyer of Paulist Press that I write a biblical meditation book for Lent. Upon the encouraging reception of that book, the project expanded to the other major liturgical seasons, *Biblical Meditations for the Easter Season* and *Biblical Meditations for Advent and the Christmas Season*. Quite a few persons wrote to me or they spoke with me at lectures or conventions, asking about the continuation of the series into Ordinary Time, the thirty-four weeks of the rest of the church year. A deacon and his wife even telephoned long distance about the matter.

The occasion to follow through came when my own life's journey took me to Korea, the Philippines and Japan for a five month stint of lecturing and preaching. For the most part deprived of books and personal files, my resources turned out to be most appropriate for composing a meditation book: my heart and memory along with stretches of silence and solitude in between assignments. These assets could have been empty and sterile, were it not for the inspiring presence of missionaries and local religious leaders, and, of course, the source of all inspiration and life for everyone, God's Holy Spirit.

The vitality of the church in these countries has contributed enormously to the insights and possibilities of these meditations. Day by day as I prayed with pen and paper or at other times with all sorts of typewriters, I may have been looking out my window upon the Korean mountains in the Green Belt around Seoul and hearing the gong of Buddhist drums, exorcising the demon; or beyond my window there may have stretched the lovely Japanese gardens at the Passionist retreat house near Osaka, Japan, and the way of the cross winding up the wooded mountainside; or I may have been lecturing at the energetic East Asian Pastoral Institute of Manila, an extraordinary school where students include capable religious leaders, catechists, bishops and a cardinal archbishop, from the Solomon Islands to Pakistan; or I may have been alone during the early morning hours, high in the mountainous area of the Tboli tribe where Fr. Rex Mansmann, C.P., is salvaging and ennobling the handcraft, folklore and customs of this most ancient people of the Philippines. These are only a few of the many stages along the way where these meditations took shape.

The journey from initial drafts to printed book followed another long path. Everyone who reads this book owes a fervent, grateful prayer to Paul I. Bechtold, C.P., long time friend and brother Passionist, founding president of the Catholic Theological Union at Chicago and a former professor of mine. During my preordination studies he had conducted a course on creative composition; this training has been most influential for the bits of clarity and insight in my writings. His editorial assistance appears particularly with the weekday meditations. At times an entire paragraph was added, sometimes just a word, but a word that turned darkness into light!

Through the long journey the pages of these meditations became tattered, strangely numbered, sometimes running backward. They were transformed into a readable script by the patient, expert typing of Sister Kay Sheskaitis, I.H.M., Sister Judy Hahn, O.P., and Sister Ann Maloney, O.P. To them I express special gratitude.

Others came to my assistance in proofreading and in preparing the indices. I gratefully recognize the careful contribution of such good friends as Sr. Julie Clare Greene, B.V.M., Sr. Jeanette Flaherty, S.P., Sr. Isabella Stokes, O.P., Sr. Rosemary Dewey, R.S.C.J., Ms. Gerry Boberg and Ms. Mary Ellen Drake.

The three volumes of these meditations cover the liturgical period of Ordinary Time, the thirty-four weeks from mid-January till the end of November, exclusive of Lent and the Easter Season. During the *weekdays* of these thirty-four weeks the first reading from Scripture runs on a two year cycle while the gospel is on a one year tract. This fact presented its own problem and challenge. In these meditations the two weekday cycles are joined and generally find their key or unifying theme in the gospel. In this way a new, sometimes creative focus is beamed upon each of the two first readings of cycles I and II. Care has been taken to identify each cycle, so that a person can separate the two and remain with the proper one for the individual liturgical year.

The *Sundays* proceed on a three year cycle, designated A, B and C. Each Sunday has its own set of readings, generally from the Old Testament, the Epistles and the Gospels of the year. Because of the prominent place of Sundays in the liturgical year, a separate meditation is proposed for each of these clusters of biblical readings. At times the ''Ordinary'' Sunday Mass is displaced by a solemnity (the highest ranking type of liturgical celebration) or by a festival honoring Jesus Christ. Each of these has a special meditation, located in the final section of the volume.

A calendar is provided as a road map through the intricacies of the liturgical year. As a friendly piece of advice, we note that the liturgical year begins with the first Sunday of Advent, not with the first of January.

At the beginning of each meditation there is a two to four line summary of each biblical selection. These are not meant to replace the reading of the entire passage from one's Bible or lectionary. The summary highlights the principal motif for meditation. Ideally, one will first read the entire passage from the Bible, then the summary and meditation in this book, again the passage from the Bible, and finally remain silent before God. The Holy Spirit will lead beyond words and even beyond thoughts into the mystery of the burning bush (Exod chap. 3) and "the tiny whispering sound" on Mount Horeb (1 Kings 19:12–13). As another biblical writer concluded a major section of his book:

> More than this we need not add,
>   let the last word be, God is all in all!
> Let us praise him the more, since we cannot fathom him,
>   for greater is God than all his works (Sir 43:28–29).

Like the three previous books in this series of *Biblical Meditations* these new volumes are not a substitute for prayer nor do they supply a homily for the occasion. If questions are raised and insights explored, they are intended to prompt the reader to stop and abide in God's presence:

> By waiting and by calm you shall be saved,
>   in quiet and in trust your strength lies. . . .
> The Lord is waiting to show you favor. . . .
>   Blessed are all who wait for him! (Isa 30:13, 18)

The purpose of these meditations, therefore, is not so much to settle upon an answer but to leave a person quietly, peacefully, in God's presence, enriched and strengthened for appreciating God's companionship in one's daily life. This life-setting is one that is shared with all men and women of faith. In this way we will pray with the larger family of God's people.

Prayer, not study, is the determining factor. Nonetheless, enough background is provided so that the reader feels at home with the biblical passages, but academic details are curtailed lest these books turn into a manual for study. On controversial issues only one position is presented, generally without proof or documentation. My own personal preference will be evident, yet these conclusions will hopefully command a respectable consensus among scholars.

These volumes are dedicated to my uncles and aunts. Some have already joined my parents in our eternal home with God; others like Emma, Albert, Ferd and Patty still grace our homeland in Hamilton, Ohio, even in their eighties and nineties keeping warm and loving homes for us. They have surrounded my life with love, concern and an exceptionally strong religious spirit.

PART ONE

Weekdays of Ordinary Time
Weeks 1—9

Monday, First Week

Heb 1:1–6. In times past God spoke in fragmented and varied ways, but in this, the final age through his Son.
1 Sam 1:1–8. Hannah was barren and ridiculed. Her husband tried to comfort her by his love and attention.
Mark 1:14–20. Jesus begins his apostolate, proclaiming the
reign of God at hand and calling his first disciples.

A number of similarities link the three readings together: 1) Jesus announces the reign of God; Hannah's son
will inaugurate the royal period of Israel and anoint the first
kings, Saul and David; 2) yet neither Jesus nor Hannah can
succeed simply in human ways, as Hannah was barren and
Jesus possessed no prestige nor position of power; 3) in each
case we see examples of strong bonds of affection: Elhanah's devoted love for Hannah; Jesus' invitation to his disciples that they should leave everything, even their parents, to
follow him; the intimate attachment of Father and Son in the
mystery of the Holy Trinity, "the Son is the reflection of the
Father's being"; 4) a decisive moment—the time of fulfillment, "the reign of God is at hand"—as Jesus begins his
public ministry; the conception of a child by Hannah; the
dawning of this, "the final age," in the opening verses of
the Epistle to the Hebrews; 5) a moment of prayer or even
ecstasy that pervades each of the readings: Hannah in the
temple, the disciples called aside to follow Jesus, the reflection upon Scripture in the Epistle to the Hebrews.

If these traits can be identified in three readings which
fall together almost by accident, and particularly if these
traits show up at the beginning either of biblical books or of
Jesus' public ministry, then evidently these five qualities are
fundamental and continuously necessary for a healthy spir-

itual, moral life. The impact of one quality upon another can be startling, certainly decisive, yet altogether they produce a balanced spirituality.

The Scriptures begin where all of us begin—within the bonds of human love and family life, within the gradual development of hopes and possibilities. The Bible always manifests a healthy respect for the normal ways of human nature.

Even if the reading of Cycle I from the Epistle to the Hebrews leaps at once into the mystery of the Holy Trinity and establishes beyond doubt the divinity of Jesus, nonetheless it acknowledges in its opening words the long, slow preparation of the Hebrew Scriptures and the Israelite people for the birth of Jesus: "in times past, God spoke in fragmentary and varied ways to our ancestors through the prophets." Those few words span almost nineteen hundred years, from Abraham to Jesus. "If a thousand years are as yesterday" in the sight of the Lord (Ps 90:4), God could have done it differently, that is, in a moment of time. God could have dispensed with Abraham, Moses and all the prophets and kings, and simply announced the presence of Jesus. Instead, God worked carefully, slowly, patiently in a way adapted to our nature. These human bonds show up in so many ways: the affection between Elhanah and Hannah, the bond of brotherhood between Simon and Andrew, James and John, and each with their father.

No spirituality can claim genuine origin with the God of the Bible if it disregards the bonds of flesh and family. Among the most important laws of this relationship we find to be the obligation to be patient and perceptive towards other people's feelings. This law is exemplified beautifully in the remark of Elhanah to his despondent wife Hannah: "Hannah!" (First of all, he repeats her name.) "Why do you weep, and why do you refuse to eat?'' (He is sensitive to her distress.) ''Why do you grieve?'' (He wants to know *her* reasons; he does not judge simply by the way it affects himself.) ''Am I not more to you than ten sons?'' (He speaks tenderly of human relationships and the value of each person, not simply of achievements and work.)

The virtues of patience and understanding are particularly relevant today; we are beginning the long thirty-four weeks of the church year. These are not the weeks of special attention like Advent and Christmas which we have just completed, nor of Lent and Easter season. These are the ''ordinary'' weeks!—the day by day weeks—the weeks that seem to get nowhere—the weeks that reflect the normal monotony of life. The bonds of friendship and family suffer their most severe tension, not so much from monumental crises (at these times, people usually rally and pull together) but from impatience, tiredness and being taken for granted. The scripture readings for this ''ordinary'' time accomplish wonders, simply by sustaining us over the long trek and desert stretches of life. ''In fragmentary and varied ways'' the Scriptures encourage and inspire us to be faithful in the small monotonies of life.

The Scriptures also induce a spirit of prayer. At times Jesus may seem only vaguely present—but nonetheless Jesus is *there* with us. In the midst of our family bonds, Jesus calls us to follow him, not with the purpose of destroying love, but to enrich it and to transform it. Even miracles take place. Hannah conceives a child, Jesus is born of a virgin, the church emerges from small beginnings.

If only we unite prayer with daily living, then the sudden change will come. Jesus will say, ''Follow me,'' and life will turn out to be far more wonderful in its achievement than we could ever have imagined.

Prayer:

Lord, the heavens will proclaim your justice and everyone will see your glory—even in my own life. What seems useless and monotonous will lead to happiness beyond my dreams and beyond my merit. We will all glory in what you have accomplished in the bonds of our family love and community loyalty. We will enter into your courts, giving thanks, and will be called home to heaven, everyone knowing that our death has been precious in your eyes.

Tuesday, 1st Week

Heb 2:5–12. Everything is subject to Jesus who is totally one with us. He was crowned with glory, after having been perfected through suffering.

1 Sam 1:9–20. Eli promises an answer to Hannah's prayer. She conceives and gives birth to a son whom she consecrates as a Nazirite.

Mark 1:21–28. People are spellbound that Jesus teaches with a new kind of authority. He even gives orders to unclean spirits.

The Scriptures, especially today, reach into the deep roots of life and therefore as the people exclaimed about Jesus, we are impressed with "a completely new teaching" and a unique "spirit of authority."

It really isn't completely new! Others before Jesus had wrestled with devils and evil spirits. We are reminded of Moses' tryst with the magicians in Egypt and his thorough command over sinister forces of wickedness and havoc (Exod 7:14—11:10, especially 7:22; 8:3, 14–15). Job too was pitted in a gigantic battle—of personal integrity—with the demon (Job 1:6–12; 2:1–10). Jesus was not the first prophet to sway Israelites with his keen perception of moral issues and with compassion for human ills and injustices. We think of the prophet Isaiah's discourse in chapter one of his prophecy: "Your hands are full of blood! Wash yourselves clean . . . cease doing evil; learn to do good" (Isa 1:15–16).

If the actions in today's Scriptures are not entirely new still they plummet into the origins or sources of life and seem to be happening for the first time when they do take place for each of us. Each conception and birth are far too personal and are related to very special circumstances—not to seem new each time. Hannah's conception of a child broke a long spell of barren married life and inaugurated a particularly creative moment for her and actually for all the people of Israel. As such it symbolizes moments in everyone's existence. We are advised, first of all, that crucial moments such as this do not happen all at once, without preparation. We must wait, not passively and indifferently, but hopefully, at times anxiously, at certain supreme moments, like Hannah, with "bitterness," with "prayer," with "weeping copiously," with "vows and promises."

Hannah advises us that great decisions cannot and must not be reached quickly and easily. As difficult as it may be, under such stress and prolonged expectation, under a barrage of criticism and doubt from other people, Hannah gives us a model of patient response:

> It isn't that, my Lord, [she said to the high priest who accused her of being drunk,] I am an unhappy woman. I have had neither wine nor liquor; I am only pouring out my troubles to the Lord . . . My prayer has been prompted by my deep sorrow and misery.

What else could Eli reply to such anguish and sincerity but "Go in peace, and may the God of Israel grant you what you have asked of him." Hannah was not driving out devils, like Jesus in today's gospel, but was manifesting the obverse of Jesus' negative action. Hers was positive, creative but just as deeply rooted in the hidden springs of human existence and dynamic hopes.

Hannah decides to consecrate her new child as a Nazirite: dedicated to the Lord in a special way and manifesting that consecration by never drinking wine and strong drink, never shaving the beard nor cutting the hair on one's head. This institution is described in Num 6:1–21, immediately before the famous "Priestly Blessing." The norms of Nazirite existence come from Israel's early life in the desert and particularly from the need of military readiness at that time. Soldiers did not cut their hair nor shave (we think of Absolom's long hair that was caught in a tree during his military revolt against David—2 Sam 18:19); neither could they compromise their sensitivity to danger or trouble by strong drink. The Nazirite, therefore, reminded Israel of her origins as a people, early days that were marked with gigantic struggles and long perseverance in the desert.

While the Old Testament deals extensively with many heroic moments of people's lives—the long, persevering wait of Hannah for a child; the exacting demands of the Nazirite; Israel's creation through flight from slavery, trek through the desert and long settlement in the land—these struggles are compressed into single moments as Jesus drives out devils and speaks with elemental authority. These same battles against evil happen in the very flesh of Jesus, as we are told in the first reading (Cycle I). God decided to bring all his children into glory through his unique Son Jesus. This work of redemption would occur not only through Jesus but also *within* Jesus: Jesus was "crowned with glory and honor because he suffered death . . . made a little less than the angels [yet] tast[ing] death for the sake of everyone [and so he was] perfect[ed] through suffering.'' In the Greek, ''perfect'' technically means: to have gone through the entire cycle of human existence and so arrive at the goal or end.

Today's Scriptures then summon us: to respect the deep, creative graces at the root of our existence; to wait actively, patiently, prayerfully; to pour out our soul before God; to interact with community and its leadership in the pursuit of our hidden goals, as in the case of Hannah and Eli; to be ready for the probing struggles with satan through our moments of ''nazirite'' existence; to realize that Jesus has experienced each of our trials and temptations so that in Jesus we arrive at our true glory and honor as children of God.

Prayer:
Lord, you have given Jesus authority over all your creatures, over each one of us. Jesus exercises that authority by becoming one with us in our flesh and blood, in our deepest struggles and finest hopes. Enable us to be so closely united with Jesus, that our truest self will be molded in Jesus' likeness and that his marvelous compassion quiet the evil within us.

Wednesday, 1st Week

Heb 2:14–18. Jesus shared our flesh and blood, our temptations and death, and so is able to help us in our trials.
1 Sam 3:1–10, 19–20. From the sanctuary of the ark, God calls Samuel, still a young man, to be a prophet.
Mark 1:29–39. Jesus cured Peter's mother-in-law, exor-

cised people with demons, withdrew to a lonely spot for prayer, and preached the good news.

We are consoled by the intimate presence of God the Father and the divine Son Jesus with our human nature. According to the Epistle to the Hebrews, Jesus "had a full share in our blood and flesh" and even plunged into the dark realm of our dying. To prove the point, the sacred author adds that Jesus "did not come to help angels, but rather the children of Abraham." This understatement indicates that God expected a less than angelic situation for the only son Jesus! As if these observations were not sufficient, we read again from Hebrews that Jesus "had to become like his brothers and sisters in every way, that he might be a merciful and faithful high priest. . . . He was himself tested through what he suffered [and so] able to help those who are tempted." Jesus, therefore, clearly was tempted as we are—with only one exception, "without sin"(4:15).

If we take these statements of Sacred Scripture literally—and there is no reason why we shouldn't—there is no temptation, too ugly or too fierce, that Jesus would not have been willing to undergo. The implications of this insight baffle our mind and will always remain, rightly and properly so, within the private or personal domain of Jesus, the incarnate Word. Our temptations are probably more embarrassing—and probably much more difficult—to discuss and understand than any other of our actions.

The human side of God's ways becomes visible in the episode from First Samuel (Cycle II). The interaction of child and adult reaches into everyone's memories. Who has not been disturbed or frightened by voices at night and run off to mother or father for help? What person has not jumped out of bed when hearing a call for help from someone in the home? The young man Samuel *ran* (he did not walk, nor spend fifteen minutes deciding whether or not to get out of his sleeping bag—beds were only for the wealthy) and said, "Here I am. You called me," not once, not twice, but three times! And each time the old man Eli patiently, even tenderly responded, as if to quiet the anxious young man:

> I did not call you, my son.
> Go back to sleep.

The Hebrew sounds quiet and mellow, like a whispering play on words: *lo' kerati beni; shub shahab.* Finally, Eli advises the young man:

> Go back to sleep.
> If someone calls out to you, you can reply,
> "Speak, Lord, for your servant is listening."

In such an intimate human setting Samuel becomes a prophet who will eventually change the entire course of Israelite history.

We are beginning to see and perhaps to become frightened by the way that God's immersion in our daily human life leads to an intense moment of decision and struggle: in Hebrews Jesus is caught within the "fear of death" and the embarrassment of "being himself tempted"; in 1 Samuel, a tranquil home at the sanctuary at Shiloh is about to be disrupted by the summons placed on Samuel to go forth as God's prophet.

These two biblical readings and their thoroughly domestic or human setting prepare us for the gospel selection from Mark. After preaching in the synagogue, Jesus retired to the home of Peter's mother-in-law. How human it was for Jesus first to notice her illness. Yet God is never present in our earthly home as another human being. ''Jesus went over to her and grasped her hand and helped her up, and the fever left her.'' Immediately, however, the needs of a hungry family close in upon the actors of this episode. The mother-in-law proceeded at once ''to wait on them.'' Yet we are not totally back to normal family life. Crowds gather, the sick are laid at the doorstep, demoniacs and mentally deranged people are freed of the demon within them.

All this may have been too much even for Jesus.

> Early the next morning, he went off to a lonely
> place in the desert; there he was absorbed in
> prayer.

But word had gone out. Jesus was tracked down by Simon and his companions who told him, ''Everyone is looking for you!'' Life can never be the same again.

> Let us move on to the neighboring villages so that
> I may proclaim the good news there also. That is
> what I have come to do.

Like Samuel, Jesus was sent on his way as prophet and redeemer. As redeemer it would lead to his death.

For ourselves, within the wrapping of our flesh and blood, within the warmth of our family, God is thoroughly present, sanctifying each action of love and concern. God's presence will lead necessarily to conflicts and temptations; we can never again be satisfied with what is half-good. God will expect decisions that can be reached only by prolonged prayer and healthy guidance. We will battle with demons and their fierce temptations, too embarrassing even to discuss, yet never too distant from Jesus' span of human existence.

Prayer:

Lord, give me time to be silent and prayerful, conscious of your personal presence, moment by moment, sustaining me in all my human life and relationships yet also summoning me to new decisions for fidelity and generosity. Whenever you call my name, may I reply: "Speak, Lord, for your servant is listening."

Thursday, 1st Week

Heb 3:7–14. Our hearts *today,* as Ps 95 advises us, are to be open, with confidence and fidelity towards God, not hardened, doubting and complaining.

1 Sam 4:1–11. Despite the presence of the Ark, the Israelites are defeated in battle by the Philistines.

Mark 1:40–45. Jesus touches and cures the leper who ignores Jesus' instruction and proceeds to tell everyone. Jesus can no longer go about freely but stays in desert places.

We are asked by the Scriptures to consider the danger of excessive reliance on externals—whether these be the visible aspects of religion like the ark of the covenant, extravagant religious services, miracles like the cure of the leper, or custom and routine in which we become set and hardened. "Today," advises the psalmist from the Old Testament, whose long passage is quoted in the Epistle to the Hebrews (Cycle I), God can bring new graces and new insights that will enable us to enter into a rest, thoroughly in God, deeply within our heart.

As we read the biblical passages for today's eucharistic liturgy, we instinctively take the side of the common folk against God. At least, we are surprised at the type of question which surfaces in our mind! In Cycle II, how can we condemn the Israelites for their trust in the Ark of the Covenant? After all, it was their principal link with the days of Moses and the origins of their religion in the Sinai desert. Their traditions acclaimed the power of God, manifested through the presence of the Ark. In the Torah of Moses we are told that each time the people set out from camp, the Ark moved with them, symbolic of God's direction of their lives. They would sing:

> Arise, O Lord, that your enemies may be scattered,
> And those who hate you may fall before you.

And when the Ark came to rest, the people would pray:

> Return, O Lord, you who ride upon the clouds,
> to the troops of Israel (Num 10:35–36).

As a result of this ancient tradition, a long psalm was composed which began with the rousing words,

> God arises: his enemies are scattered,
> Those who hate him flee before him (Ps 68:2).

Why shouldn't the Israelites believe that with the ark in their midst, their new enemies, the Philistines, will be scattered?

And why shouldn't the leper, once healed by Jesus, "proclaim the whole matter freely, making the story public?" Somehow or other, Jesus shunned these public demonstrations. As a result of new notoriety, Jesus "stayed in desert places [where] the people kept coming to him from all sides."

Despite how sacred the Ark may be, no matter how wondrous the miracle of healing the leper, the Scriptures insist upon the supreme attitude of *faith*. As the first reading

(Cycle I) from Hebrews repeats, today we must not harden our hearts. Today our heart must be open to new graces and most of all to God's personal presence. The external aspects of religion, even the most sacred doctrines and holiest objects, are meant to facilitate our interior communion with the Lord. Our hearts, where silence prevails and distractions are absent—our hearts that seem like ''desert places''—are the true ark of the covenant and place of wonders.

Somehow or other, God will allow the externals in each person's life seemingly to collapse. The Ark will be captured by the enemy. The tried and true of religious practice and belief will seem inadequate to our needs and leave us lonely, almost helpless. We must traverse this desert to find Jesus.

The Scriptures bring another, somewhat fearful warning to our attention. As mentioned already in this meditation, the common folk are hardly to blame. They are enthusiastically rallying around traditional centers of their religion—the Ark of the covenant and the miraculous power of God. *Who* then is to blame? It seems that religious leaders carry the burden of fault. Earlier in First Samuel, in a section not read in the liturgy, Eli's two sons, Hophni and Phinehas, were guilty of serious offenses. They were reserving the best part of the people's sacrifices for themselves and offering to God only the remnants; there were other scandalous actions. Mysteriously enough, religious leaders bear the brunt of blame if superstition and selfishness are rampant among the people—or if the people cannot distinguish true from false forms of religion.

Each one of us is a religious leader in one way or another: as parent or teacher, as priest or minister, as neighbor or friend. In all of these capacities we influence others and are responsible for the moral attitude and strength of faith in others.

The Scriptures put serious questions before us. Do I use my position of authority to dominate others or to acquire personal benefits or to further personal career? Do I seek to slip away from the center of attention, so that my words and actions lead others to prayer and recollection in God's presence? Do I avoid the temptation of bragging about religious accomplishments (perhaps the leper's fault, once he was healed by Jesus) and consider favors as signs of the Lord's personal love and concern?

Prayer:

Today, Lord, you are speaking with us. Do not let our hearts be hardened by selfishness but anxious to acknowledge your goodness and be in wonder of your presence within us. Never permit religion to distract us from you nor to be a false, external support for our rigid externalism. Do not, Lord, hide your face beneath the visible aspects of religion. We seek you, our Lord.

Friday, 1st Week

Heb 4:1–5, 11. Through obedient faith, directed especially towards Jesus, we enter into a rest similar to God's on the seventh day.

1 Sam 8:4–7, 10–22. When the people demand a king like the other nations, the Lord tells Samuel to acquiesce. Samuel points out how demanding such a king will be.

Mark 2:1–12. A crowd gathers round Jesus, at home within Capernaum; he heals a paralytic after first forgiving his sins.

Many interesting details converge in today's readings, balancing and correcting one another. We need this multifaceted view in order to achieve a harmonious spirituality in our personal lives and in our ministry towards others, whether in family, neighborhood or church.

We begin with the more historical, or less theological information in First Samuel (Cycle II) and in the Gospel of Mark.

(1) In the days of Samuel, the political scene shifted and Israel's existence was seriously threatened by the Philistines. The older ways, inherited from Moses, Joshua and the first followers of these heroes, were no longer sufficient to meet the united threat of the Philistines. Israel could not survive if the people remained separate and divided into individual tribes and loosely united under a system of sanctuaries and prophet-priests.

(2) God directs Samuel to accept a king for Israel. Now as in the past God works through human means within human situations—like the Hyksos and then the native Egyptian dynasties in the land of the Pharoahs; like the chastening problems of the desert; like the uniting of slaves and oppressed people in the drive to wrestle control of the promised land from the petty king tyrants. God is not tied to any single form of government for Israel; Samuel is told to seek and anoint a king.

(3) Any major movement, like royalty in Israel, was bound to lead to excesses in power and prestige, and therefore to new forms of oppression. No human institution, even when sanctioned by God and functioning within a religious system, is immune to human failure and sin. It must be reformed, reinvigorated and even at times changed.

(4) The harmony of God's creation promised us in the sacred books is always a hope and a promise, ever since the creation of the world. From Cycle I we learn that there is always an open invitation to enter into this beautiful rest. Yet we cannot take a step in the right direction nor remain within

the lovely paradise of peace, unless we are guided by obedient faith, not just in important moments like choosing a king, but also in many other, minor moments of life: obedient to the inspiration to forgive, to pray, to share, to encourage—all the inspirations which enable marriage, neighborhood and church to be happy and holy institutions. These are the virtues that guide us and our society, whether in secular government or in church, so that we can make proper transitions, blessed and guided by God.

(5) Jesus exemplifies at Capernaum how to ready ourselves for dramatic change and to settle peacefully in God's rest. There is a gathering of many persons at the home of Peter's mother-in-law, presumably Jesus' headquarters at Capernaum. We may see here a symbol of church unity, a bond that does more than unite us among ourselves but enables all of us together to be one with Jesus. From Jesus, within the setting of Peter's home, *God's word* came *to them*. Yet an unusual incident then takes place, which manifests extraordinary ingenuity and persistent determination. The four persons who are bringing a paralytic to Jesus and cannot get through the crowd, proceed to carry the man to the roof, make a hole and lower the mat on which the paralytic was lying directly before Jesus. The incident not only manifests creative tenacity but also a lovely form of helpfulness and dependency. Without the paralytic the healthy people would never have gotten this close to Jesus, and without his friends the paralytic was unable to get anywhere.

The supreme moment comes, when Jesus re-creates paradise in healing the paralytic and inducing a new state of innocence:

> Which is easier, to say to the paralytic, 'Your sins are forgiven,' or to say, 'Stand up, pick up your mat, and walk again'?

To enter into God's rest and to avoid the temptation of grumbling and jealousy, there must be forgiveness—not only from Jesus, but also from each of us. We are all commanded (it is not a choice) to forgive our neighbor if we wish to be forgiven by God. Such is the prayer each day in the *Our Father*. With such forgiveness, we remain united as one people of God and we avoid the excesses of our greatness. We can be one people, strong in our opposition to any "Philistine" threat and yet never succumbing to jealousy, power plays, sensuality and excessive materialism. We can cross the bridge of change and support one another in the difficulties of change, patient with weakness, forgiving towards deliberate sins, capable of rallying round again in a bond of love and hope.

Prayer:

Lord, we sing your goodness forever, through all the changes and transitions of our lives. You are king, not only of each space and place, but also of each moment in time. Enable us always to be patient and forgiving, with a spirit faithful to you.

Saturday, 1st Week

Heb 4:12–16. God's word is a two-edged sword, penetrating soul and spirit; Jesus is a compassionate high priest sympathizing with our weakness, tempted even as we are, without sinning.

1 Sam 9:1–4, 17–19; 10:1. Saul, an attractive and attentive young man, is anointed king upon the inspiration of the Lord.

Mark 2:13–17. Jesus calls Levi, a tax collector, to be a disciple, and eats with him and other transgressors of the law—to the scandal of some Pharisees. ''I have come to call sinners, not the self-righteous.''

Each one of us, through God's special gifts in our lives, is called to religious leadership. We are asked to inspire other members of our family, neighborhood, work-force, community or parish with enthusiasm for goodness, forgiveness, truth and patience—in precisely those virtues where we are gifted by God. As we meditate upon today's biblical readings, God instructs us through the vocation of Saul and Matthew. We are provided further theological reflection through the Epistle to the Hebrews. We can observe the *types of people* whom God calls, the *norms* for effective leadership, and the *aids* or *helps* for living up to these ideals.

From the example of Saul and Matthew (we learn from Matt 9:9–13; 10:3, that Levi the tax collector is the same as the apostle Matthew), we see that Jesus calls the most likely person, Saul, and the least likely person, Matthew. We are informed:

Saul . . . was a handsome young man. There was no other Israelite handsomer than Saul; he stood head and shoulders above the people.

Yet Matthew, as a tax collector under the hire of the Roman occupation force, was not permitted to enter a synagogue nor to go up to the temple. He was excommunicated for all contact, even at table, with law-abiding Jews.

It is not so much that God can choose any riffraff for religious leadership. In a way God can, but that is not the way God goes about it. Rather, God, whose word ''penetrates and divides soul and spirit, joints and marrow, [judging] the

reflections and thoughts of the heart'' (words from the first
reading, Cycle I), recognizes far more value and potential in
people whom we too quickly call riffraff! How many people
we may have injured psychologically or whose growth we
have stunted by our failure to second their ideas, to perceive
their hopes, and to place trust in their hidden ability. While
other people may have seen only a non-observant, irreli-
gious person, hobnobbing with the foreign oppressors, Jesus
recognized someone with a compassionate heart, unper-
turbed by human weakness, optimistic and hopeful towards
others—in fact, the very dispositions which God attributes
to himself as he led the Israelites out of Egypt and prepared
for the covenant on Mount Sinai.

As Moses stood atop Mount Sinai and held in his hands
the two stone tablets of the law, God passed by and a voice
was heard:

> The Lord, the Lord, a merciful and gracious God,
> slow to anger and rich in kindness and fidelity,
> continuing his kindness for a thousand genera-
> tions, and forgiving wickedness and crime and
> sin; yet not declaring the guilty guiltless (Exod
> 34:6–7).

''Not declaring the guilty guiltless''—these words remind
us that Jesus did not canonize Matthew on the spot. Realist-
ically, Jesus was conscious of Matthew's faults. When Jesus
explains his choice to the grumbling Pharisees, Jesus said:
''I have come to call sinners, not the self-righteous.'' Jesus
was quite conscious that the apostles needed a training period.

Our meditations have already drifted into the norm for

leadership and into the attitudes for sharing our gifts with others. We ought to recognize and second the good but hidden qualities in others. We need to be honest and practical in our appraisal, so that we enable others to gain strength where they are weak, wisdom where they are mistaken and most of all confidence where they feel slighted and overlooked. Neither do we act this way or speak this way *once;* we must interact continuously. Jesus gives us a hint of this persevering help. Jesus not only calls Matthew but also accepts an invitation to dine in Matthew's home with all his friends and fellow tax collectors. The extensive training period is already underway, the friendship is being deepened, understanding is setting up more points of contact.

To help us to perceive goodness where we thought to see only faults and sins, we need continuous insights from Scripture. Today's selection from the Epistle to the Hebrews reminds us how "God's word is living and effective, sharper than any two-edged sword." Not only does God penetrate the depths of our psyche, but Jesus himself shared each moment of our existence, even our temptations—again according to the Epistle to the Hebrews. The Scriptures combine a pure insight into ideals and a compassionate understanding of human nature, two essential qualities for religious leadership.

Prayer:

Lord, your words are spirit and life, rejoicing our hearts, enlightening our eyes, giving wisdom to the simple and trustworthy. Through your words grant that I may be your instrument in summoning others into religious leadership, so that they may gratefully acknowledge their gifts from you and turn these gifts into helpful programs for others.

Monday, 2nd Week

Heb 5:1–10. Jesus, like every high priest, is taken from the human family, shares their weakness and prays with reverence and obedience. For these reasons Jesus "became the source of external salvation for all who obey him."

1 Sam 15:16–23. Because Saul disobeyed the Lord in not exterminating all the Amalekites, the Lord rejected Saul as king. "Obedience is better than sacrifice."

Mark 2:18–22. Jesus' disciples do not fast as long as the bridegroom is with them. No one puts new wine into old wine skins.

Upon first reading, today's biblical selections raise too many problems for a quiet time of prayer, and so we are tempted to look elsewhere for inspiration. The Epistle to the Hebrews (Cycle I) begins with a strong confession of faith in the divinity of Jesus. As we read from the opening verses of this epistle: "To which of the angels did God ever say, 'You are my son; today I have begotten you'? (Monday of the First Week in Ordinary Time) Or again, 'I will be his father, and he shall be my son'?" Yet in today's reading from the same epistle, Jesus is compared to all other high priests "beset by weakness and so must make sin offerings for himself as well as for the people." We are reminded of last Saturday's reading from the same epistle, that Jesus "is able to sympathize with our weakness [as] one who was tempted *in every way that we are,* yet never sinned."

Perhaps less theological in scope and far closer to the moral scene of peace and justice, the episode about the Amalekites is all the more baffling, if not downright scandalous. Saul feels compelled under divine command to exterminate these neighboring people, a tribe hostile towards Israel (1 Sam 15:1–3). Up to this point we might think that

Saul's feelings may be swayed by Israel's long hatred for the Amalekites and confused with God's will. Yet, when today's passage clearly attributes Saul's rejection from the position of king over Israel for not destroying the Amalekites to the last person, we are left aghast.

The problem in the gospel is not as taxing on our theological or moral ingenuity, yet we are a bit surprised that Jesus' disciples do not show up as pious and edifying as those of John the Baptist and the Pharisees!

Rather than turn our meditation into theological research about the extermination warfare, sometimes undertaken by ancient semitic people, or about the interaction of Jesus' humanity and divinity, it may be spiritually more profitable at this time of prayer to reflect on the answer of Jesus in the gospel and from this vantage point return to our difficulties.

Jesus does not allow himself to be trapped into a theological discussion about the purpose of fasting and its long tradition in the Scriptures—something well and good in itself but not proper at this moment. Jesus reaches beneath theology to common sense and homespun examples. He asks: what normal person calls for fasting and mourning, so long as the bride and bridegroom are celebrating their marriage? Long experience has taught the maker of wine, never to put unfermented wine into an old wine skin. The old, shrunken skin will explode! No one who makes clothing and cares for the family garments sews a new piece of leather upon an older, shrunken piece of leather. The new patch will naturally shrink and as it pulls away produce a larger hole.

Jesus' appeal to common sense has a leveling effect: everyone can participate in the discussion. Sometimes the poorer, less learned a person may be, the fewer hindrances there are that block a clear, honest answer! Jesus is advising all of us. unless theology can stand the test of common sense and blend fittingly with the accumulated wisdom of good people over the ages, that theology is suspect. Is it true theology—meaning by that, is it truly (as the word signifies in its Greek origin) *theou-logos, God's word?*

Theology and common sense must blend and support each other—on the firm foundation that God is *one*. We do not worship an entirely transcendent God, distinct from the God of nature. Neither are there two separate gods, one for the learned theologian and another for the unschooled lay person. At the heart of all theology is the doctrine that God created the universe and saw "how good it was" (Gen 1:12). Moreover, when God created the human family, the Book of Genesis emphasizes God's pleasure all the more: "God saw that it was *very* good" (Gen 1:32). Our God is immanent in his creation. In the harmonizing of theology and common sense, theology certainly clarifies the vague, instinctive impressions and feelings of common sense, but at the same time common sense challenges theology to come down from its ivory tower, mingle with the sweat and tension of daily work and like Jesus the high priest admit to being "beset by weakness" and even to be humiliated by temptation.

What kind of questions would common sense put to theology? Perhaps, our question about the extermination warfare in the First Book of Samuel. Did God *really* order it? Are we sure that Saul was rejected precisely for not exterminating the Amalekites literally and completely? Was Samuel correct in thinking that *God* ordered this military expedition? Is the Bible short-circuiting the steps between God's condemnation of sin among the Amalekites and Israel's barbarous response?

Common sense will probably be consoled to find Jesus beset by our weakness and learning obedience from what he suffered. We can easily find God-with-us (the meaning of the word *Immanuel*) in our good deeds and virtuous habits. It is far more helpful and redeeming to experience the close presence of Jesus in our weakness and temptation. As Jesus remarked at the end of last Saturday's gospel:

> People who are healthy do not need a doctor; sick people do. I have come to call sinners, not the self-righteous (Mark 2:17).

Perhaps the result of today's meditation lies in the need to be humble in our theology and persistent in our common sense.

Prayer:
To the upright, Lord, you show your saving power. Enable me to find your way of sincerity, patience and respect for the persistent voice of good tradition. Enable my faith to be suffused by the supreme virtue of charity.

Tuesday, 2nd Week

Heb 6:10–20. After patient waiting Abraham obtained the promise. We have another source of encouragement to wait faithfully: Jesus, who has gone our way ahead of us and is already behind the veil.

1 Sam 16:1–13. Samuel went to Bethlehem, presumably for a family dinner and religious service, and while there anointed Jesse's youngest son, David, as king. The Spirit rushed upon him.

Mark 2:23–28. Jesus defends the disciples who were pulling off heads of grain on the sabbath. Jesus appeals to David's example and then comments: the sabbath was made for the human family, we were not made for the sabbath.

The Scriptures put us on the alert that wonderful possibilities and profound truths lie hidden, mysteriously, within the most ordinary events and our closest household people. These routine matters, like family and friends whom we meet each day, can seem so insignificant that not even God (we think) pays any attention to them. Yet we all know that they hold the key to our peace and holiness in God's sight. The reading from Hebrews (Cycle I) puts it plainly: "God . . . will not forget your work and the love you have shown him by your service, past and present." God notices each action and each thought—so that how we comb each hair on our head comes under divine attention (Matt 10:30, "As for you, every hair of your head has been counted, so do not be afraid of anything").

The Epistle to the Hebrews enunciates another, encouraging truth. The imagery derives from the ancient biblical tradition of pilgrimages to the Jerusalem temple and of a veil separating the Holy Place from the Holy of Holies. We are told that Jesus is "our forerunner," who has followed the same route that we are taking through life, or to reverse the image, we walk in Jesus' footsteps in our daily routine. And so do our family and friends. Jesus has already arrived at the goal and is at home within the Holy of Holies. If we continue faithfully and perseveringly, we too will pass beyond the veil in paradise. In another text from Hebrews, the image is extended still further. By his death, Jesus has rent open the separating veil so that all have access into the Holy of Holies (Heb 10:19–22). The most human of any human activity—death—becomes the means of full union with the divine!

When the same Epistle to the Hebrews alludes to the faith and perseverance of Abraham, we are reminded of the serious ups and downs in Abraham's marriage, yet always leading to the conception and birth of the chosen and predestined one, Isaac (*cf.*, Gen 15; 18:1–15; 21). In a marriage that seemed to get nowhere, unless to injustice against Sarah when in Egypt Abraham called her only his sister (Gen 12:10–20) or against Hagar whom Abraham dismissed and sent into the wilderness with only ''some bread and a skin of water . . . [her] child [Ishmael] on her back'' (Gen 21:14). Through it all, an extraordinary mystery of human salvation was disentangling itself for our salvation.

Another family episode comes to our attention in the reading from First Samuel (Cycle II). Jesse presents his sons before the prophet-priest Samuel. Jesse, of course, lets David, just bordering on puberty, remain out in the fields. He wouldn't know what is going on, and would care less— so thought Jesse! But not God, nor Samuel, who said: ''Send for him; we will not begin the sacrificial banquet until he arrives.'' What impresses us about an incident that contains all kinds of mysterious leads is the normal family actions and reactions in this episode. As we realized from yesterday's meditation, unless we act as normal human beings, we will be poor instruments for God's divine work of human salvation.

Finally, we come upon the episode in the gospel. The disciples of Jesus are walking through a field of ripe grain. They pluck some of the grain, rub it in their hands, blow away the chaff and have a bit of nourishment. The human reaction of hunger makes them forget, not only that it is the sabbath day but also that there are rules about the sabbath.

These reflections upon the biblical passages could propel us in many directions. Perhaps the response most congenial to these readings comes from a determination or resolve never to despise our most human needs and actions, never to dismiss those people who seem dull or unimportant to us, never to conclude (in the words of the Letter to the Hebrews) that God ''will forget your work and the work that you have shown by your service, past and present, to his holy people.''

As a challenging examination of conscience, we should ask ourselves about the people whom we have underrated or ''used'' for small jobs. Have we allowed routine to spoil what once was exciting and joyful? Do we treat some people like children and leave them ''out in the field'' when more important people come into our lives? To the extent that this happens, we will be missing our way towards the Holy of Holies. We will miss the presence of God's special instrument for the messianic kingdom in our lives, as Jesse overlooked his young son David. We will become so formal and legalistic as to make ourselves the slaves of protocol and pompous behavior rather than the humble servants of Jesus.

Prayer:

Lord, we hear you say, ''I have found my servant, David,'' as you enable us to perceive the hidden goodness and extraordinary potential in others. This moment of respect, Lord Jesus, becomes my rock and my salvation and renews your holy covenant within me. Marvelous are your deeds, holy and awesome your name—in these daily occurences of my life.

Wednesday, 2nd Week

Heb 7:1–3, 15–17. Jesus is high priest forever according to the order of Melchizedek in virtue of a power of life that cannot be destroyed.

1 Sam 17:32–33, 37, 40–51. In a duel of right against might, freedom against oppression, David kills the giant Goliath.

Mark 3:1–6. Jesus asks: is it permitted to do a good deed on
the sabbath? to preserve life? He cures the man with the
shriveled hand.

Each biblical reading for today begins on a battle ter-
rain. According to the Epistle to the Hebrews, "Melchizedek . . . met Abraham returning from his defeat of the kings
and blessed him." The First Book of Samuel is taken from
the long account of David's duel with the Philistine giant
who had been taunting the Israelites and ridiculing "the
armies of the living God." In the gospel the Pharisees kept
an eye on Jesus to see whether he would heal on the sabbath,
"hoping to be able to bring an accusation against him." Jesus, we are told, "looked around at them angrily, for he was
deeply grieved."

As we allow ourselves time to reread the biblical passages, there emerges ever more clearly an overriding concern for life—despite the context of battle and death. The
Epistle to the Hebrews concludes that like Melchizedek, Jesus too is a priest forever "in virtue of the power of life that
cannot be destroyed." David replies to King Saul's fear, for
"The Lord, who delivered me from the claws of the lion and
the bear, will also keep me safe from the clutches of this
Philistine." In the discussion of the sabbath with the Pharisees, Jesus asks: "Is it permitted to do a good deed on the
sabbath—or an evil one? To preserve life—or to destroy it?

God, therefore, is the Lord of life, not of death; of
peace, not of violence; of justice, not of oppression. For the
record, the Bible often runs into difficulty when it discusses
death, warfare and suffering. The statement is repeated in
the Bible: "Return, O Lord, and save my life; . . . For
among the dead no one remembers you" (Ps 6:6). Israel
came to a clear belief in the resurrection very late, at the

time of the writing of the Book of Daniel, around 165 B.C. (*cf.*, Dan 12:1–3). Only then could Israel begin to talk about death with calmness and peace. Death could begin to be accepted trustfully only when it led to new life and the resurrection of the body.

Warfare, too, is another serious biblical problem. True, from a quick reading of the early books of the Old Testament—or from John the Baptist's remarks to soldiers in Luke 3:14—war is an accepted fact of life. A strange sentence: war or death, an accepted fact of life! Yet, use of military force ricocheted against Israel, bounding back with such catastrophes as the collapse of the large empire of David and Solomon in the devastating attack by King Shishak of Egypt (1 Kgs 14:25–26) and finally with the leveling of Jerusalem to the ground by the Babylonians in 587 B.C. (2 Kgs 25). For this and other reasons there developed the position in the late apocalyptic literature that only God can truly undertake warfare in favor of the chosen people. Finally, suffering too remained inexplicable, as is so evident in the Book of Job.

In the Bible, consequently, we cannot find an adequate answer to such major questions as war, suffering and death. Yet, we also discover in the Scriptures an attitude of living one's life energetically, fully, responsibly, in the cause of community welfare and our neighbor's peace. We do not sit back and let evil carry the day unopposed. In the gospel Jesus could have sidestepped the issue by healing the man with the shriveled hand in private, after the sabbath service was over. Jesus decided to face the issue squarely: "He addressed the man with the shriveled hand, 'Stand up here in front!' " In the reading from First Samuel (Cycle II) David pleaded with King Saul to be granted royal permission to fight in the name of Israel. The Epistle to the Hebrews, one of the most theological of all New Testament books, deliberately chooses its examples and locates the eternal priesthood of Jesus in the context of Abraham's return from battle and his being blessed by Melchizedek. Abraham rallied his forces in order to retrieve his relative Lot from the invading army of the five kings (Gen 14).

Some important questions are put to each of us by our meditations upon today's readings: 1) do I love my life fully and energetically?—at the service of others?—seriously seeking the peace, welfare and justice in the life of others? 2) am I appreciative of life everywhere and aware of the wonderful potential of life in people who are handicapped? and in my own handicaps and disabilities? 3) do I avoid using might to set up and safeguard my own selfish kingdom? If so, it will sooner or later come crashing down on my head as did the military kingdom of David. 4) am I minister of life, delighted in all of its expressions, dedicated to its preservation and extension?

Prayer:

Lord, may I always turn to you as my refuge and my fortress, my stronghold and my deliverer, my shield in whom I trust. May Jesus always be high priest in my life, consecrating my life for life eternal and uniting my life in a community of faith.

Thursday, 2nd Week

Heb 7:25–8:6. In Jesus we have a high priest, holy, innocent, separated from sinners, minister of the true tabernacle in heaven.

1 Sam 18:6–9; 19:1–7. Saul becomes jealous of David, but through Jonathan's intercession, the two are temporarily reconciled.

Mark 3:7–12. Great crowds from Galilee, Judea and even
   from Gentile areas press upon Jesus. Unclean spirits cry
   out in his presence.

Despite the temporary reconciliation between Saul and
David, despite the enthusiasm of the crowd pressing upon
Jesus, if only to touch him, despite too the transcendent portrait of Jesus the High Priest in the Epistle to the Hebrews,
still we sense a serious tension on all sides. The peace between Saul and David cannot remove the roots of jealousy
and irrational fear in Saul's heart. In the gospel reading we
remember very well yesterday's account of the Pharisees
who "began to plot with the Herodians on how they might
destroy" Jesus. This intrigue will be fanned to ever more
fierce jealousy and hatred by the crowd's enthusiasm for Jesus. Finally, we are more than a little baffled by the portrait
of Jesus the High Priest in the Epistle to the Hebrews. On
previous days Jesus was a compassionate high priest, able to
sympathize with us in all our weakness, even in our temptations, for he has shared our human life totally, but without
sin. Now we are given a glimpse of a transcendent high
priest, lifted above us, "separated from sinners [that is,
from ourselves], higher than the heavens."

As men and women of faith, we will always find ourselves caught in these tensions and seeming contradictions,
similar in many ways to the overwhelming mystery of Jesus,
truly God and truly human, eternal before the dawn of creation and limited in time by circumstances of birth and
death. Our life is a pilgrimage whose destiny lies beyond the
horizons of this earth, in heavenly places where Jesus has already gone behind the veil. We are continually being asked
to achieve humanly what is beyond our unaided human ability. Each of us is a strange mixture of excitement for Jesus

and embarrassment in his presence, or at times just plain tedium about Jesus and all religion. Often we are reconciled with relatives and neighbors, even with members of our family, yet we know deep in our heart that seeds of jealousy or resentment still lie hidden.

It is helpful to recognize that these tensions are the inherent problems of people of faith. By faith we accept as real what we cannot prove nor see; we not only accept but we even risk our life and our eternity on the conviction that the purpose of our earthly life lies beyond the present form of our earthly existence. By faith we are continually challenged not to succumb to what is often taken for granted to survive on earth. Must I presume that people are liars, that they are always hiding half the truth from me and that they are using me for their own advantage? Faith directs our eyes heavenward and gives us a glimpse of Jesus, our high priest, "holy, innocent, undefiled, separated from sinners, higher than the heavens." There in the Holy of Holies Jesus is making intercession for us that we be conformed to his holiness. Faith insists that our enthusiasm for such goodness is not flimsy as the clouds racing across the sky; such deals are more real than the earth beneath our feet.

Today's readings, then, tone up our life, put a fresh appearance around us and renew the power of the spirit. In the Epistle to the Hebrews (Cycle I) we are reminded that we have in Jesus a "priest . . . made perfect forever." Here is true security, eternal reality. Anger, jealousy, moodiness—all of these reactions in King Saul (Cycle II) have their ups and their downs and eventually collapse from sheer exhaustion. Saul ended up committing suicide! What we see before us is "only a copy and shadow," and at times a very imperfect copy, a wavering shadow.

The enthusiasm of the crowd for Jesus is not a passing

sort of excitement. It is an echo of heaven, where people from all nations unite in turning with love and loyalty and gratitude to Jesus.

Tension and conflict bring about a deeper understanding of our complex lives, even a mature wisdom. The Scriptures advise us to look carefully. What we think is real may be only a passing shadow; what we think is strong and effective (like King Saul) may only destroy itself; what we think is just the blind excitement of the crowd may be voicing the deepest everlasting instincts of faith. One day we will be with Jesus behind the veil and like Jesus we will be holy, innocent, undefiled, separated from sinners, higher than the heavens. Jesus, our God made human, functions as priest that our human nature be made like God's. Jesus is our pledge that this will truly happen. The tensions of faith help us to discern these all important facets of our life.

Prayer:

Lord, in you we trust and you will not allow this trust to be in vain. You will rescue us from death, from stumbling so that here on earth we will walk in the light of your hopes and in the strength of your grace. May we always through faith hear your voice and be ready to do your will.

Friday, 2nd Week

Heb 8:6–13. Jesus, our high priest is mediator of a new and better covenant, as announced by the prophet Jeremiah.

1 Sam 24:3–21. David refrained from killing Saul. Even Saul then acknowledged that "you are in the right" and will one day be king of Israel.

Mark 3:13–19. Going up a mountain, Jesus commissioned the twelve to preach the good news and to expel demons.

The statement that "Jesus went up the mountain and [there] summoned the men he himself had decided on," evokes memories of Moses who went up Mount Sinai to receive God's law and covenant (Exod 19) and on Mount Sinai Moses solemnized the covenant, surrounded by chosen leaders (Exod 24). Even though the reading from Hebrews (Cycle I) declares "the first [covenant to be] obsolete and . . . close to disappearing," the Scriptures see a strong continuity between the two covenants.

In fact, when Jeremiah announces the "coming days . . . when I will make a new covenant with the house of Israel," he was not inferring that the Mosaic covenant would be annulled and that God would make an entirely new covenant. If that had been the case, Jeremiah's book would never have remained within Judaism and its sacred traditions. Jeremiah's discourse about the new covenant, which turns out to be the longest single quotation from the Old Testament in the New, is best interpreted as a call to a *new spirit* in living the Mosaic covenant. Israel was not to be obsessed with externals and legalistic conformity to the letter of the law. Jeremiah was insisting upon an approach towards the covenant that had become prominent in the Book of Deuteronomy, the approach of loving obedience, persistent loyalty, especially within the bonds of family and neighborhood, and gratitude for many undeserved benefits.

The Book of Deuteronomy was the center of a vigorous reform during the days of Jeremiah. Jeremiah's "new" covenant would be a challenge to return to the ancient, genuine spirit of Deuteronomy, where we read:

Hear, O Israel! The Lord is our God, the Lord alone! Therefore, you shall love the Lord, your God, with all your heart, and with all your soul, and with all your strength. Take to heart these

words which I enjoin on you today. Drill them
into your children. Speak of them at home and
abroad, whether you are busy or at rest. Bind them
at your wrist as a sign and let them be as a pendant
on your forehead. Write them on the doorposts of
your houses and on your gates (Deut 6:4–9).

This stirring call of Deuteronomy was certainly inscribed on
the heart of Jesus. Jesus could not improve upon it and
called it the first and greatest of the commandments (Mark
12:28–34).

What is obsolete in the old is not what it says but how
we obey. The letter kills, the spirit gives life. We must seek
to be conformed to the least desire of God, not as slaves but
as children, not for seeking reward as much as for express-
ing love and gratitude, not for external show but for interior
peace. Even the smallest demand of the law is fulfilled in essence when a Christian lives in that spirit (Matt 5:18).

We can understand David's action toward Saul in this
way (Cycle II). The letter of the law would have permitted
David, in defense of his life, to repel Saul's attack even to
the point of killing him. Self-defense, especially under re-
lentless oppression, is permitted in the Bible. The interchange between David and Saul reveals the deep reverence
of David for his king. David calls out to Saul, "I will not
raise a hand against my Lord, for he is the Lord's anointed
and a father to me." Saul replies, "Is that your voice, my
son David?" The text then records that Saul, having realized
David's magnanimity, "wept aloud." David's respect for
the person of Saul was determined not only by a high regard
for the Lord's anointed but also by an affectionate spirit for
one who was like a father to him. What pain when father and
son, friend and neighbor are set at odds. The covenant is
lived amid these vicissitudes of human life.

The new covenant insists upon a divine spirit within the human area of life. This aspect may be aptly symbolized by the statement that "Jesus went up the mountain and [from there] summoned the persons he himself had decided on." Throughout the Bible the mountain has been a favorable place for prayer and for erecting temples and sanctuaries. For this reason, one of the important titles or epithets for God in the Bible is "rock," which passed into Hebrew prayer most probably from the prominent rock upon which the Jerusalem temple was built (*cf.,* Ps 18:2–3, "I love you, O Lord, my strength, O Lord my rock, my fortress, my deliverer. My God, my rock of refuge . . ."). Here is an excellent example of combining the external symbols of strength with the interior spirit of love. In order to acquire the new spirit of love for living the new covenant, we need to ascend the mountain—to be alone often in prayer, to find our one security in the Lord. "Alone in prayer"—so important is this attitude that the Gospel of Luke states that Jesus spent the entire night in a prayer-vigil before he called the twelve.

Mountain then conveys to us the clear message: alone in prayer, alone with God's sovereign majesty over our lives, total in our obedience that reaches to our hearts and interior motivation. These are the ingredients that make our old life into a new undertaking, our old covenant new and vibrant with the presence of Jesus.

Prayer:

Have mercy on me, God, for I take refuge in the shadow of your wings. As I contemplate your wonder from the mountain peak of prayer, grant that kindness and truth shall meet, justice and peace shall embrace, so that I may be your instrument in establishing the new covenant of your love on earth.

Saturday, 2nd Week

Heb 9:2–3, 11–14. Jesus enters the more perfect Holy of Holies, one not of human making, in order to atone for us with his own blood, and so to cleanse our conscience to serve the living God.

2 Sam 1:1–4,11-12,19,23-27. David mourns the death of Saul and Jonathan with tears, fasting and a dirge composed in their honor.

Mark 3:20–21. Jesus and the disciples retire into his own home, and again he is overwhelmed by the crowd. His family fear that he is out of his mind!

We watch as Jesus retires, either into the Holy of Holies, his home with God the Father, or into his home at Capernaum to rest and to obtain nourishment. In each case Jesus attends to human needs, in the heavenly Holy of Holies with our continued purification and redemption and at Capernaum with crowds who assembled for instruction and healing.

In heaven and on earth Jesus offers his blood as a source of life. The heart of Jesus had to beat with more intense fervor and to impel life-sustaining blood throughout the body, so that Jesus might maintain his all-consuming ministry. As Mark's gospel remarks, it was "impossible [for Jesus and the disciples] to get any food whatever." The activity turned out to be so incessant that "his family, when they heard of this, came to take charge of him, saying 'He is out of his mind.' "

The blood of Jesus again becomes the source of life, this time liturgically, according to the Epistle to the Hebrews (Cycle I). The author is comparing the death of Jesus with the Yom Kippur ceremony at the Jerusalem temple. On this day of atonement the high priest entered the Holy of

Holies and sprinkled blood towards the Ark of the Covenant and the "propitiatory" or "mercy-seat" which rested on top of the Ark. Here God was thought to be enthroned, invisibly but effectively (Exod 25:17–22). The sprinkled blood signified a flow of life between God and the people Israel. Just as blood that moves from heart to limbs unites each member of the body in one living organism, likewise the sacrificial blood intimately bonded God and the people together in a shared life—life in its full expression, life in its everlasting pledge of happiness.

We are told in the Epistle to the Hebrews that we are united with God through the blood of Jesus. The basic symbolism of blood looks towards life, not towards death—yet we cannot help but remember the death of Jesus by which the veil of the temple was rent apart and Jesus entered into the most holy place. Even this death, however, is remembered as a sign of Jesus' love and dedication to us, even as a surety that Jesus shared every moment of our life, especially that moment which is the most human of all, the moment of our death. If Jesus is so completely bonded with us—for we share the same life-carrying blood—then we are where Jesus is; and Jesus is where we are. As Jesus' blood mystically flows through our veins, its purity and strength cleanse our consciences from dead works. As a result, every action of ours becomes an act of worship of the living God.

The reading from 2 Samuel and from the gospel provides a new insight into the intensity of our union with Jesus. Jesus is so caught up in the needs and sorrows of our human existence, according to the gospel of Mark, that he has no time even to eat. His family think that he is no longer responsible for himself and plan to "take charge of him." They remark that "He is out of his mind." The two sides of Jesus' humanity become very visible. First, Jesus is neglecting his health and must be forced to take some rest and nourishment. From the flip side of the coin, Jesus is seen to be overcome by the sight of human misery and need and lost within this surging sea of flesh and blood. The flow of life-giving blood between Jesus and ourselves cannot be more vibrant and incessant.

As we reread the selection from 2 Samuel (Cycle II), we realize that Jesus was not a superactive individual, never stopping, never thinking, just doing. At the base of his existence Jesus was experiencing strong love and overwhelming compassion. We can hear Jesus repeating the words of David's dirge:

> I grieve for you, my brother and my sister!
>   most dear have you been to me;
> More precious have I held love for you
>   than love for women.

The last line may strike us as awkward. Yet it must be said that Jesus freely renounced the possibility of marriage so that he might give himself to each person, man and woman, more completely and more intimately than man and woman give themselves to each other in marriage.

The Scriptures ask us to follow Jesus and to enter the two homes that are united as one living presence through his life-giving blood. In the footsteps of Jesus we are drawn into the Holy of Holies and caught up in the mystical and contemplative wonder of God's presence. Here we find ourselves cleansed already by the strong blood of Jesus and enabled ''to worship the living God.'' Again we follow Jesus into his home at Capernaum and allow ourselves to be absorbed within the mass of humanity, all our brothers and sisters, crying out for love, understanding, healing and new life.

Prayer:

Lord God, you are seated on your throne within the Holy of Holies and through the cleansing, life-giving blood of Jesus we find ourselves in your presence. We acclaim your greatness over all the earth. We can turn again to our earthly existence with new hope that your anger will cease, tears will be wiped away, mourning over the dead will end, for all are alive in you through the blood of Jesus.

Monday, 3rd Week

Heb 9:15, 24–28. Jesus offered himself as a sacrifice the one time of Calvary for all people and so he renders unnecessary the many sacrifices of the Jerusalem temple.

2 Sam 5:1–7, 10. David is anointed by the elders of the northern part of the land and then he establishes Jerusalem as capital of the north and south, of Israel and Judah.

Mark 3:22–30. Jesus does not cast out devils by the prince of devils; a divided household cannot survive. However sins against the Spirit cannot be forgiven.

Unity, its high cost and its great reward, is the centerpiece of today's readings from Scripture. Jesus, according to the Epistle to the Hebrews (Cycle I), unites and finalizes all the temple sacrifices, even the yearly Yom Kippur ceremony, by his one sacrifice on Calvary and his resurrection to the right hand of the heavenly Father. David, as we read in Second Samuel (Cycle II), creates a single kingdom out of the rival and jealous groups, the people of southern Judah and those of northern Israel. Finally, Jesus summarizes our thinking in a very practical way: ''A household, divided according to loyalties, cannot survive.''

The high cost of unity is particularly evident in the Epistles to the Hebrews. Through the blood of Jesus, poured out on the cross, we are united as one single community of faith and united with God in the heavenly Holy of Holies. Today's reading returns several times to the subject of death and of blood. What the epistle states succinctly in refined theological language, the two Books of Samuel extend over many chapters as they tell of David's gradual rise to power and his suave way of gaining the loyalty of the north. We need to remember that David came from the southern tribe of Judah, an area seldom to the forefront of biblical attention up till now; Mosaic leadership and tradition had been concentrated in the northern region of Israel. Unity then required a strong theological synthesis as well as persistent political expertise. These conditions are clear enough in the first reading of Cycles I and II.

In the gospel Jesus puts the cost of unity in terms of a strong and continuous loyalty to the Holy Spirit and an unswerving rejection of Satan. In fact, with fearful solemnity, Jesus warns of the one sin which ''will never be forgiven,'' namely ''Blasphemy against the Holy Spirit.'' Those who sin against the Spirit will ''carry the the guilt of their sin without end.'' Persons who sin against the light, blinding themselves to the evident goodness of others, ascribing the good deeds of others to unworthy motives, closing their heart to the call for compassion and forgiveness—such persons close themselves to the presence of the Holy Spirit. In other words, then, there must be a unity and integral wholeness about ourselves: our intellect united with our eyes that see the goodness in others; our intellect united with our memory and so arriving at the solid wisdom of good experience; our intellect united with our flesh and blood and so judging sympathetically and compassionately and able to forgive others.

There cannot be a bond of union and trust in a family, community, church or nation, unless each individual strives to be peacefully united in the complexity of one's character. We must be possessed by the Holy Spirit and through this Spirit find our interior peace, our sincere and kindly awakening to the world around us. We will not attribute the good deeds of others to Satan even if their good deeds threaten us in some way and seem difficult to harmonize with some of our own ideas.

Once we have achieved interior peace and unity in the Holy Spirit, then we are disposed to reach outward and strive for peace and unity in the smaller world of our family and neighborhood, and to support those good causes that work for peace in the larger world of Church and among nations. The reading from Second Samuel provides some hints about this pursuit of peace. When the elders of the northern tribes of Israel come to David and sue for peace (it is helpful to recall that civil war flared up between Israel and Judah for a brief period after Saul's death), their first and only appeal was to the common bonds of human existence: ''Here we are, your bone and your flesh.'' They cut through all kinds of arguments and reasons, justifications and clever dealings, to the basic union of flesh and bone. An extraordinary statement when people are divided by race or wealth (and lack of it), even by religion and politics: ''Here we are, your bone and your flesh.'' Further, even though the elders of Israel come to David, who is actually their only hope of decent human existence, David does not take advantage of them. Rather he chose a new city for the capital of the united kingdoms of Israel and Judah, a neutral city where each group would be equally represented. Our union with others then should reach into the roots of our existence, our bone and our flesh, where no person is better or different than another person. Secondly, union cannot be to anyone's selfish advantage but for the common good and shared happiness of all.

Finally, from the Epistle to the Hebrews we learn that all attempts at unity must be founded, renewed and sustained *in Jesus,* the "mediator of a new covenant." Jesus died that we may be united as brothers and sisters in the same family. The blood of Jesus becomes the bond of life that circulates in the veins in all of us and brings us into a bond of life with God the Father and the Holy Spirit. In fulfillment of the symbolic rite of Yom Kippur, when the high priest sprinkled blood toward the Holy of Holies, the blood of our High Priest Jesus now flows between us and the Father. In the mystery of this divine life, we become one family, all of us. As in a family, blood is thicker than water and holds its own secrets of love and reconciliation. In the blood of Jesus, by which we are drawn into the Holy of Holies and become one with God, there are secrets which we will never understand on earth. Through Jesus we can learn to trust the most basic instincts of life and unity and reach out to our neighbor who is our bone and our flesh.

Prayer:

Lord, we find ourselves breaking into song at your wondrous deeds. Through the mystery of the death of Jesus, we come into contact with a reality that unites all of us as one body. Grant that we always respect this mystery in ourselves and in others and so never sin against the Holy Spirit.

Tuesday, 3rd Week

Heb 10:1–10. The sacrifices and temple ceremonies turn out to be a shadow of the good things to come, when Jesus offered himself, once, for all time and for all people, perfectly accomplishing God's will and sanctifying us in the new covenant.

2 Sam 6:12–15, 17–19. David dances before the ark during the festival procession bringing it into Jerusalem. Through David's generosity the celebration ends with a sacred banquet.

Mark 3:31–35. Turning to the crowd, Jesus declared: these are my mother and my brothers and sisters—whoever does the will of God.

Fidelity to God's will, in the declaration of today's gospel, forms a family of all followers of Jesus. Jesus identified the true disciple, not by special privileges acquired at birth, nor by rank or position, certainly not talents, gifts and financial resources—only by conscientious fidelity in the day by day routine of life. Jesus is asking us to undertake each action as though it were done in the context of a family. The other party is my sister or brother, my mother or father.

In order to know God's will, therefore, Jesus did not turn to the giants of apostolic activity, the twelve apostles, nor to his immediate earthly family, not even to Mary his mother. Jesus is declaring that God's will is not to be identified with great achievements but with faithfulness in the daily routine of life, with sympathy and understanding as shown in a family, with such virtues as patience and forgiveness which keep a family together.

At first reading it may seem that Jesus is breaking a family tie rather than forming one. When Jesus' mother Mary and other members of his family and relations come to him, one would think that Jesus would drop everything else and run to meet them. This eagerness to join one's parent, by contrast with Jesus' distancing of himself from Mary, is very evident in the action of the patriarch Joseph in Egypt. When word was brought to Joseph that his father Jacob had arrived "in the region of Goshen" and was already approaching the royal palace, we are told that:

> Joseph hitched the horses to his chariot and rode to meet his father. . . . As soon as he saw him, he flung himself on his neck and wept a long time in his arms. And [Jacob] said to Joseph, "At last I can die, now that I have seen for myself that Joseph is still alive" (Gen 46:29–30).

The contrast between the action of Joseph and that of Jesus startles us. Yet we also recall the way by which Joseph too distanced himself from his brothers when they first came to Egypt for grain. Evidently, there are moments when we reach inward to our intimate family circle; the one by birth and upbringing; other moments when we turn outward not to form our own family or community but to share family love with outsiders.

Jesus shows us examples of both moments: in today's gospel he is conscious of his world family; later from the cross he uses up what little strength is left in his dying moments to provide for his mother Mary (John 19:25–27). Yet even this last tender moment between Jesus and Mary becomes a lesson or type of Jesus' relation with the entire church. Here as elsewhere in the gospels, Mary is often representative of the church, the center of a praying community (Acts 1:12–14).

The will of God is directing us in each moment as we reach inward or reach outward. How difficult it is to distinguish which moment is at hand in our long series of relationships with family and outsiders! The true and godly decision is reached through a combination of courage and tenderness, a blend that is seen in each action of Jesus.

The first readings are enlightened by our reflections on the gospel. If God's will is normally found and fulfilled in the small events of family life and in our sharing of family love and tenderness with outsiders, then we can see in the selection from the Letter to the Hebrews that God is not disparaging the daily sacrifices of the old covenant. This is no put-down! Yet we are asked to sustain our daily, small actions by the strength and goodness of Jesus. Repeatedly we need to turn to Jesus, to purify our motives, to see our goals more clearly, to infuse more sympathy and tenderness into our actions and to form an ever greater circle of love. The one offering of Jesus sanctifies all of our daily actions. The essence of his sacrifice is the gift of his will:

> Sacrifices and offering you did not desire,
>   but a body you have prepared for me;
> Then I said, ''As is written of me in the book,
>   I have come to do your will, O God.''

God's will can be reached carefully and tenderly; it can also break upon us suddenly by surprise. At times it summons us to rejoicing and celebration.

> David, girt with a linen apron [as a sacred minister] came dancing before the Lord with abandon, as he and all the Israelites were bringing up the ark of the Lord with shouts of joy and to the sound of horn.

The spontaneity of children can teach grown-ups that such is the Kingdom of God. Children too can huddle up with warm embrace in the close family circle; they can also run through the neighborhood and wave at total strangers. They are teaching us the meaning of Jesus' words as he gazed at the wide circle of people from all parts of the land:

> These are my mother and my brothers. Whoever does the will of God is brother and sister and mother to me.

Prayer:

Whatever be the moment, Lord God, be it a serious decision that seems to tear apart my family attachment and desires, or a spontaneous shout of joy and round of dancing, let it always be that "Here I am, Lord, I come to do your will." I will always react with a blend of courage and tenderness. Then the doors of my heart will be opened to receive the King of glory.

Wednesday, 3rd Week

Heb 10:11–18. Jesus offered one sacrifice for sin and has forever perfected those who are being sanctified. He has inaugurated the new covenant with the law inscribed on their hearts.

2 Sam 7:4–17. While David is not to build a house for God, he is promised an everlasting house or dynasty by the Lord.

Mark 4:1–20. Parable of the sower and the mystery of Jesus' words about the Kingdom of God.

God's hopes are present within us, fully in all that they can ever promise or achieve, mysteriously in that we must always struggle to comprehend. The letter to the Hebrews

(Cycle I) assures us: "Jesus offered one sacrifice for sins. . . [and] by [that] one sacrifice he has forever perfected those who are being sanctified." This Jesus, who is our hope, our way, our truth and our life (John 8:12, "I am the light of the world"; 11:25, "I am the resurrection and the life"; 14:6, "I am the way, and the truth, and the life"), this Jesus lives in us as vine and branches are united in one flow of life. For if we continue with the citations from John's gospel, we come to another image that casts much light upon the parable of the sower and of the seed within the ground: "I am the vine, you are the branches. The one who lives in me and I in that one, will produce abundantly" (15:5). Such is not only the promise of life, but the actual pulse of life within us, the life of Jesus, with all of its plans and potential for life, yet nonetheless hidden in darkness and accepted in faith.

The reality of such divine potential within us is expressed in still another way by the Epistle to the Hebrews:

> This is the covenant I will make with you
>   after those days, says the Lord;
> I will put my laws in their hearts
>   and I will write them on their minds.

This law which is inscribed within us is Jesus our light and our life.

This law, this seed, this sap that flows between vine and branches—different figures of speech for the same mysterious reality means that Jesus is truly within us—yet hidden as deeply in darkness as sap in the vine, as seed within the dark earth, as delicate hopes within our heart. We are not able ahead of time to dictate how it will develop. The mystery of fulfillment is further emphasized by the reading from Second Samuel. Divine reversals seem to cut across the text.

At the beginning of chap. 7, David wants to build a house or temple for Yahweh. At first Nathan agrees: "Go, do whatever you have in mind, for the Lord is with you" (2 Sam 7:3). The next day the prophet Nathan returns with the opposite instructions from the Lord. Appealing to the ancient traditions that the ark was always enclosed in a shepherd's tent that can be easily dismantled and reassembled, Nathan declares that the Lord never asked, "Why have you not built me a house of cedar?" Instead, Nathan announces, God will build a house for David, an everlasting dynasty:

> Your house and your kingdom shall endure forever before me; your throne shall stand firm forever.

The obvious meaning of these words would seem to be: the Davidic dynasty would always possess the right to be the kings of God's chosen people and their throne shall stand firm at Jerusalem forever. That would seem to be the unquestionable sense of the passage. But it was not so. This prophecy, like any word from God, contains mysterious possibilities which we cannot anticipate simply from study of the ancient meaning of the text. The dynasty was removed by the Babylonian conquerors in 587 B.C. and even the devout Israelite who composed Ps 89 could not understand God's word and its fulfillment at that time:

> How long, O Lord? Will you hide yourself forever?
> Where are your ancient favors, O Lord,
>   which you pledged to David by your
>   faithfulness (Ps 89:47, 50).

Strange that even God's inspired word can be only a series of questions! Even the devout psalmist was left in darkness, questioning the base of faith, questioning God. And in this relation with God, the psalmist remained in contact with the One who inspires the message and speaks the word.

The gospel adds its own share of mystery. It quotes some of the most difficult words of Old Testament prophecy, those of Isaiah:

> They will look intently and not see, listen carefully and not understand, lest perhaps they repent and be forgiven (*cf.,* Isa 6:9–10).

The passage from Isaiah, however, ends with hope—still couched in mystery yet nonetheless hope:

> As with a tenebinth or an oak
> whose trunk remains when its leaves have
> fallen (Isa 7:13b).

Life still remains, hidden beneath the earth, waiting as Isaiah will declare in chap. 11, for the spirit of the Lord to rest upon it, so that a shoot shall sprout from the stem and a bud blossom from its roots. As we continue to read in chap. 11, new life reaches out within a new paradise where "the wolf shall be a guest of the lamb [and] the calf and the young lion shall browse together [and] the baby shall play by the cobra's den" (Isa 11:6–8).

The gospel assures us that fulfillment will come to every prophecy and that every hope will blossom in its time. The gospel also insists upon the human factor, the condition of the soil, the environment of thorns or rocks or pathways. We are not to wait passively and do nothing as God brings the mystery to fulfillment. While we believe firmly that the mystery is beyond our control and that we will eventually be taken totally by surprise, nonetheless we are expected:

To be mindful that others do not walk over our
   hopes and stamp them out in the pathway of life;
to persevere through persecution and difficult times;
to discipline ourselves against "anxieties . . .
   the desire for wealth, and cravings of
   other sorts."

Salvation then is the interaction of God's mystery and our earnest dedication. Thereby we will humanly achieve what is humanly impossible, because (to paraphrase Paul's words) even if "I planted the seed and Apollos watered it, God made it grow" (1 Cor 3:6).

Prayer:

Lord Jesus, you are a priest forever, offering a perfect sacrifice, your own sacred self, that your hopes and the seed of life within us will reach the fulfillment of God's word. Your covenant with us will last forever. Enable me to co-operate with faith and energy.

Thursday, 3rd Week

Heb 10:19–20. We are assured of entrance into the Holy of Holies by the new and living path Jesus has opened for us. We must rouse each other to love and good deeds.

2 Sam 7:18–19, 24–29. David prays gratefully for the everlasting promises to his house.

Mark 4:21–25. Everything hidden will be revealed at a later time. To those who have more will be given; from those who have not, what little they have will be taken away.

"The new and living path [which] Jesus has opened up for us," according to Cycle I, leads to the cross and through this means to the heavenly sanctuary. These reflections in the Epistle to the Hebrews are overladen with rich biblical allusions which enable us to see "the new and living path" as it extends through the earthly life of Jesus and earlier as it reaches back into Old Testament liturgy. These references, moreover, enable us to peer more deeply into the mystery of Jesus' life with God behind the veil in the Holy of Holies.

The larger context of this reading from Hebrews is the Old Testament ritual of Yom Kippur, the Day of Atonement, when the high priest entered, this one time of all the year, behind the veil into the Holy of Holies. There, clouded with the smoke of incense, he sprinkled blood towards the place of the Ark of the Covenant (the Ark had been missing since the destruction of Jerusalem in 587 B.C.). The ceremony signified the purification of the people Israel by a flow of new blood—new life—between them and God; such is the symbolism of the sprinkling of blood (see Lev 16 and 17:11, "blood as the seat of life makes at-one-ment").

This ceremony takes on a new, poignant meaning on Calvary. Jesus is the high priest, the blood is his own precious blood, the cross is the altar and place of the Ark. With a slight shift of symbolism, common enough in the Bible, the veil which guards the Holy of Holies is the flesh of Jesus. Both were torn open when Jesus died upon the cross. When Jesus "gave up his spirit, suddenly the curtain of the sanctuary was torn in two from top to bottom" (Matt 27:50–51).

The death of Jesus not only reveals the mystery of God's faithful love for us—the flow of one life between us—but it also enables us to enter into the Holy of Holies. One with Jesus we stand before the holiest of all mysteries. The death of Jesus also provides us with new insight into his entire earthly life. Each step was leading to Calvary, and it reminds us that each step of our earthly life follows "the new and living path'' of Jesus' example. Each moment we are entering into the Holy of Holies.

Through Jesus' example and the words of Scripture, the lamp is no longer hidden under a bushel basket or under a bed. We see new meaning in our daily actions, particularly in those which are difficult and seem to draw blood. These enable us to complete the ritual of at-one-ment; our blood flows from ourselves, through our sincere and dedicated actions, towards the place of the Ark, the cross, the eucharistic table, the tabernacle of God's special presence. We see a new holiness in each act of our daily life. Each leads to the cross and through the cross and the torn veil of Jesus' body (our suffering body too?) into the Holy of Holies.

If we have this kind of faith and dedication, then ''to those who have, more will be given.'' If we do not have this kind of faith, then ''what little they have will be taken away'' and be lost in meaningless exhaustion.

From this background we can approach David's prayer in Cycle II. David is thanking God for the everlasting promises of royalty confided to his family. Little did David realize that these promises would truly become everlasting and permanent in their deepest meaning when Jesus through death reentered the Holy of Holies to take his place at the right hand of the Father (see Acts 2:29–36). In a way that could not have been understood at the time—when the fall of Jerusalem 587 years before Jesus seemed to deny God's promises—new meaning comes by the words of Jesus:

> Listen carefully to what you hear. In the measure
> you give you shall receive, and more besides.

Only by giving in full measure—giving up one's interpretation and appreciation of divine promises yet continuing in the faith that God is straightening the crooked lines of history and of life, will we "receive, and more besides." By uniting our sense of fulfillment with the death of Jesus, the lamp is taken from underneath the bushel basket and placed on a stand. If we can apply the figure of speech according to the symbolism of Hebrews, the lamp is placed on a stand in the Holy of Holies and we see the wonderful mystery of God's love in the torn body-veil of Jesus and we experience a new flow of life in our one blood and at-one-ment.

Prayer:

Grant, Lord, that we may ascend the mountain of the Lord where your holy temple and the Holy of Holies are established. The new and living path to this mountain will be marked by the blood of Jesus. Join my blood with that of Jesus, so that together we may enter into the Holy of Holies. Then we will find our resting place forever.

Friday, 3rd Week

Heb 10:32–39. Do not surrender your confidence. You need patience to do God's will and to receive what he has promised. My just one lives by faith.

2 Sam 11:1–4, 5–10, 13–17. David's sin of adultery and murder of Uriah.

Mark 4:26–34. Deep within the earth, the seed sprouts and grows without the farmer knowing how it happens. The mustard seed springs up to become the largest of shrubs.

The work of God is so enormous and so full of promise, that it comes to fulfillment only after much time, much patient waiting in the darkness of the earth, much suffering as the seed breaks apart and loses itself for the new sprout to develop, much careful attention to the tender development of the first shoots which appear on the surface of the earth. It is illuminating to the long process of the gospel growth if we unite Jesus' parable about the seed sown within the dark earth with the life-experiences behind the two readings from the Epistle to the Hebrews (Cycle I) and the Second Book of Samuel (Cycle II).

We are not following standard parable interpretation, to take an incidental detail of a story as a major element in its explanation, yet an occasional lapse from the rules may be forgiven, so long as we know that the infraction is not our normal practice! The element of ''earth'' where the seed nestles, breaks apart and begins its new life appears in its dark, difficult character within the first readings of Cycles I and II. The Epistle to the Hebrews could have been written for converts from Judaism, likely former Jewish priests (Acts 6:7, ''many [Jewish] priests . . . embraced the faith''). These could easily remember the glorious moments of temple worship—with tears and regret—as they participated in the house services, the eucharist in upper rooms, with little ritual and no grandeur (Acts 2:42). Their family ties had been disrupted; many of their own household persecuted them (Luke 11:51–52; 21:12).

The Epistle to the Hebrews is continually facing the problem of discouragement over the long trek of following Jesus on our earthly journey to be with him behind the veil in the Holy of Holies. In today's selection we notice the admission of persecution and delay. The following phrases are addressed immediately to the reader: *you* are that one who—

> endured a great contest of suffering after you
> had been enlightened;

publicly exposed to insult;
in prison and the confiscation of your goods.

There is also the continuous need to persevere:

do not surrender your confidence
you need patience
just ''a brief moment . . . he will not delay''
''the just person lives by their faith''
do not draw back and perish; be with those
    who have faith and life.

The dark, damp earth takes on a new significance in the reading from Second Samuel. Here we read the account of David's adultery: the king's attempt to make Uriah think that he was the father of the child after making him drunk so that he would go home and sleep with his wife, and David's treacherous plan to have Uriah killed in battle by the king's enemies! How the word of God seems to break apart in the dark earth of human misery. This initial episode begins a long series of murders, sexual excesses, military adventures and revolts within the household of David in 2 Sam 11 to 1 Kgs 2. We ourselves are at a loss for an adequate explanation why God should accept such a dark and even intolerable way for the fulfillment of his promises to David about an everlasting dynasty. The one through whom those promises would be immediately fulfilled turned out to be Bathsheba and her future son Solomon.

Most of us cannot explain how the seed which falls into the ground becomes stalks of wheat to provide grain and bread or becomes ''the largest of all shrubs with branches big enough for the birds of the sky to build nests in its shade.'' Nor can we understand God's ways in the history of

David. Yet just as wheat provides bread and the mustard tree shade, so also the story of David consoles us secretly and says: God too does "not surrender confidence" in us and does not abandon "patience" in us that the divine "will [be accomplished] and [we] receive what he has promised." God practices what he preaches and preaches what he practices!

Salvation then is a common undertaking of patience and confidence between God and ourselves. It ought to be also the way by which we creatures encourage the salvation of one another—by manifesting patience and confidence in members of our family, community and neighborhood—especially through the long dark hours when the seed is in the earth, breaking apart and showing little or no sign of what it will become.

Prayer:

Lord, you will make justice dawn for us like the light and your bright promises will be fully realized. In this extraordinary way you show yourself faithful in doing what you promised. Enable us to imitate your patience and so to be people of confidence in ourselves and in others. In this way, you will graciously wipe out our offenses and let us hear the sounds of joy and gladness.

Saturday, 3rd Week

Heb 11:1–2, 8–19. Faith is confident assurance and conviction that we await a better, heavenly home, a city whose designer and maker is God. God who makes the promise is worthy of trust.

2 Sam 12:1–7, 10–17. Nathan rebukes David not simply for a sexual offense but for offending against the respect due

to the love and tenderness of another person. David will be punished and purified by the sword in his own family. Mark 4:35–41. Jesus quells the storm at sea. Humanly, he manifests divine power in overcoming superhuman forces.

We ourselves are human beings, not angels, certainly not gods; we live on planet earth, not in space nor yet in our heavenly mansions. We deal with hopes and we struggle against opposition through our human resources and in our human family, with our eyes and ears and mouths, our imagination and memory and intellect, our emotions and will power, faculties that function only so long as we are physically awake, that operate only according to the strength and resiliency of our body.

While these facts are obvious and are accepted by everyone, nonetheless, another set of facts also stare us in the face and clamor more and more for attention. These latter come from the Scriptures and from daily observation of human existence, our own and others, personally seen or discovered through newspaper, TV and radio. We see handicapped people, physically impaired and yet accomplishing more than many people who can see, walk, hear, reach out and touch. All of us know our own personal handicaps and disabilities, sometimes secretly withheld from others, even in the same family, which we have overcome by an inner dynamism and vision of hope. We know others who are faithful, day after day, to their family obligations, their neighborhood duties, their dedication to assist others in health services and social rights. These people carry on as though such routine is normal. For ourselves it would be heroically demanding to persevere for a month in such a set of circumstances.

As we reflect upon daily life, we see that each person is

expected to achieve humanly what is beyond human strength, to reach for goals beyond the horizons of planet earth and yet to journey towards their goals not by flying on the clouds but with feet pressing the sidewalks, the dirt and the wooden floors of earthly pilgrimage. Today's scriptural readings enable us to reflect upon these same questions and impossible dreams through the lives of men and women who people the pages of the Bible. These are ordinary folk, with our temptations and discouragement—yet living with "confident assurance concerning what we hope for, and conviction about things we do not see . . . looking forward to the city with foundations, whose designer and maker is God . . . searching for a better, a heavenly home. Wherefore God is not ashamed to be called their God . . . [they have even] reasoned that God was able to raise from the dead." These lines from the Epistle to the Hebrews (Cycle I) help us to identify a cloud of witnesses who hover over us and belong to our human family, beckoning us also to be men and women of faith.

Even in death, "all of these died in faith. They did not obtain what had been promised but saw and saluted it from afar." What heroic faith and inspiring hope! In dying, when our eyes have grown dim and our hearing fades away, in our hearts we see the lights of our "heavenly home" and hear its joy "from afar."

Even kings share the human condition of common folk. How evident is this fact in the readings from Second Samuel (Cycle II). David's infatuation with Bathsheba can be humanly explained, and according to royal protocol and prerogatives in the ancient Near East absolutely normal. Yet the prophet Nathan speaks God's judgment which cuts through human explanations and excuses to state dramatically: "You are the one! Now, therefore, the sword shall never depart from your house, because *you despised me* in taking the wife of Uriah to be your wife.''

This statement of Nathan provides the most important cue for our meditation and proper understanding of hopes. Ideals are more than statements in a book, even if this book is as sacred as the Bible; nor are they philosophical deductions, reached by calm, objective deliberations. God is immediately and personally involved. In acting as he did, David is told by Nathan, in the name of God: ''*You despised me* in taking the wife of Uriah to be your wife.'' God is to be identified with our hopes, so that in acting as we know we should, we seek God and love God; as on the contrary, when we hurt others, we repudiate and despise God. We hear Jesus' words:

> I assure you, as often as you did it for one of my least brothers or sisters, you did it for me (Matt 25:40).

Jesus then is with us always. We are not alone during the storms at sea, when buffeted by raging wind and by waves breaking against our ''boat.'' Jesus says to us, as to the disciples in today's gospel, ''Why are you so terrified? Why are you lacking in faith?'' Jesus revives the kind of faith by which our worst sins are forgiven, our greatest inabilities are suffused with new strength and our eyes see again a vision of our heavenly home, a vision that enables us while still on earth to forgive, to be patient, to remain faithful, and to share ideals.

Prayer:

Lord, I believe in you and in your fidelity. You will always remember your covenant with us, even when we are

most unworthy. You will give back the joy of salvation and
sustain us with your own strong, willing spirit. Lord, I believe that even the wind and the sea obey you.

Monday, 4th Week

Heb 11:32–40. After a litany of heroic men and women who
    endured all kinds of hardships, the author states that we
    too must be included: ''Without us they are not made per-
    fect.''
2 Sam 15:13–14, 30; 16:5–13. David is forced to flee Jeru-
    salem because of Absalom's revolt. Along the way David
    is cursed by one of Saul's clan, yet accepts it as God's
    will.
Mark 5:1–20. Jesus cures the demoniac (the devils fell into
    a herd of swine that rush into the sea and drown) and then
    commissions the man to proclaim the good news to the
    ten cities.

The Scriptures respect the human situation, yet they
also make us realize that while on earth we are engaged in a
dynamic struggle with evil spirits and are expected to respond heroically. Not that every day of our existence is to
measure up to such dramatic expectations. If that were the
case, we would collapse under the tension and lose emo-
tional control like the demoniac in today's gospel. Yet at
key moments of our life that struggle between good and evil
spirits absorbs all of our attention and to survive we must be
heroic. Even at such times, however, the Scriptures call us
to homey virtues like patience and hope.
    In the readings from Hebrews (Cycle I) we are coming
to the end of one of the most theological documents in the

New Testament, composed by a disciple of Paul and John who was able to blend Paul's insistence on faith with John's concern for Jesus' incarnation and earthly life and for the liturgy. The author of Hebrews portrays Jesus' life as a long pilgrimage through human life, stepping into the footprints of every kind of human existence and even sharing our temptations and discouragement, leading eventually after the struggle against death on the cross into the Holy of Holies. The Epistle to the Hebrews has been continually drawing upon Old Testament passages, but mostly of a liturgical or highly doctrinal nature. Now, however, in chap. 11 it summarizes the earthly pilgrimage of Jesus in another way, by a litany of Old Testament saints, all of whom struggle heroically to be faithful to God's will in their life.

Women and men are canonized for their extraordinary fidelity to the Lord in very difficult circumstances. These saints, upon closer examination, are a motley assortment— some unnamed as the woman who received the dead back to life (2 Kgs 4:8–37), another the prostitute Rahab (Heb 11:31). No class is passed over, low or high station in life, male or female, individually or members of communities. The Epistle to the Hebrews seems to be insisting that by following daily in the earthly footprints of Jesus, as Jesus did in ours, we will be ready for the moment of great trial.

The trial struck King David from within his own family, or as David expressed it to his nephew Abishai, ''[from] my own son, who came forth from my loins.'' The family history of David in Second Samuel is long and complicated, sordid and pathetic at times, brilliant and successful at other times, yet reaching back to David's sins of adultery and homicide in the case of Bathsheba and Uriah. No matter how guilty David has been, we cannot help but admire his humility and compunction when confronted by the facts, his

loyal love even towards a son in revolt and seeking his life.
When David advises restraint—that the clansman related to
Saul should not be executed for cursing the king—and attributes the situation to God's providence, no one can blame
David as a super-spiritualist, out of touch and incapable of
practical decision. David's entire life would refute such an
evaluation. Yet, he is declaring:

> Let him alone and let him curse, for the Lord has
> told me to. Perhaps the Lord will look upon my
> affliction and make it up to me with benefits for
> the curses he is uttering this day.

David is manifesting another form of heroic action.

The same tenderheartedness, often manifest in David is
now visible in Jesus' reaction to the demoniac. This man
ran up to Jesus who had come by boat on the southeastern
shore of the Lake of Galilee and was now walking inland.
Jesus responds with exemplary patience and respect. When
the unclean spirits ask to be sent into the herd of swine, Jesus "gave the word." When the local inhabitants begged Jesus "to go away from their district," he proceeded to get
into the boat. When the man, now cured of his mental illness
and strange ways, wants to follow Jesus, Jesus accepts his
offer but sends him forth as a missionary-disciple "to proclaim throughout the Ten Cities what Jesus had done for
him." Jesus did not enter into the causes of the mental illness nor worry about the consequences of being associated
with a former demoniac. Jesus saw a brother of good will
and fervent enthusiasm. This type of action is also heroic.

We begin to see how the heroic actions of God's saints
knit them ever more closely as a family, and this family includes ourselves, each of us with our gifts of hope and in-

spiration. David respects bonds of family and the larger pattern of God's providence. Jesus willingly receives the demoniac into the larger group of those who believe in him. The Epistle to the Hebrews sums it more theoretically and theologically:

> [The Old Testament heroes and heroines] did not obtain what had been promised. God had made a better plan, a plan which included us. Without us, they were not to be made perfect.

Our acts of heroism are never intended to set us apart but to reunite us in an ever larger family. Even when we are at our best, like the Old Testament saints, we still need others to support and encourage us. Perhaps we can understand this final position of today's scriptures by rereading St. Paul's hymn to charity:

> If I have faith great enough to move mountains, but have not love, I am nothing. If I give everything I have to feed the poor and hand over my body to be burned, but have not love, I gain nothing. . . . There are in the end three things that last: faith, hope, and love, and the greatest of these is love (1 Cor 13:2–3, 13).

Prayer:

Lord, comfort our hearts with hope—hope that enables us to be heroic at crucial moments of our lives, hope that sharpens our vision to see the good in others. With the hope that you place in us, you will make us a fortified city, sustaining all kinds of opposition. I will never fear. Lord, you will rise up and save me.

Tuesday, 4th Week

Heb 12:1–4. We have before us a cloud of witnesses, and at
   their head is Jesus who endured the cross. We should
   keep our eyes fixed on him and not abandon the struggle.
2 Sam 18:9–10, 14, 24–25. Absalom is executed by Joab.
   David mourns the death of his son instead of celebrating
   the victory.
Mark 5:21–43. Jesus cures the woman long afflicted with a
   hemorrhage and raises to life the twelve year old daughter
   of Jairus.

In today's reading, the Letter to the Hebrews (Cycle I)
tells us to fix our gaze on the cloud of heavenly witnesses.
The very word *cloud* directs our attention beyond the limits
of our earthly life (Heb 10:19–20, the reading for last Thurs-
day), beyond even the veil of the Holy of Holies. The other
two readings for this day, from the Second Book of Samuel
(Cycle II) and the Gospel of Mark, waken us from our heavenly vision and abruptly settle us back again on this earth
with our brothers and sisters. Perhaps no passage in Scripture is moistened with more tears and is more revelatory of
the loving attachment between parent and offspring than
David's mournful words over Absalom:

> My son Absalom! My son, my son Absalom! If
> only I had died instead of you, Absalom, my son,
> my son!

The bonds and frailty of human life appear again in the gospel account of the woman, for twelve years seeking a cure,
submitting to treatments ''of every sort and [having] ex-
hausted her savings in the process,'' and then of the twelve

year old daughter of the synagogue official named Jairus. With enduring tenderness he asks Jesus to come and simply lay his hand on "my little daughter."

If there is any clash of thought and images between the Epistle to the Hebrews and the other two readings, it resolves at once as we recall that nothing is more human than death. As the proverb expresses it, the old will die and the young *shall* die. It is normal for the elderly to pass away and there seems to be a divine sentence that many young shall also die. As we blend the three biblical passages, we are also reminded that the process of life-death is to be surrounded with a full outpouring of human emotion and human energy. Life, therefore, and not death remains the center of everyone's concern, even of God's concern. This life is not some rarified existence in the clouds (despite the use of this word in the first reading) but it is life throbbing in flesh and blood, in deep emotion and at times uncontrollable passion. General Joab could not understand how David would weep over the death of Absalom, a son who had revolted against David and had not only sought to kill his father but had even claimed David's wives as his own "in view of all Israel" (an incident omitted from the liturgical reading, 2 Sam 16:21–22). Joab directly approached David and stated bluntly, "You have put all your servants to shame today by loving those who hate you and hating those who love you" (2 Sam 19:6–7).

Perhaps we begin to realize why biblical people, even when they came to a clear acceptance of life after death, could think of this existence only in terms of a resurrection, with their body and all of their human relationships restored. Many aspects of the heavenly way of life either remain unknown or else are seen in a very different way (husbands and wives will no longer beget children) but the Bible still situates our future life in a resurrected body. We will continue to manifest and enjoy the happiness of every human bond established on earth.

This fact about heaven becomes clear if we look back upon today's readings: David does not want to see alive just any young man among the Israelites; he longs for his son. Jairus would have been deeply hurt if someone had suggested that he adopt another twelve year old girl in place of his dead daughter. In the case of the woman, afflicted for twelve years with a debilitating illness, Mark's gospel provides us with details that reflect a very human concern. Matthew and Luke will edit them out of the text for their own special reasons, yet they remain in Mark, one of the inspired passages of the Bible, for

> Everything [that was] written before our time, written for our instruction, that we might derive hope from the lessons of patience and the words of encouragement in the Scriptures (Rom 15:4).

When, therefore, the Epistle to the Hebrews speaks of the martyrdom of Jesus who "for the sake of the joy that lay before him . . . endured the cross, heedless of its shame," and of ourselves who are called upon to resist "to the point of blood," the Scripture is certainly not endorsing a calloused disdain for earth and a reckless disregard about health nor a cold, passionless approach towards family and friends and other loyalties. We are being encouraged to consecrate our entire selves, body and soul, flesh and blood, to our love and loyalty. To such a person Jesus will say, *"Talitha, koum,"* arise—as he takes them by the hand. In heaven he may not say to the attendants, as he did to others in the household of Jairus, "Give her [or him] something to eat," but then again he might. Who knows? We may be uncertain about food in heaven, but we are not left in the dark that each of us will live eternally as a full human person, spirit and resurrected body inseparably one.

Prayer:

Listen, Lord, and answer. We are poor and afflicted; you are good and forgiving. With confidence, inspired and strengthened by your inspired word, we ask you to hearken to our prayer and attend to the sound of our pleading. Your love will reach us in the grave and unite us with a people yet to be born.

Wednesday, 4th Week

Heb 12:4–7, 11–15. Suffering disciplines us and brings forth the fruit of peace and justice. It strengthens our drooping hands.

2 Sam 24:2, 9–17. In punishment for numbering the people, the Lord sent a pestilence. David prays that the Lord strike himself, the shepherd who had done wrong, not the people who are innocent sheep.

Mark 6:1–6. The people of Nazareth find Jesus "too much" and he could work only a few cures there. He preached elsewhere.

Three faults seem to cluster together: jealousy, pride and stubbornness. Each finds a cure in the bond of love within the family and in the bond of faith within the Church. The evil of jealousy flares up in the gospel: the people of Jesus' hometown, the men and women who as boys and girls grew up with the child Jesus, now find him "too much" for them. Why should he have more wisdom than they themselves, they ask. And why should he work miracles while they cannot? In the Epistle to the Hebrews, "the bitter root . . . through which many have become defiled" turns out to be stubbornness, and the recommended cure is discipline. The reading from Second Samuel describes many difficulties but pride seems to be at the bottom of all of them.

Perhaps the Scriptures are making too big a case out of such "ordinary" faults as stubbornness, pride and jealousy. We take them for granted in ourselves and others, and presume they belong to the normal inconveniences of life, like headaches or the common cold. The beauty and power of Scripture lie precisely in its unwillingness to take sin or a mediocre life for granted. Scripture combines a continual dedication to ideals with a practical sense of living on planet earth. The Bible, moreover, reflects the wise perception that most people are bothered and hurt more by such day-to-day sins as pride, stubbornness and jealousy than they are by the heinous sins of murder, bribery and adultery. "The fruit of peace and justice," to which Hebrews refers, is prevented from growing to maturity in our families and personal lives—if we can cross to Second Samuel for a moment—by the pestilence of pride or jealousy or stubbornness.

The pain of jealousy is manifested many times over by the frequency with which people repeat Jesus' words: "No prophet is without honor except in his [or her] native place, among his [or her] kindred, and in his [or her] own house." If the phrase "his or her" bores us by its repetition, it also insists that no person is exempt from jealousy, man or woman, Jew or Gentile, wealthy or poor. And jealousy hurts most the person who surrenders to it.

In the first reading (Cycle II) we have been following the career of Saul and David, and we saw how Saul became moody, undependable, fearful and finally driven to suicide; David seemed to possess an extraordinary reservoir of energy, a clarity of judgment, a love that charmed all opposition and extended even to the son in revolt. David received the promise of an eternal dynasty. Like a pestilence Saul was destroyed by jealousy. We read, already in 1 Sam 18:9, "From that day on, Saul was jealous of David."

The people in the gospel who suffered most and were lost sight of were the people of Nazareth. We are told:

> He could work no miracle there, apart from curing
> a few who were sick . . . so much did their lack of
> faith distress him. He made the rounds of the
> neighboring villages instead.

What a sad commentary on jealousy: Jesus made the rounds of the neighboring villages *instead*. Nazareth is left behind in silence; nothing is more unbearable than the silent treatment, particularly the silence of God. Jealousy is the incurable disease—"he could work no miracle there."

Close to jealousy in its symptoms and effects is the fault of stubbornness. God tries in many ways to heal this disease:

> Whom the Lord loves, he disciplines:
> he scourges every child he receives.

The cure for stubbornness is not to be found in suppression, anger and coercion. The first condition is: "whom the Lord loves." Throughout the discipline the force and intention of love ought to be manifest. Discipline seeks to show or reveal the pain already being suffered by the stubborn person within themselves. The Hebrew word for discipline means just that: to learn wisdom from one's suffering in the hard road of experience. Wisdom reunites the child within the family, the adult within the home and relationship.

Finally, today's biblical passage from Second Samuel

(Cycle II) points out the pestilence let loose by pride and excessive control. The Scriptures are not condemning a census of the people; the first part of the Book of Numbers records the results of another census, undertaken with God's blessing. It must have been David's motive that made this one evil in God's eyes. Yet, as mentioned already, an understandable fault! Why shouldn't a ruler be proud of the nation? Yet from a more extensive reading of the Bible and wider experience of human life, we see how a census *can* lead to government control, heavier taxation and affluence at the top. The pestilence is stayed by David's prayer, a prayer in which he accepts the blame and begs God to be merciful to the sheep, for ''what have they done [wrong]?'' Again, it is the bond of love and loyalty with the family and community that brings the solution and that heals the disease.

Prayer:

Lord, I humbly pray, forgive the wrong I have done. You, Lord God, who form a covenant and family, are my shelter from distress. Within your virtues of love and loyalty, you let me hear again the sound of joy and freedom. Let me always remember that when you discipline, you are actually my father and mother with compassion and concern.

Thursday, 4th Week

Heb 12:18–19, 21–24. We draw near Mount Zion, the city of the living God, the assembly of the first-born, to Jesus, the mediator of a new covenant whose sprinkled blood speaks louder than Abel's blood.

1 Kgs 2:1–4, 10–12. Before dying David exhorts Solomon

to be courageous and to remain faithful with whole heart and whole soul.

Mark 6:7–13. Jesus sends forth the twelve, two by two, preaching repentance, expelling demons, anointing the sick, working many cures.

A phrase from the first Book of Kings (Cycle II) neatly sums up and centers our reflections: remain faithful with whole heart and whole soul. Even for our human equilibrium we cannot afford to be off center, to be divided in our loyalty, to be maybe and maybe not. If we are not dependable, sooner or later our loyalty will fail. If we are divided, partially this way and partially that way, our house is built on sand and when the floods come, we will be swept away (Matt 7:24–27). If we leave the back door always ajar we will one day step outside and slip away from responsibility or even from those we love most. "Every kingdom divided against itself is laid waste" (Luke 11:17).

"Remain faithful to me with whole heart and with whole soul." Fidelity to our friends and loved ones as well as to our community and church demands courage, another expectation which David makes of his son Solomon in today's reading. Courage does not mean that each moment is fraught with tension and worry; nor does it turn life into a continuous battle. Once our house is built on rock, once our loyalties are well directed, once there is an integral wholeness about ourselves, then our life settles down with a peaceful and relaxed spirit.

The Epistle to the Hebrews reinforces the need of an integral completeness about ourselves and our family and community. It refers to

the spirit of just people made perfect,
Jesus, the mediator of a new covenant,

the sprinkled blood of Jesus which speaks
   louder than the blood of Abel.

These allusions introduce us to important Old Testament
passages. A just person in the Hebrew Scripture is someone
of faith, like Abraham, who firmly believed that God would
accomplish every promise. Abraham's justice reflects God's
justice, that is, God's way of living up to each and every
good hope and divine promise. Justice did not depend upon
Abraham's strength and ability. In fact, the promise of an
heir is made to the patriarch in Gen 15 where he and Sarah
seemed to be blocked by their advancing years from ever begetting their own child. Yet, as Scripture says, "Abraham
put his faith in the Lord who credited it to him as an act of
righteousness" (Gen 15:6).

"Mediator of a new covenant" resonates some of the
most beautiful texts in the Bible. We think of Deut 6:4–5:

Hear, O Israel! The Lord is our God, the Lord
alone! Therefore, you shall love the Lord, your
God, with all your heart, and with all your soul,
and with all your strength.

In seeking a revival of this ideal, Jeremiah declares that
everything will become new, if only this basic commandment of the Lord is fulfilled:

I will make a new covenant . . . I will place my
law within them, and write it upon their hearts; I
will be their God, and they shall be my people (Jer
31:31, 33).

The new covenant was sealed in the blood of Jesus, not with
the mere blood of animals as on Mount Sinai. It is the blood

of Jesus, as it were, that flows through our veins, and unites us with one, integral life with Jesus, and through Jesus with the Godhead. Like the blood of Abel, this blood cries out from the earth, from Calvary, begging not for vengeance but for mercy. Through forgiveness and compassion God will be just and fulfill every divine promise.

Life in such abundance cannot be a selfish life. It must be shared. Though written on the heart, it asks us to reach out to the neighbor whom we are to love equally as ourselves. These two commandments, love of God and love of neighbor, are the basis of all the commandments, the source of stability and integral wholeness. Therefore, Jesus sent his disciples two by two, to preach, to anoint, to work miracles, to expel demons. What they have received from Jesus must become the property of all men and women. What they share is given so freely that they move onward, without food, without traveling bag, without coins in the purse. Sandals are allowed, so that they can move all the more quickly in their mission of sharing the good news of Jesus.

David asked for a complete dedication; the Epistle to the Hebrews shows how deeply interior is this consecration; the gospel of Mark insists that our interior love be shared with all of our neighbors.

Prayer:

Within your holy city, Lord God, you bestow security and love; it is our castle and our home. We pray that your loving strength always have dominion over us and that we find our strength within your world family.

Friday, 4th Week

Heb 13:1–8. Recommendations to good morals, hospitality, contentment, to be mindful of prisoners and the persecuted. Jesus Christ is the same, yesterday, today, and forever.

Sir 47:2–11. David is praised, as a warrior and defender of Israel, as the sweet singer of Israel, as penitent sinner, as receptor of eternal promises.

Mark 6:14–29. Herod, curious about John the Baptist and then about Jesus, considers Jesus to be the Baptist risen from the dead. Mark recounts the martyrdom of the Baptist.

Today commemorates great precursors of Jesus, people like John the Baptist in the gospel, David in the reading from Sirach (Cycle II), and the long series of leaders in the Epistle to the Hebrews (Cycle I). As it is summarized in Hebrews: "Remember your leaders who spoke the word of God to you; consider how their lives ended, and imitate their faith." As the author of this document looked backward over the two millennia of Israelite history and the magnificent "cloud of witnesses," as they are called in Heb 12:1 (Tuesday of this week), everyone merges into the mystery of Jesus and in some way reflects the features of Jesus' character and mission. Those stirring words ring out: "Jesus Christ is the same, yesterday, today, and forever."

These portraits of Jesus are not still photos, silent and changeless, forever declaring their immutable message and eternal truth in words as everlasting as those chiseled on stone (Job 19:24). Statements of that kind are found in Scripture, but the portraits which we find in Hebrews, even in the reading for today, are living people, in the midst of problems and temptations, struggling and deciding as best they can under the circumstances. We are told of prisoners and persecuted people, of people humiliated by sexual temptations, of others jealous of wealthier neighbors. We do find here the eternal truth that "God will judge fornicators and adulterers" as committing evil, yet the section is concluded more generally:

> The Lord is my helper,
>   I am not afraid;
> What can anyone do to me?

This quotation from the Old Testament reminds us that the trials and questions continue and that there is no single solution revealed ahead of time by God—only the assurance that "the Lord is my helper." The importance of this quotation is assured, not only from its citation as a summary statement in Hebrews, but also from its presence several times in the Old Testament (Ps 27:1; 118:6).

The passage from Sirach in honor of David indicates the presence of God through a long career, from youth when he battled the Philistine giant, as king when he extended the boundary of Israel and overcame all opposition, as a private individual when he became guilty of adultery and murder yet repented humbly and publicly. We also witness moments when David sang "with string music before the altar, providing sweet melody for the psalms." God was present through every moment, as helper, as one who forgave, as one who inspired ideals, as one who overcame all opposition to the fulfillment of the divine will in the life of David.

That goal and purpose sublime and sure, which the presence of God assures for us, seems to collapse beyond recognition in the gospel account of the martyrdom of John the Baptist. It ends dramatically, even hideously, when the daughter gave to her mother "the head of John the Baptist on a platter.'' No wonder John haunted the memory and un-easy sleep of King Herod. No wonder that he hoped that somehow John's death was not final, but that Jesus was John raised from the dead. And we know that in a way Herod could not comprehend, John was not dead, but alive in Jesus who ''is the same yesterday, today and forever.''

''Today, and forever.'' ''Today'' means in the prob-lems and temptations, in the tensions and hopes, even in the collapses and failures. Jesus is here! Jesus is not providing a quick answer—a few, yes, as it becomes very clear that adultery is condemned—but most of all Jesus is ''my helper; I will not be afraid; what can anyone do to me?'' If there was still hope for King Herod, to recognize John the Baptist still alive in Jesus and therefore still leading to Jesus; if there was hope for David who was swept by passion into adultery and murder—then no collapse in our lives is a final defeat. Mys-teriously, it leads to repentance, humble compassion to-wards others, a renewed dependence upon Jesus.

Jesus is present in our prisons and among the perse-cuted people of the world—as Jesus was the reason for the Baptist's imprisonment and persecution. We must seek Je-sus in these areas that are enclosed, narrow, dark, lonely and seemingly hopeless—in prisons, and among the lowest mi-grant, unwelcome people in our midst. To seek Jesus in all of these abandoned people and places is reexpressed mag-nificently in Hebrews:

> Love your fellow Christians always. Do not ne-glect to show hospitality, for by that means *some have entertained angels* without knowing it.

It amazes us that if we reread all the episodes in today's scriptures and if we review all the moments in our own personal lives, we can conclude that we may "have entertained angels without knowing it!"

Prayer:

Lord you are my light and my salvation. Whom should I fear? Whatever be the tension or temptation, even if these encamp about me like an army, my heart will not fear. Let me always, in every circumstance, seek your face. Then I will realize how unerring are your ways, how fire-tried are your promises. I will proclaim you, O God, among the nations.

Saturday, 4th Week

Heb 13:15–17, 20–21. May the God of peace who brought up from the dead the great Shepherd of the sheep in the blood of the eternal covenant, Jesus our Lord, furnish you with all that is good that you may do his will.

1 Kgs 3:4–13. Solomon prayed: "Give your servant an understanding heart to judge your people and to distinguish right from wrong."

Mark 6:30–34. Jesus invites the apostles to come aside and rest. Yet when this solitude is invaded, he pities the people, sheep without a shepherd.

The theme of peace in today's readings is very fitting for Saturday, the sabbath, an ancient Hebrew word that itself means to stop, to rest, to take or give a holiday. This is the day that "God blessed and made holy, because on it he rested from all the work he had done in creation" (Gen 2:3). Earlier in the Epistle to the Hebrews (Cycle I) heaven was called by the name of sabbath:

A sabbath rest still remains for the people of God.
And the one who enters into God's rest, rests from
their own work as God did from his. Let us strive
to enter in that rest (Heb 4:9–11, Friday, 1st
Week).

We turn to the Scriptures for advice in arriving at that peace
on earth which reflects the heavenly peace.

First of all, the opening sentence in the selection from
Hebrews (Cycle I) advises a sincere and close relation between our private prayers and liturgical action on the one
hand and our secular pursuits and external behavior on the
other hand. The phrase, ''sacrifice of praise,'' resonates
many biblical passages which almost seem to condemn liturgical actions in their insistence that attitudes at prayer reflect attitudes towards our family, neighbor and even the
stranger. We recall:

Not for your sacrifices do I rebuke you,
   for your holocausts are before me always. . . .
Offer to God praise as your sacrifice
   and fulfill your vows to the Most High (Ps 50:8,
      14).

To a text like this one we can unite another with a strong
prophetical ring:

Do you call this a fast,
   a day acceptable to the Lord?
This, rather, is the fasting that I wish:
   unleashing those bound unjustly,
   untying the thongs of the yoke;
Setting free the oppressed,
   breaking every yoke;

> Sharing your bread with the hungry,
>   sheltering the oppressed
>   and the homeless (Isa 58:5–7).

Perhaps we can turn to the following sentence in today's reading from Hebrews for the best commentary on the acceptable sacrifice of praise:

> Do not neglect good deeds and generosity;
> God is pleased by sacrifices of that kind.

This line can be connected with another in Hebrews, just a few verses earlier:

> Jesus died outside the gate. . . . Let us go to him
> outside the camp, bearing the insult which he bore
> (Heb 13:12–13).

With striking contrast, we are advised to seek Jesus "outside the camp" where the outlaws, the lepers and the unclean cluster. With these Jesus was crucified as a common criminal. "Outside" is at a distance from the sacred temple and the ritual sacrifices which were "inside."

Peace means that we go out to the poor and needy and thereby be able to transform our prayers and ritual into a worthy sacrifice of praise. "Do not neglect good deeds and generosity."

Peace also requires a good relationship between ourselves and our leaders, be these in civil society or in the church: "Obey your leaders and submit to them." This admonition certainly must not be interpreted that we obey even to the point of committing sin! Therefore, we obey with sincere seeking of what is best for the entire community. "Submit to them"—again by putting the common good before private desires, certainly before selfish whims, even before personal ambition. The peaceful relationship here should bring "joy, not . . . sorrow, for that would be harmful to you."

To seek first the kingdom of God, that is, the common good of the entire community, united in Jesus, is exemplified for us in the reading from First Kings (Cycle II). Solomon is rewarded:

> because you have asked for this—not for a long life for yourself, nor for riches, nor for the life of your enemies, but for understanding . . .

It is interesting to note that this interchange between God and Solomon came "in a dream at night." Dream implies a mystical perception, a moment when we settle into the mystery of our better self, a time when we are not distracted by selfish wants and petty concerns. Rather a time with God.

Such a time was necessary—as Jesus remarked to the disciples: "Come by yourselves to an out-of-the-way place and rest a little." The peace which we are seeking is not a human creation; it is God's special gift. The rabbis considered the sabbath, along with the Torah, as God's supreme gift to his chosen people Israel. We need the long stretches of silence, undictated and unprogrammed, when God can appear "in a dream at night" and speak the right question to the best part of ourselves.

Yet, even this solitude was discovered by the people who "from all the towns hastened on foot to the place." When "Jesus saw a vast crowd, he pitied them, for they were like sheep without a shepherd and he began to teach them at great length." Jesus fulfills the injunction of Hebrews: to go to those outside the camp, to those wandering and in need. Jesus leaves behind the solitude and the sacred, to find the word of God while mingling with the crowd.

Peace means the integral harmony of all these aspects of our life, centered in the mystery of God's presence with us.

Prayer:

Lord, on this day of peace we turn to you, our shepherd. Led by you, even in dark valleys, there will be nothing that we want. In this solitude teach us your decrees so that with all our heart we will seek you in every moment of our lives.

Monday, 5th Week

Gen 1:1–19. God creates light, the sky, the earth and the sun, moon and stars on the first four days of creation.

1 Kgs 8:1–7, 9–13. Solomon brings the Ark into the newly constructed temple amid a magnificent ceremony. A cloud fills the sanctuary to symbolize the Lord's awesome presence.

Mark 6:53–56. Wherever Jesus went in Galilee, the sick were brought to him. Whoever touched him got well.

The reading from Genesis (Cycle I) provides the wide lens setting of the universe, the real sanctuary or throne room for God's majestic presence. The temple at Jerusalem, whose dedication is celebrated in First Kings (Cycle II), was considered a mirror of God's heavenly home, a reflection of the Lord's wondrous presence throughout the universe, the place for reenacting the redemptive acts of God in the history of his chosen people. These redemptive acts become

concentrated with strength and compassion in the acts of Jesus, the first and third reading—from Genesis and Mark—
speak about the *real* world, the same one that our eyes be-
hold and our feet walk upon, the very one where our bodies
feel aches and pains and reach out for healing. In between
the first and third reading there is the selection from First
Kings about the *symbolic* world of the temple. Symbol does
not mean unreal but rather acts as a sign of a deeper meaning
within the real and a means, therefore, enabling us to plummet into the mystery of God's presence in the ''real'' world
round about us.

It is important then to note that the sacred ceremonies
of the sanctuary—whether this sanctuary be the Holy of
Holies of the Jerusalem temple or the central area of our
churches with eucharistic table and tabernacle—lose their
meaning if they lose contact with the physical world of earth
and sky (even with the adornments of each, like stars or animals or fishes) or if they are no longer vivid reminders of
God's redemptive acts, healing us in our sickness, forgiving
us in our weakness, inspiring us with hope. At the same
time, we see that without sanctuary services and church liturgy we easily lose sight of the mysterious presence of God
in our universe and in our daily secular living.

This close interaction, as intimate as soul and body in
forming a human being, is emphasized in the verse that is
omitted from the reading today of Cycle II. Verse 9 is de-
leted, perhaps as an irrelevant detail that might distract us
from the magnificent dedication for the Jerusalem temple. It
reads:

The poles [by which the ark of the covenant was
carried throughout its long journeys from the days
of Moses, through the desert, into the promised
land, till this day of enthronement in the Holy of

Holies] were so long that their ends could be seen
from that part of the holy place adjoining the sanctuary; however, they could not be seen beyond.
They have remained there to this day.

This verse may reflect the impatient discontent of the priest-
scribe unhappy over the architectural blunder that did not
provide adequately for the poles of the Ark; they protruded
from the Holy of Holies into the adjoining room of the Holy
Place. The verse also reminds us of the extraordinary respect
of the scribes for sacred scripture, never to remove what
seemed unnecessary and certainly archaic. Yet divine wisdom might be informing us about an essential element of liturgy and church services. Just as the poles remained on the
side of the ark of the covenant, ready to carry it into the
streets and daily lives of the Israelite people, likewise our
church services should always be on the edge of moving into
our own personal lives, down our neighborhood streets, into
our city, state and international politics and business. All of
us are consecrated as levites to carry the Ark, to bring the
eucharist and our church services into our homes and activity, to be the living temples of God's presence.

We can find other indications for worthy liturgy and
faith-filled lives in the relationship of today's readings: Genesis (Cycle I) and Mark (Cycles I and II) coming from the
"real" world of secular life, First Kings (Cycle II) from the
symbolical world of the temple and church. Genesis declares clearly that the world where we look out to see the
light of the sun and where our ears strain to hear melodies
from the wind, is a world of beauty, indeed a sacred world.
Each activity is a response to God's word: "Let there be
light . . . let there be a dome in the middle of waters called
the sky . . . let there be luminaries in the dome of the sky."
The result of his creative word is always a delight for God.

After each creative moment, the text of Genesis records that "God saw how good the light was . . . and God saw how good it was [the earth with every kind of vegetation]." Too often we forget "how good" God sees it to be and we think of our world as a bad place, an ugly place or a place of temptation. We need the liturgy in which light, bread, wine, sound and music are all reconsecrated by the word of God, to tell us symbolically how good *all* light is, how good is *all* our food and drink, how good is *all* our sound and music.

In order that these physical objects be cleansed and reconsecrated they must be touched by the word of God and be obedient to the touch of Jesus, as in today's readings from Genesis and Mark. We are the instruments of God to cleanse and reconsecrate our good world. Our touch of kindness and love is the touch of Jesus; our word of forgiveness and encouragement is the word of God. Each touch heals; each word is creative. The liturgy then brings us to the heart of the mystery of our real world.

Prayer:

Lord, you have clothed our world with majesty and glory; through its splendor you yourself are robed in light as with a cloak. May we always enthrone you as our God, present all around us. May this faith in your daily presence in our everyday life be enkindled by the wonderful presence of your son Jesus in the Eucharist.

Tuesday, 5th Week

Gen 1:20—2:4. After forming man and woman to the divine likeness which God saw to be very good, God rested and blessed the seventh day.

1 Kgs 8:22–23, 27–30. Solomon concludes the temple ded-

ication ceremony by a prayer of faith (no God like you), of confidence (listen to our prayers), of humility (grant pardon).

Mark 7:1–13. The crime of nullifying God's word and of disregarding fundamental obligations by recourse to human traditions and practices.

Even more clearly than yesterday the Scriptures for today proclaim the sacredness of the created world. In concluding the work of creation, God first crowns his efforts across the universe by forming humankind to the divine image: "male and female he created them." While God saw that all his other works were good, after creating humankind, "God looked . . . and found it *very* good." Marriage, home and family become the most perfect image of the Godhead, and here God must continue to be present so as to maintain the divine image and the divine hope in every human thought and action. After this most divine of all works on the sixth day, God proceeded to "rest from all the work he had done" and so "blessed the seventh day." God does not withdraw from his newly created world in order to rest, but rather God rests in the midst of all its beauty and goodness. The world is temple and church; the sound of wind and surf, of bird and animal, are the hymns of praise.

From this background (Cycle I) we can reread the scriptural passages from First Kings (Cycle II) and from Mark's gospel. We begin to understand why Solomon or Jesus spoke as they did.

Solomon: "Can it indeed be that God dwells among us on earth? If the heavens and the highest heavens cannot contain you, *how much less this temple which I have built?*"
Jesus: "You have made a fine art of setting aside God's commandment [that the world, as blessed by God, is to be

respected and appreciated] in the interests of keeping your traditions!''

Solomon's prayer reminds us that God's normal temple is the universe, and for that reason the king asks how a human construction can contain God. Jesus argues that the produce of the world, its fruits and vegetables, are all clean because they have been created and blessed by God.

Nonetheless, Solomon *did* build the temple; Jesus *did* sanction fasting and abstinence from food. In this one book, the Bible, we read these diverse statements about eating and about fasting, about the entire world as God's temple and about constructing a temple or church for prayer. This diversity is not meant to cancel out and neutralize but rather to balance, nuance and enrich.

We construct a temple or church for the same reason that we build a home for a family. A home is necessary, at least for the large majority of humankind, in order to remain closely knit in love and intimacy, in order to share sorrow and joy and thereby support one another, in order to nourish and protect during sickness and old age. We need the home in order to learn how to love properly. Only then are we capable of extending our genuine love to the larger human family. Likewise, we benefit greatly from a church. Here we learn to be family or covenanted people, bonded to one another and to God. Through the church, we have a place for prayer and instruction and a community where people undertake various offices of teaching, of leading in prayer, and of prophetically challenging. Without the church we would have been deprived of the Scriptures, of the sacraments and the memory of saints.

Some of Solomon's most stirring words come from traditions that were preserved and handed down in the ancient sanctuaries of Palestine. His words reflect the Mosaic understanding of the covenant, first solemnized on Mount Sinai and preached thereafter by the levites in the sanctuaries:

> There is no God like you . . . You keep your covenant of kindness with your servants who are faithful to you with their whole heart.

These lines echo the first commandment: "I, the Lord, am your God . . . You shall not have other gods besides me," as well as the famous *shema‘* prayer of Israel: "Hear, O Israel! The Lord is our God, the Lord alone! Therefore, you shall love the Lord, your God, with all your heart, and with all your soul, and with all your strength." This interaction between temple and world, or in our case, between church and world, can be restated this way: we are not to live our entire life in church, but through the church we learn how to live our entire life, just as a child learns through the privacy of the home how to share love and fidelity in the public domain of the outside world.

To wash ourselves or our food before eating is good, if it induces respect, cleanliness and a relaxed spirit. Yet if it divides, leads to arguments and a better-than-thou spirit (as seems to have happened in today's gospel), then it violates the plan of God to form one large human family and the blessing of God to keep everything good in his eyes.

The Scriptures induce a total dedication and an integral service. The Bible is continually cutting down the barriers which we raise. If the word of God sanctions walls for temple and home, it is with the intention of training us to live in the world outside those walls. When we are thoroughly at home in the outside world, then we are ready for heaven, "the highest heavens," where all God's children are at home. Therefore, Jesus could not tolerate separations that divide and split apart. People who favor such divisiveness are the hypocrites condemned by the Scripture:

> This people pays me lip service
> but their heart is far from me.

Prayer:

Lord, how lovely is your dwelling place. Here we find a home and here we learn how to transform the entire world into a home where your sacred presence is ever more manifest. You have put us in charge of your world, help us always to love and respect this, your holy temple.

Wednesday, 5th Week

Gen 2:5–9, 15–17. God creates Adam and places this first human being in the garden to cultivate it. There is a prohibition not to eat of the tree of knowledge of good and bad.

1 Kgs 10:1–10. The Queen of Sheba visits Solomon to find out for herself about his wisdom, riches and good judgment.

Mark 7:14–23. That which enters into us does not render us impure; it is rather the wicked designs from the deep recesses of the heart that constitute impurity.

Within the story of creation (Cycle I) and the account of the visit to King Solomon by the Queen of Sheba (Cycle II), our attention may be first attracted by the external grandeur of the scene, yet upon further reflection we discover at the heart an interior element of discipline and wisdom.

The Lord God planted a garden with all kinds of things

"delightful to look at and good for food," and placed Adam within it "to cultivate and care for it." Within the garden was the tree of knowledge of good and evil whose fruit Adam was not to eat. Adam was expected to exercise self-control and a humble regard for the wisdom of God's instructions.

When we turn to the reading from First Kings, at the center of all the glitter and wealth was Solomon's "great wisdom." We remember Solomon's prayer at Gibeon that God "give your servant an understanding heart to judge your people and to distinguish right from wrong" (Saturday, 4th Week). Because Solomon requested wisdom rather than wealth or a long life, God declared: "I will give you what you have not asked for, such riches and glory that among kings there is not your like." Wisdom then remained at the heart, integrating and balancing all the external wonder.

Jesus' words to his disciples in today's reading from Mark develop this same, traditional idea. That which is outside is good. Whatever we eat or drink is clean and healthy. Evil comes from the human heart, and from a wicked heart flow those crimes and offenses which corrode and corrupt the world about us.

The universe is not only good, but it is much better than we deserve. According to the ancient Book of Genesis we perceive this fact as we carefully follow the steps by which Adam is placed within the garden of paradise.

1) The earth was barren, for the Lord God had sent no rain;
2) The Lord God sends rain and opens the springs of water beneath the earth;
3) The Lord God formed Adam out of the clay and blew into his nostrils the breath of life;

4) The Lord God planted a garden . . . and there he placed the man whom he had formed.

The story teller wants to impress upon us—for every story has a point which a careful reader will not miss—that the creation of human life needed a special intervention of God who breathed the breath of life into man; that the garden was not the result of human labor and ingenuity but was prepared ahead of time by God. We can conclude that the goodness inside of each human person and the goodness outside are both "supernatural," in that it exceeds what we can do by ourselves and what we deserve.

The wisdom, then, to make the best use of the world also lies beyond the reach of our intelligence. It comes from the vigorous activity of our intellect, of course, but also from our intellect illumined by God's assisting grace. It is a type of wisdom that includes a kindly regard for others, a humble attitude to care for the needs of our neighbor, a strength not to be selfish. This wisdom also results from living ever more frequently and for ever more prolonged periods of time with God in prayer. A sensitivity towards God, a remembrance of God's gracious acts for us in the Scriptures, a joy from offering praise and adoration to such a God—these all belong to the wisdom by which good judgment is formed.

Without this interior wisdom, wicked designs begin to take shape within our heart. Jesus names these evil actions, almost the reverse of the ten commandments: fornication, theft, murder. With these offenses he also includes others that seem less malicious: greed, arrogance, an obtuse spirit. Perhaps Jesus is reminding us that we cannot stop with greed, arrogance and an obtuse spirit. If we tolerate these bad habits and unsavory attitudes, we will easily slip into worse sins.

The wisdom by which we direct our lives must be sincere and fully supernatural, open always, as we read in the creation of the first human being, to the breath of God's Holy Spirit. At the base of our existence lies that intuitive, secret wisdom, the fruit of living prayerfully in God's presence and of responding humbly and obediently to the movements of God's spirit within us.

Prayer:

Lord, we commit our ways to your guidance. Do not allow our steps to falter. Through your providential care let justice dawn for us like the morning light. Then we can join the chorus of the universe, praising you for gifts beyond our merit, beyond our dreams.

Thursday, 5th Week

Gen 2:18–25. God forms woman who alone of all earth's creatures stands equal to man. Both from the same substance, man and woman are to be united as one body.

1 Kgs 11:4–13. Solomon's sins are traced to the influence of his pagan wives; as punishment his kingdom will be divided.

Mark 4:24–30. A Syro-Phoenician woman, by her humble, persevering faith, induces Jesus to cure her daughter despite his reluctance.

Women occupy the center role in today's biblical readings: in Genesis (Cycle I) the first woman heals the loneliness of man, measures up equal to him in a way that no other creature could, and the two are united, as the text declares, as one body. While woman brings joy and stability into the life of the first man in Genesis, we find that women are held responsible, at least in part, for the apostasy of Solomon (Cycle II). These are pagan women. Finally, in the gospel a pagan woman surprises Jesus with her faith and humble perseverance.

This convergence of biblical passages leads to important insights not only about the relation of the sexes but also about healthy tensions in family, friendship and community. Their differences as man and woman along with diversity in personality, talents and interests help people to complement one another and challenge one another to grow. No matter how we interpret the text of Genesis, from a literalist to a very metaphorical way, we must always maintain that woman and man, when separated from each other, are each lacking important gifts and qualities. The union by which they complement one another is to be intimate, permanent and total. Most of all, it is to enable the image of God, divine goodness, strength and fidelity, to be manifest. In this way marriage sets the pattern for all human friendship and community. It is created in the first paradise. It is completed only in the second and everlasting paradise of heaven.

Our reflection has led us away from the initial insight, the role of women in today's biblical passages. It is helpful to note that women in the Scriptures are modeling for both men and women, and men are modeling for both women and men. Scripture has a universal message. And what is scattered and fragmented must be reunited in Jesus. We are reminded of the familiar passage of Paul to the Galatians:

> There does not exist among you Jew or Greek, slave or free person, male or female. All are one in Christ Jesus. Furthermore, if you belong to Christ, you are the descendants of Abraham, which means you inherit all that was promised (Gal 3:28–29).

Faith in Jesus, then, even overcomes biological laws of generation. People whose ancestors were not Jewish are made children of Abraham by their union with Jesus, the new Israel, and so share in the promises.

The reading from Genesis challenges us to place no lesser earthly creature or goal before another human being, particularly before our spouse, friends, neighbor or community member. We read how God led Adam through the universe to see all of its life and beauty, but "none proved to be a suitable partner." Like Adam each of us ought to be willing to drop or forego every other desire and ambition for the sake of the other person. Adam exclaimed: "This one, at last, is bone of my bones and flesh of my flesh." If a spouse is to leave father and mother and cling to the other, then each of us has a divine mandate to put nothing before our love and loyalty for the other person. Jesus put it still more heroically and totally:

> There is no greater love than this:
> to lay down one's life for one's friends (John 15:13).

In this context we understand Jesus' other words:

> Whoever tries to preserve their life will lose
> it; whoever loses it will keep it (Luke 17:33).

Therefore, not only do we refuse to put any other object before our spouse, friend or community member, but we do not even place ourselves in preference to them.

The reading from First Kings (Cycle II) expresses the same demand of total loyalty and intimate love, but this time in a negative way. Solomon's heart is said to have turned to other gods by the coaxing of his wives. Love and friendship make many demands upon the other; we need one another badly. In the intimacy and immediacy of living together, we do not normally cross-question and suspect the other party. We are generally acting correctly when we tend to say "Yes!" A positive answer would always seem more in accord with God's will then a divisive, negative reply. Under such circumstances we can take advantage of the other person and hurt them badly. When suspicion and division erupt, the healing process is long and difficult.

How long and difficult is shown in today's gospel. Jesus is reluctant to divert attention away from his own chosen people, Israel, to attend to the pagan woman. There is no way by which we can soften and explain away the harsh reply of Jesus. Listening to Jesus' reply in the setting of today's other readings, we understand that Jesus would not repeat the mistakes of Solomon and interact closely and disastrously with the gentiles. The division is healed by humility, perseverance and love for another, her child. Not for selfish pleasure or personal gain, but for the sake of her daughter, the woman diverts Jesus' harsh words by replying:

> Please, Lord! Even the dogs under the table eat the
> family's leavings.

This answer was too much for Jesus to deal with. He heals the daughter but he also says to the woman: "Be off now!" Jesus needed more time before he could deal with the old separation and the new bond of union.

Prayer:

Lord, husbands and wives, friends in a neighborhood, brothers and sisters in religious communities, these are like fruitful vines in the recesses of your home; the fruit of this love like olive plants around your table. May we always find our union with one another in you, Lord Jesus, and in this love may you always preserve us from the idolatry of preferring other pleasures and ambitions to the ones we love.

Friday, 5th Week

Gen 3:1–8. Woman and man disobey God's directions and attempt to hide from God in the garden. They realized that they were naked and made clothing for themselves.

1 Kgs 11:29–32; 12:19. The prophet Ahijah announces the breakup of David's kingdom; ten of the twelve tribes will align themselves with Jeroboam as their king.

Mark 7:31–37. Jesus cures a deaf man also suffering from a speech impediment; the people's ''amazement went beyond all bounds.''

The first reading (Cycle I) tells of paradise lost; the gospel, of paradise regained. The passage from First Kings (Cycle II) situates us in the long stretch of time in between the first and last moments of salvation history. Even though paradise lost and regained holds our attention, we are reminded even here of the human, physical aspects of this paradise. In Genesis man and woman become ashamed of their nakedness; up to the time of their sin, they experienced no shame nor fear before one another. Every aspect of themselves was created to the image of God and was seen by God and themselves as very good. These same earthly, physical aspects of paradise show up again in the gospel. In order to cure the deaf man who also suffered from a speech impediment, we are told that Jesus ''put his fingers in the man's ears and, spitting, touched his tongue [with saliva]; then he looked up to heaven and emitted a groan. He said to him [in their native Aramaic language], 'Ephphatha!' '' Jesus' words and action, even his *groan* in distress over the man's disability and in wonder over God's miraculous action, all manifest the *human* way by which the man was led back into paradise.

That Mark intends paradise, or we may say, the final eschatological age, becomes clear to us as we read the gospel passage more carefully. The phrase, ''he makes the deaf hear and the mute speak'' is drawn from the prophecy of Isaiah, where ''those whom the Lord has ransomed will return and enter Zion singing, crowned with everlasting joy.'' The fulfillment of all messianic prophecies is at hand:

> The desert and the parched land will exult;
>> the steppe will rejoice and bloom. . . .
> They will see the glory of the Lord,
>> the splendor of our God. . . .
> Here is your God,
>> he comes with vindication . . . to save you.
> Then will the eyes of the blind be opened,
>> the ears of the deaf be cleared (Isa 35:1–5).

In fulfilling the prophecy, however, Jesus reaches beyond the vision of Isaiah. The prophet concludes this vision, abounding with light, music and dancing (v. 6, ''Then the lame will leap like the stag''), by the joyous procession entering ''*Zion* singing and crowned with everlasting joy.'' Zion will now receive foreigners as well as Israelites, someone like this gentile man who lived in the Greek settlements of the Decapolis or ''Ten Cities.'' Jesus is flashing a hint of universal salvation, something which we already observed in yesterday's gospel about the Syro-Phoenician woman.

We can contrast the two paradises, lost and regained. In Genesis man and woman, once they had sinned, realized that they were naked and felt ashamed. In the gospel, once the man is healed of his deafness and speech impediment, every other impediment is dropped. With joyful spontaneity he forgets at once the injunction from Jesus "not to tell anyone." Not only the man himself but everyone else announces the good news of what Jesus has accomplished. The gospel has almost a playful interaction here:

> Then he enjoined them strictly not to tell anyone;
> but the more he ordered them not to, the more they
> proclaimed it!

The text implies: as often as Jesus kept on [continuously] telling them [the form of the Greek verb indicates repeated, unsuccessful attempts!] all the more abundantly and frequently did they keep on announcing the good news.

The first parents left paradise and at once felt compelled to surround themselves with defenses against the other person. Fear of themselves and of others inhibited the spontaneity and trust of their relationship. The man cured of deafness and speech impediment seems to toss all restrictions to the wind, dancing, singing, leaping "like a stag," shouting and proclaiming the good news. We lose paradise and we reenter paradise as human beings with physical bodies as well as with spiritual souls. In fact, the Scriptures seem to focus more upon the earthly expressions of joy rather than upon its spiritual source.

In between the two scenes of paradise stands the reading from First Kings (Cycle II). The kingdom of David is to be rent apart and ten of the twelve tribes will transfer their loyalty from the house of David to Jeroboam. We could advance any number of human reasons for this schism. For the moment we observe that God is sanctioning this division. The northern ten tribes will not only punish David and Solomon, but they will also be God's instrument for preserving some of the most important traditions from Moses and for advancing the prophetic movement. Within the northern kingdom there will emerge the first two of the classical, writing prophets, Amos and Hosea. In fact, the section from Isaiah, chap. 35, quoted earlier in this meditation, comes from a northern influence. We are learning more each day how the foreigner is not simply converted but brings a richness of insight into the mystery of God which we may have been overlooking.

Prayer:

You, Lord, our God, bring us forth from our sins and oppression; you heal all of our disabilities. You are our shelter, our home where we sing glad cries of freedom. We confess our faults and come again to you for healing. We remember your promise of paradise, where with body and soul we will dance in your presence.

Saturday, 5th Week

Gen 3:9–24. The Lord God interrogates man and woman, and then issues a sentence of condemnation against serpent, man and woman. Death is one of the penalties and also expulsion from the garden.

1 Kgs 12:26–32; 13:33–34. Jeroboam, the first king of the north, makes his own sanctuaries, priests and feastdays.

Mark 8:1–10. Jesus, out of compassion for hungry people, multiplies bread and fish for about 4000 people.

We find a cycle of life in today's scripture. In Genesis (Cycle I) we have already heard how God created human-kind out of the earth, and this day our first parents are con-demned to "return to the ground from which you were taken." The gospel seems to repeat this cycle on a different, more optimistic note. Men and women are tired, in fact so weak, comments Jesus, that "if I send them home hungry, they will collapse on the way." People are returning to the earth by reason of their earthly origin. Jesus, however, mul-tiplies bread and fish, and everyone returns not to the earth but to their homes with renewed vigor. In Genesis Adam and Eve ate the forbidden food and die; in the gospel their children eat the heavenly food and live! The reading from First Kings (Cycle II) offers another clue why life so often leads to death rather than to a new life. King Jeroboam acts out of personal ambition and false fear.

The difference between life and death lies within our-selves and our motives for acting. Earth is not evil. Cer-tainly not, if it provides God with the material for molding man and woman—and if in the days of Jesus it produced the bread and indirectly the fish, the subject of Jesus' miracle and the food of new life for the people. Even in the First Book of Kings the break of the northern tribes from the Da-vidic dynasty at Jerusalem was not in itself an evil act. Yes-terday the prophet Ahijah announced that it would happen in the name of the Lord God. As we reread the Scriptures for further direction, we begin to see the way that leads, not to death, but to life:

1) to receive whatever we possess as a gift from God;
2) to look upon the abundance of good things which surround us on earth as blessings to be shared;
3) to avoid selfish ambition and the unhealthy, suspi-

cious fear which always accompanies such ambition;

4) to be honest and admit our failures and learn from them, rather than put the blame on someone else, as did Adam and Eve.

As we ponder the Scriptural passages for today, we will be able to hear God's word revealing a personal message for each of us.

The ways that lead to death can entrap us in the secular world and in the religious realm. In Genesis we find man and woman living thoroughly with the secular—by that we mean, living before the organization of religion with its sanctuaries or church, priests or ministers, ritual and ceremonies. Driven by pride, by a desire to master the world and by an ambition to control others, man and woman sinned. These are the sins of secular society. In the Book of Kings, the way to death comes from the religious realm. Jeroboam uses the instruments of religion to commit his sin. He deals with priesthood, sanctuaries and feastdays to control the riches of the northern kingdom and to prevent peace and reunion with the south. By jealousy he kept north and south, which both professed the same religion, at each other's throat.

Again we see that the difference between life and death is not *out there* but inside ourselves. Perhaps, we need to add—not entirely within ourselves but how we react to God—with trust, love, and gratitude, with obedience and hope, with the godly spirit to share as God has shared, even with indifference to personal ambition. It is amazing how quickly and simply the gospel ends. After the magnificent miracle of feeding ''about four thousand'' from seven loaves of bread and a few small fishes, the gospel ends abruptly:

He dismissed them and got into the boat with his disciples to go to the neighborhood of Dalmanutha.

Acting out of compassion, not ambition, Jesus did not make a living from miracles. The happiness of seeing others restored to life and strength was its own joy!

Prayer:

Lord, teach us to number our days aright that we may gain wisdom. The riches and beauty of this earth come and go quickly, yet with your blessing they can become a means of new life for ourselves and for others. Never let us forget your wonders, accomplished out of compassion for us. Then we will share your gifts generously and gain eternal life.

Monday, 6th Week

Gen 4:1–5,25. Cain kills Abel out of jealousy and becomes a restless wanderer. Yet even then God put a mark of protection on Cain.

James 1:1–11. Trials test and strengthen our faith. Whatever we ask, believing and not doubting the word, will be given to us. Riches fade away.

Mark 8:11–13. Jesus refuses to accede to the Pharisees who demanded a sign. He gets into the boat and goes to the other side.

Faith is at the heart of today's word from God. In two of the most theological, in-depth presentations of the New Testament, the Epistle to the Romans and the Epistle to the Hebrews, faith becomes both the basis and the conclusion of the Christian life on earth. In Romans chap. 1, Paul writes:

''The just person lives by faith''; and the Epistle to the Hebrews summarizes not only its own understanding of Jesus but the entire Old Testament in chap. 11 by stating:

> Faith is the confident assurance concerning what we hope for, and conviction about things we do not see. Because of faith our ancestors were approved by God (Heb 11:1).

Twice, in fact, Hebrews refers to the incident of Cain and Abel, the subject of the first reading (Cycle I):

> By faith Abel offered God a sacrifice greater than Cain's. Because of this he was attested to be just, God himself having borne witness to him, on account of his gifts; therefore, although Abel is dead, he still speaks (Heb 11:4).

Later in the same Epistle, we read where faith has brought us:

> You have drawn near . . . to Jesus, the mediator of a new covenant, and to the sprinkled blood which speaks more eloquently than that of Abel (Heb 12:24).

We see how faith, indeed, is the centerpiece of biblical religion, yet we must inquire further and see what is the heart of faith. Negatively, we learn from the gospel that faith does not revolve around miracles. When jealous and suspicious people test Jesus and look for some heavenly sign, Jesus sighs in the depth of his spirit. He must have thought to himself, so I must work miracles to prove myself!

The greater the miracle, the greater the love! Human beings can then judge for themselves and measure God!

The Epistle of James takes our reflections in the opposite direction—not in the way of miracles that overcome all barriers and difficulties but in the way of "pure joy when you are involved in every sort of trial." James adds:

> When your faith is tested this makes for endurance. Let endurance come to its perfection so that you may be fully mature and lacking in nothing.

Faith then is linked with loyalty, steadiness, dependability. Faith is not self-confidence so much as it is confidence arising from God's fidelity. Faith means that our love for God and for others will peer through darkness and see hope and new life. Faith means that the blood of Abel like the blood of Jesus cries out from the earth for compassion and forgiveness and for the sealing of a new covenant. Trials unto death which even wring this price of blood from us seal the covenant of love and loyalty—and the bond of one, shared life—all the more securely.

Such faith is not "devious and erratic." It does not "disappear 'like the flower of the field.' " It also catches up with us in our restless wandering and persistent guilt. Cain might run away from his family but he could not run away from God. "The Lord put a mark on Cain," a mark of divine protection, a pledge of God's faith. Abel's blood calls out from the earth, so that the bonds of family and life can be reinstated.

When some people responded to Jesus with suspicion, fear and jealousy, "he left them, got into the boat again, and went off." Jesus becomes the wanderer! Such dispositions do not bring Jesus into our midst; he remains only with people of faith, compassion and forgiveness.

Prayer:

Once I went astray, Lord, but your love caught up with me, comforted me and enabled me to pray, "Be kind to me, O Lord, and I shall live." You will let your voice resound through thunder and trials and I will be brought into your holy temple where "all say, 'Glory!' "

Tuesday, 6th Week

Gen 6:5–8; 7:1–5,10. The beginning of Noah's flood, caused by human wickedness and the Lord's regret at creating the human race.

James 1:12–18. God tempts no one but rather is the giver of every good gift. He wills to bring us to birth with a word spoken in truth.

Mark 8:14–21. Be on your guard of the yeast of the Pharisees and the yeast of Herod. The disciples remained blinded to Jesus' wonderment. "Do you still not see or comprehend?"

At first reading today's biblical passages seem to be concerned entirely with externals. We are fascinated by the story of Noah and the flood that covered the earth. We hear James speaking about heavenly luminaries and earthly temptation, about gifts of life and penalties of death. In Mark we read about the disciples who have but one loaf of bread as they embark on a hard pull across the Sea of Galilee.

Our discussion, even our theology, must begin with externals. It is the sight of the poor, the oppressed or the persecuted that stirs us into considering the purpose of suffering in God's providence. The behavior of the people in the days of Noah evoked regret in God's heart and that statement from Genesis raises all sorts of theological problems: how can God regret? did God make a mistake? does God change the divine mind? Similarly in the gospel Jesus' response to the disciples turned into a volley of questions which certainly evince surprise on Jesus' part that his followers would act as they did:

> Why do you suppose that it is because
>   you have no bread?
> Do you still not see or comprehend?
> Are your minds completely blinded?
> Have you eyes but no sight?
> Ears but no hearing?
> Do you remember when I broke the five loaves . . .?

The gospel passage ends on a question:

> Do you still not understand?

It is important that we remain alive to our external world and even by intuition or keen awareness pick up on events around us. Jesus shows that type of delicate perception on many occasions: the gospel will say that he reads the hearts of others. Each small external movement in another person—even the raising of an eyebrow or the far-away look in someone's eyes—was perceived by Jesus and read for its meaning. We are told in today's gospel: "The disciples concluded *among themselves* that it was because they had no bread," but in the meanwhile Jesus was "aware of this" and knew what they had been quietly discussing in their closed ranks. Not only does the Bible show how God in the Old Testament and Jesus in the New discerned the least movement of life in the human family, but this astuteness led to profound religious or theological conclusions.

We begin with the externals but we must not remain with them. For this reason it is not a good method of biblical interpretation, as in the case of Noah's flood, to exhaust ourselves, arguing about the externals: did it really cover the earth? could all those animals really be contained within the ark? In fact, archaeological studies show that mammoth floods swept across large areas of land in Mesopotamia and gave rise to flood stories, from which the biblical narrative drew some of its details—yet each of these flood stories, whether in the religious annals of the Akkadians or Sumerians or Hebrews stresses the religious meaning and adapts the externals to show the writer's struggling with theological issues.

The flood story in Genesis begins with the interior dispositions of the human heart; these were immediately apparent—to the perceptive person—from externals:

> When the Lord saw how great was the human
> wickedness on earth, and how *no desire that his
> heart conceived* was even anything but evil, *he re-
> gretted* that he had made the human family on
> earth, and *his heart was grieved.*

The Scriptures move from external actions to the desire of the human heart and to regret in God's heart.

Likewise in James' Epistle the initial moment is located in the externals, whether it be holding out to the end through trial . . . or passions that lure a person into sin . . . or worthwhile gifts and genuine benefits from the Father of the heavenly luminaries. Yet already we perceive the movement of the spirit and the silent beating of the heart. How else can anyone persevere till the end unless by God's special gifts of fidelity and long-suffering patience and deeply rooted hope in others. In this context we can interpret James' final sentence:

> God wills to bring us to birth *with a good word spoken in truth* so that we may be a kind of first-fruit of his creatures.

God's word, placed deeply within our heart, induces the good fruit in our lives.

If at times, we are left with a question, or as in today's gospel with a whole series of them, God wants us to remain within our hearts, listening, contemplating, wondering, seeking, correcting and most of all just *being* in God's presence.

Prayer:

Lord, help me to be delicately aware of the least moment of sorrow or joy in my neighbor and especially in members of my family or community, so that from these small external manifestations I may be attentive to their heart and secret needs and hopes. Then from such charity within our hearts and in our midst we can truly give you "Glory!" in the temple of human life and sustain one another with your kindness and comfort.

Wednesday, 6th Week

Gen 8:6, 13, 20–22. From the dove Noah learns that the flood is over and offers sacrifice to the Lord who "smelled the sweet odor [and] said, 'Never again will I doom the earth because of humankind.' "

James 1:19–27. Be a doer of the word, not an idle listener.

Humbly welcome the word that has taken root in you, with its power to save you.

Mark 8:22–26. Jesus cures the blind man in stages—privately, with spittle and the touch of his hands.

The gospel alerts us to the long, gradual process by which we come to the light of truth and to the persistent strength to follow the way of truth. The reading from Genesis (Cycle I) points out dramatically that the period of the flood must run its full course and that the period of the earth's return to normal existence cannot be rushed. James' epistle (Cycle II) appears like concentrated vitamins or a compressed dictionary of moral instructions; we know instinctively that time is needed to comply with a list as long as this one.

The miracle story in today's gospel occurs only in the Gospel of Mark; it was not repeated nor even adapted by Matthew and Luke, even though these evangelists relied heavily upon Mark. This is also the only miracle which Jesus worked in stages. Jesus even uses such lowly human substance as spittle!

Jesus' condescension to live and even to work his miracles on our human level offers great comfort. There is first of all the delicate consideration for the blind man. Jesus does not make a public exhibition of him but "took the blind man's hand and led him outside the village." We must picture the incident to realize its gentle compassion: to take by the hand and lead away from the crowd. "Putting spittle on his eyes" and touching the closed eyelids with his fingers, Jesus is bonding himself all the more closely with the blind man. After all, the man cannot see the tender sorrow in Jesus' eyes at the sight of this disability, but he can *feel* the clasp of Jesus' hand and touch of his fingers, even the warmth and smoothness of Jesus' spittle over his eyelids.

Jesus, it seems, is not so much conforming to pagan ritual practices but rather adapting himself to the human condition which he began to share in the womb of Mary, his mother.

The stages of the miracle are noteworthy: first, people looked like walking trees; then, "he could see everything clearly." These too are the stages of our growth in faith. At first, a new insight into God's goodness and its expectation that we gently "look after orphans and widows in their distress" (as we read in James' epistle) may appear like "walking trees," really not a part of our real world. We argue that we do not have the time, nor the material or financial resources to help the poor, the needy and the hungry. Jesus, however, presses the bond of our human flesh and family, places spittle again over our eyelids, gently presses and strokes and to our amazement—to paraphrase the gospel words: "we can see perfectly; our sight is restored and we can see everything clearly." We have the light to see our way for helping, for finding time and for locating resources to be of service and "look after orphans and widows."

The admonition of James no longer seems too difficult, too sudden and abrupt:

> Strip away all that is filthy, every vicious excess.
> Humbly welcome the word that has taken root in
> you, with its power to save you. Act on this word.
> If all you do is listen to it, you are deceiving your-
> selves.

Jesus never deceived himself, he acted on the word that was his very life and so possessed the power to save.

God respects our human condition, even when we ask for time because the word may still seem awkward and unnatural for us, like human beings who walk around like trees! Not only does this divine understanding of our human

situation appear in the length of the flood—the cleansing of
the world could not be rushed but must continue for the full
forty days—but in God's actions at the end of the flood. We
are told that "the Lord smelled the sweet odor [of Noah's
sacrifice and swore] 'Never again will I doom the earth.'"
God is said to understand our weakness, our "heart, evil
from the start," and so allows time for our conversion and
transformation through the seasons of our life:

> As long as the earth lasts,
>   seedtime and harvest,
>   cold and heat,
> Summer and winter,
>   and day and night
> shall not cease.

We are grateful to Mark for preserving the memory of Jesus'
respect for the stages of our life and its growth to sanctity.
The steps to sanctity follow the path of human existence,
only we cannot walk the path alone but must be like Jesus
who "took the blind man's hand and led him outside the village." We take the hand of our neighbor in need—and to
our surprise the hand that we clasp is leading us to our salvation—just as the blind man led Jesus into an episode that
preached redemption to us today.

Prayer:
    Lord, lead me to your holy mountain, so that I may
walk blamelessly, never with slander on my tongue nor with
reproach in my heart towards my neighbor. Then I can offer
a sacrifice of praise, take up the cup of salvation and call
upon the name of the Lord. When death comes and my eyes
open onto eternity, I will hear your sweet words: precious in
the eyes of the Lord is the death of his faithful one.

Thursday, 6th Week

Gen 9:1–13. The rainbow, a perpetual sign of God's covenant with Noah and the human race. Blood and life belong to God.

James 2:1–9. Show no favoritism. Love your neighbor as yourself.

Mark 8:27–33. Peter confesses Jesus as the Messiah but is reprimanded when he rejects Jesus' announcement that the Son of Man must suffer.

We are reminded of two signs of the covenant between God and the entire human race: the rainbow and the cross. And just as each spans the universe, likewise the covenant levels all men and women to an equal status with no favoritism in God's eyes. We are invited to reflect upon the glories and hopes of forming one human family and to realize the cost in suffering and sharing.

The rainbow and the cross symbolize God's bond of union with the human family. Each spans heaven and earth vertically; each reaches out over the world horizontally. Each presumes its full share of suffering and purification; each offers a strong promise of joy and completion. The rainbow appears after the rain has cleansed the atmosphere; it marks the end of the dark, massive clouds across the sky and is a herald of bright sunlight. In the reading from Genesis (Cycle I) the rainbow announces not only the end of Noah's flood but also gives a divine promise that such a flood will never again sweep the earth. Despite its lightsome beauty and ethereal cast, the rainbow will not let us forget the devastating sorrow of the flood. Only now, the flood is seen as a purifying force, washing the human race clean of its wickedness.

The same remarks are inspired by the cross. No one can

look at a cross, no matter how bejeweled and ornate it may be, without remembering the excruciating death of Jesus. Yet the cross is lifted high upon our churches and is worn as the sign and emblem of our victory over sin and hopelessness—Jesus' resurrection, the pledge of our own resurrection.

Both cross and rainbow, moreover, carry a message of universal salvation. Neither symbol is immediately linked with any particular religion, not even with the religion of Israel. Neither carries the connotations, specific to Israel, like the manna, symbol of the Eucharist, or the Ark of the covenant, symbol of God's presence in the temple of our bodies, or the holy city Jerusalem, symbol of heaven. Cross and rainbow belong to the world and in fact come to our attention first from the secular sphere of life. The cross was a Roman form of execution; the rainbow, visible to every human eye, no matter whether a person be a believer or not. At the heart of biblical religion, whether this religion be Judaism or Christianity, lies this secular, universal sign!

The Epistle of James (Cycle II) examines our conscience whether or not the universal sign of the cross and sign of the rainbow are genuinely operative in our own lives. The reading begins straightforwardly:

> Your faith in our Lord Jesus Christ glorified must
> not allow of favoritism.

We are not permitted to distinguish one person from another by external indications of wealth, power, prestige, rank or name. If we operate under these false standards, we are liable, as James reminds us, to "hand down corrupt decision." If we return for a moment to the symbol of the cross and the rainbow, we find that each reduces Jesus and ourselves, in fact, everyone, to a human being created by God to the divine likeness. On the cross, Jesus died naked; through the rainbow we look upon a world washed clean and appearing in its naked beauty. Returning to James' epistle, we find that we are not to judge other persons when

- they enter the assembly fashionably dressed, with rings on their fingers;
- they enter the assembly dressed in shabby clothes.

In God's eyes we are all poor and naked, beautiful and naked. *We are* what we have grown to be by our faith in God's goodness and fidelity, by our imitation of God's generosity and forgiveness.

Before James concludes his remarks, again returning to the topic of favoritism (''If you show favoritism, you commit sin and are convicted by the law as transgressors''), we read the biblical injunction:

You shall love your neighbor as yourself.

This rule was called the second commandment by Jesus; the first, of course, is to love God with our whole mind and heart and soul (Matt 22:36–40). It is repeated again by Paul in Romans:

Any other commandments there may be are all summed up in this, ''You shall love your neighbor as yourself'' (Rom 13:9).

These beautiful words are hard statements to put into practice. Little wonder that ''Peter then took Jesus aside and began to remonstrate with him''! Peter was truly ''tempting''

Jesus, who had to reply abruptly and sternly (sometimes, the only way to deal with temptation): "Get out of my sight, you satan!" Jesus' final words in the gospel seem to resonate again in James' epistle for today: "You are not judging by God's standards but by human standards."

The cross and the rainbow are beautiful and demanding, hopeful and distressing, dark/grim and open/fragile, deeply personal and fully universal. In this way we can truly answer Jesus' question to the disciples: "And you! Who do you say that I am?"

Prayer:

Lord, look down from your holy heights and wrap us round with the rainbow of your love and fidelity. Gather all of us into the one family of your compassion and forgiveness. You will care for me through the goodness which you spread abroad in the hearts of all men and women. Do not let us wander from the embrace of the cross, from the outreach of the rainbow.

Friday, 6th Week

Gen 11:1–9. At the tower of Babel, where people presumed to be independent of God, their language is scrambled and they themselves scattered in all directions.

James 2:14–24,26. Faith without works is as dead as a body without breath.

Mark 8:34–9:1. One must lose one's life for Jesus' sake and for the gospel, to save it. What advantage is it to gain the whole world and lose oneself?

Interesting parallels and enigmatic contrasts strike our attention. We see the human endeavor to construct the tower of Babel and the human agony to carry one's cross after Jesus up the hill of Calvary—the tower of Babel and the hill of Calvary, two ways of approaching heaven and being with God. One is evil, the other is good. In building the tower of Babel human works destroyed peace and harmony; in the epistle of James works become the proof that God is present within us and through faith these works unite us with our neighbor. The gospel too contrasts two forms of human activity: taking up one's cross and following Jesus; or acting for selfish, personal aggrandizement. Again one is good; the other is evil. The action which seems to destroy us is the one which heightens the vitality and permanence of our life; the action which seems to affirm and build us up turns upon us and destroys us.

> Whoever would save their life will lose it, but whoever loses their life for my sake and the gospel's will save it.

As we reread the biblical selections for today, we find clear evidence for this enigmatic statement of Jesus. The people who built their tower of Babel to protect and secure their life, actually lost everything in the process. Abraham who was willing to sacrifice his only son Isaac is blessed with promises of eternal offspring. The Epistle of James offers another example in v. 25, which is omitted from the liturgical reading for this day:

> Rahab the harlot will illustrate the point. Was she not justified by her works when she harbored the messengers and sent them out by a different route?

The Epistle of James includes two rather unusual examples from the hundreds available in the Hebrew Scriptures: first, Abraham, ignorantly thinking that he must worship God as heroically as any of his Canaanite neighbors and so be willing to kill his son of promise, Isaac: second, there is Rahab the harlot, also misguided in her profession! Scripture is telling us that God can see a brighter future and even a purer holiness in people who are basically sincere, honest and dependable than in others whose external behavior wraps them in mantles of splendid display, yet whose heart is shallow with its treasure located in esteem and reputation. These people can always say the proper religious formula to "the brother or sister [who] has nothing to wear and no food for the day," but do "not meet their bodily needs. What good is that?"

It is helpful to see that James bases the spirit of divine faith upon a firm and genuine human sincerity. Even if it seemed in Abraham's day to sacrifice one's best—even one's only child—to God, sincerity and common sense, the bonds of human flesh and loyalty, shouted "No!" and this religious insensitivity to the bonds of life was corrected ever after.

Yet the wisdom of the flesh and the natural bonds of life are not sufficient. They can lead to such pompous manifestations of strength and independence as to build a tower of Babel. This protective tower can be military build-up for an entire nation, unions or corporations that selfishly guard the rights of the privileged insider, elaborate religious ritual that make anyone look pious and good, or just personal excuses and private ways of avoiding responsibility so that we never risk making a mistake.

To act against our selfish inclinations and pious camouflage, to reach out spontaneously with practical assistance to the "brother or sister [with] nothing to wear and no food for the day" means to take up one's cross. To stand by someone in need and disgrace is to follow the way of Jesus who befriended prostitutes and tax collectors. It means to lose one's life.

As we lose our life, our security, our appearance of holiness by these good actions, we are manifesting extraordinary faith. We are being prompted to reach beyond human wisdom. We are being led by faith. In the depth of that faith we will have a glimpse of the true "reign of God established in power." Where we think to have lost everything and to have died, we are fully alive and so can never taste death. No one can take that vision from us, the memory of being with Jesus and sharing life with the most destitute. What can anyone offer in exchange for life such as this, happy in its ecstasy of wonder like Abraham's joy in the return of Isaac, self-restoring in dignity, like Rahab the harlot in saving the lives of the messengers.

Prayer:

Lord, you look down from heaven and peer in our hearts. May you not only see but also encourage true sincerity and honest helpfulness, so that what you have created us to be may become a full reality by our following the way of Jesus. May we be just as generous in sharing our life as was Jesus in carrying the cross of our sorrows.

Saturday, 6th Week

Heb 11:1–7. The incidents in Gen 1–11 manifest that "faith is the confident assurance concerning what we hope for, and conviction about things we do not see."

James 3:1–10. Guarding the tongue from inflammatory

speech that strikes a forest fire, lest "blessing and curse come out of the same mouth."

Mark 9:2–13. Jesus' transfiguration; Elijah has already come.

The necessity of faith is not removed even by the experience of visions! The experience of Jesus' transfiguration led to further questions, for it made the disciples—Peter, James and John, who were with Jesus on the mountain— perceive a still greater depth of meaning than they ever thought was present in their daily life. Visions do not stop the clock and freeze reality but are a momentary insight that will tend to leave us more restless and unsettled than before and will hurry us onward, not to another vision but to the reality of what God is promising us.

The transfiguration of Jesus, like his baptism and prayer in the garden of Gethsemane, enables us to see for a moment the intimate personal relation between Jesus and the Heavenly Father. We also see the close contact of Jesus with an earthly way of life, a life ending in death, and the overlapping of future glory with present difficulties in one profound mystery. At the beginning of his ministry, when Jesus was baptized by John, the heavens were split open and a voice was heard to say in a loving and approving way: "You are my beloved Son. On you my favor rests" (Mark 1:11). Yet this message of endearment was fraught with heavy responsibility: it resonated Ps 2 and the enthronement of the Davidic king along with Isa 42 and the vocation of the suffering servant. The transfiguration scene again presents Jesus in close bonds with God the Father—if the awesomeness is more profound as a cloud overshadows everyone and Jesus is flanked with Moses and Elijah, likewise is the fearful sense of impending doom more accepted. Coming down from the mount Jesus speaks of his death, and in Luke's gospel Jesus discusses his "exodus" or passage from this world to the next with Elijah and Moses during the vision (Luke 9:31). Finally, when the time for that passage was at hand, Jesus is once again wrapped in awesome prayer in the garden of Gethsemane, this time pleading over and over again:

> Abba (O Father), you have the power to do all things. Take this cup away from me. But let it be as you would have it, not as I (Mark 14:36).

The vision of God the Father plunged Jesus ever more thoroughly into a mystery—not just the mystery of divinity, nor simply the quiet of contemplative prayer, but the more profound mystery still of God's presence and hopes within the path of human life as it proceeds through many trials and triumphs to death. Death will be the supreme mystery of God's most intense, intimate presence with us as it was with Jesus. Only after we have traveled that passage from life through death to eternal life, only after "the Son of Man [or better translated, the child of earth] has risen from the dead," can we really tell what we have seen in the fleeting vision of Jesus' transformation before us on the mountain.

Visions then reenforce faith, in that they make faith all the more necessary and difficult. Yes, more difficult, because between surface reality and God's hopes, between our intuitions and what we can explain to ourselves and to others, the distance seems to widen even into an abyss.

The reading from Hebrews, chap. 11 (Cycle I) not only summarizes what we have been perusing from Genesis but also warns us: what you thought you understood is only half or less than half of the truth.

> *Through faith* we perceive that the worlds were created by the word of God. . . . *By faith* Abel of-

fered God a sacrifice greater than Cain's. . . . *By faith* Enoch was taken away.

Always by faith, and ''faith is confident assurance concerning what we hope for, and conviction *about things we do not see.*'' These opening words of today's reading base ''confident assurance'' upon ''things we do NOT see.'' When we think we see and understand, we should be filled with new questions. The wonder of God is certainly (not doubtfully!) so great that we know with ''confident assurance'' that it is far beyond what we think to see and understand.

The reading from James (Cycle II) brings us down to earth, with a jolt, no doubt about it. It can be linked with the theme of faith and the wonder of vision in this way: what we know about others is so little compared to the goodness and hope which God sees in them. Therefore, how careful we ought to be in talking about others, in spreading gossip and half-truths. If we aspire to teach others, then with what patience and humility. Perhaps, in the example of Jesus, our instruction ought to give insights which raise still more questions about the extent of God's goodness and about the heroic expectations of God for our human lives—even death.

Prayer:

Lord, I will praise your name forever! The mystery of your glorious majesty lies hidden in all your wondrous works around me. Keep me from speaking poorly of the most beautiful work of your creation, my brothers and sisters.

Monday, 7th Week

Sir 1:1–10. All wisdom comes from God and remains with
him forever. It produces true fear of the Lord that warms
the heart and gives length of days.

James 3:13–18. A wise spirit is not characterized by jealousy but by innocence, leniency, sympathy and peace.

Mark 9:14–29. The mute spirit which convulses the boy is
driven out by faith and prayer.

Three great and related moments in Mark's gospel—
Jesus' baptism, transfiguration and prayer in the garden (see
yesterday's meditation)—are each followed by struggle: Jesus' baptism by the Lord's wrestling with Satan in the
wasteland (Mark 1:12–13); the transfiguration by the disciples' futile contending with a demon in the mute boy; the
prayer in the garden where Jesus struggles with the will of
the heavenly Father amidst ''fear, distress and sorrow to the
point of death'' (Mark 14:34). Even though Mark is not
characterized like Luke as a gospel of prayer, nonetheless
each of these episodes is either surrounded or concluded by
prayer: Jesus spends the forty days in the wasteland in prayerful seclusion ''with the wild beasts and angels'' (1:13),
caught between heaven and earth, between overwhelming
goodness and demonic evil, in the grip of contemplative
prayer of the most fearful type. Today's episode of the mute
paralytic and demonic possession ends with the statement,
''This kind you can drive out only by prayer.'' In the garden
Jesus admonishes his disciples, ''Be on guard and pray that
you may not be put to the test'' (14:38).

In each case prayer carries a note of fear. Such fear can
turn into anxiety and worry, so that we are paralyzed. Fear
can reduce us to the condition of the mute boy, overwhelmed by some demonic force—either paralyzed or

thrown into a panic. That type of prayer is not healthy; it is not genuine comtemplation; it does not lead truly to the biblical understanding of fear of the Lord. Here we are assisted by the reading from Sirach, an Old Testament book introduced into Cycle I. As we learn from the last chapter of Sirach, this elderly gentleman conducted a "house of instruction"—in Hebrew, *beit midrash*—for noble youths (Sir 51:23). With serene strength and sure touch Sirach spoke about every aspect of human existence, ranging from the home into the business world, from study of the law to the entertainment of guests. Yet he always settled in a spirit of wonder, prayer and the true fear of the Lord.

> Extol God with renewed strength,
>   and weary not, though you cannot reach the
> end . . .
> It is the Lord who has made all things,
>   and to those who fear him he gives wisdom (Sir
>   44:32,35).

Today's reading from the opening poem also ends with the fear of the Lord which "is glory and splendor" and "warms the heart."

For this kind of fear to emerge in the midst of prayer, we need to meditate further upon the opening poem from the Book of Sirach: God's wisdom is spread across "heaven's height [and] earth's breadth," so great that no one can explore them. God "has poured her forth upon all his works [and] upon every living thing. He has lavished her upon his friends." This wonderful wisdom exists at the depth of our being and is also with God where "it remains forever." At the depths of our selves is a perception, an intuition, a divine spark of wonder, a godly way of holding everything together in harmony. Yet this wisdom is also so magnificent that "you cannot reach the end" of it. This type of wisdom leads to a fear that is "glory and splendor" and that "warms the heart."

The reading from James (Cycle II) provides us with another aspect of true prayer, linked also with the wisdom about which Sirach spoke. A "wise and understanding" person manifests "humility filled with good sense." James adds:

> Wisdom from above . . . is first of all innocent. It is also peaceable, lenient, docile, rich in sympathy and the kindly deeds that are its fruits, impartial and sincere. [It reaps] the harvest of justice [that has been] sown in peace.

When we review these qualities of prayer, we too cry out with the father of the mute and epileptic boy: "I do believe! Help my lack of trust!" The biblical appreciation of prayer may seem far beyond us. In fact, it is and we remember again Sirach's healthy advice: "weary not, though you cannot reach the end." What we strive to reach, we already possess at the depths of ourselves. Through Jesus we discover who we are, provided we persevere long in prayer and provided we balance our prayer with true and healthy fear, with humility and good sense.

Prayer:

Lord, as I look across the world, I find myself in your presence, as you are robed in the majesty of what I see. I believe. I trust. I seek your holy wisdom that will give joy to my heart and refresh my soul. In this prayerful spirit, I confidently struggle with demons.

Tuesday, 7th Week

Sir 2:1–11. Study the generations long past and understand; has anyone hoped in the Lord and been disappointed? Has anyone persevered in the fear of the Lord and been forsaken?

James 4:1–10. Recommendations to sincerity, humility and fidelity—shunning worldliness and selfishness.

Mark 9:30–37. Whoever welcomes a child such as this for my sake welcomes me. And whoever welcomes me welcomes, not me, but him who sent me.

The gospel directs us to welcome Jesus as one welcomes a child. In this way, Jesus adds, we welcome God our Parent and the Holy Spirit. Putting it this way, we are reversing the sequence yet not (let us hope) turning around the true meaning. How do we welcome Jesus as though Jesus were a child? In no way does Scripture want us to deny our adulthood: God's word is too close to earth and to reality for such masquerading as that.

The recommendation to welcome Jesus as one would welcome a child comes as a conclusion to today's gospel. Earlier in Mark we encounter Jesus' advice, rather his warning to his disciples:

If you wish to rank first, you must remain the last one of all and the servant of all.

We welcome or find Jesus then among the servants and the least important of all people. Just as children easily find other children in a group and quickly begin to play and enjoy themselves, so too we ought to gravitate towards the servants and the least. Childhood is not a matter of age only. A person who is lonely may be someone who not only feels isolated, perhaps rejected, but who also treasures beautiful memories and buried hope. Buried beneath many frustrations, yet these hopes are still genuine possibilities, waiting for the healing touch of kindness. A lonely person then is like the child who possesses tremendous possibilities within its life yet remains incapable of articulating them, maybe of even knowing what these hopes are.

To welcome Jesus as a child, then, is to open one's arms to the infinite possibilities that lie before us in life.

As we continue to move backwards in the gospel, we come upon the fearful, really un-childlike statement about being put to death and rising again after three days. Yet, isn't there a reckless spontaneity about children? If a child runs after a ball that has been thrown across the field, the child never looks at the ground. It has its eyes fixed on the falling ball. If the child trips and falls, it collapses upon the ground with such ease and freedom, that the child at once bounces up again. What we seem to lose for the sake of being a disciple of Jesus' we regain "after three days," that is, with the confidence that the loss will come to an end and will be returned to us a hundredfold.

In the passage from the Epistle of James (Cycle II), we seem to have left the child's world for ever. There is talk of "conflicts and disputes," of "inner cravings that make war within your members," of murder and envy. If we seem to have abandoned even the memory of receiving Jesus as one would receive a child, then we seriously need to reconsider our situation. We can find the way towards this conversion in the words:

God resists the proud
but bestows his favor on the lowly.

This quotation is drawn from the Greek version of the Book of Proverbs, 3:34. The other quotation which "Scripture says" strangely enough cannot be found in our extant Bible:

> The spirit he has implanted in us tends towards jealousy.

Evidently, James is drawing upon ancient traditions and bits of wisdom, from which the Bible was drawn but which the Bible did not exhaust, traditions that give true meaning and good sense to what has been written down in the Bible. The adult spirit, then, which tends towards jealousy needs to be turned back to the childlike spirit in its innocence and spontaneity.

It is often enough a difficult journey for adult persons to go backward to the memory and goodness of their childhood. It will cause them "to lament, to mourn and to weep. [It will seem that] laughter be turned into mourning and joy into sorrow," as James writes towards the end of today's reading. Yet as we get closer to our childhood, we are ever more relaxed and free and we bound upwards again. James ends with the assurance that the Lord "will raise you on high!"

As we reach still further back—not only coming to the first reading from Sirach (Cycle I) but also to our ancestors, in a sense our pre-childhood days, we realize how true it is:

> Study the generations long past and understand;
> has anyone hoped in the Lord and been disappointed?

We all possess the memory of great hopes joined with faith in the Lord's fidelity. This Lord, we are told, is "compassionate and merciful . . . he forgives sins, he saves in time of trouble.'' Sirach beautifully combines fear with confidence:

> You who fear the Lord, hope for good things,
> for lasting joy and mercy.

As we see any child, we think of the opening words from today's Bible passage in Sirach: ''prepare yourself for trials.'' Yet as we find again the child in each of us, we welcome Jesus. Our trials are united with Jesus' cross and resurrection, and we rebound with firm hope ''after three days.''

Prayer:

Lord, I commit my life to you and so I trust that I will dwell in your land and enjoy your security. You will not allow me to remain in shame. You will find the child in me. As you find me, I pray that I will turn to you as a little child and find my peace in you.

Wednesday, 7th Week

Sir 4:11–19. The long, delicate and sincere way of interacting with wisdom which brings happiness and reveals secrets.

James 4:13–17. Arrogant and pretentious claims are reprehensible. We do not know what kind of life will be ours tomorrow.

Mark 9:38–40. Jesus corrects the apostles who complain about someone, not of their company, casting out devils in Jesus' name.

Sirach, the wise and aged teacher of a Jerusalem school, tends towards caution and prudence (Cycle I); the gospel for today reaches outward almost with abandon: "Anyone who is not against us is with us." We begin to bridge the distance between the two readings from the advice given to us by James against arrogance and pretension (Cycle II).

It is generally agreed that wisdom is not easily acquired, principally because it depends upon human experience. What is wise seems at times distant and impersonal, difficult and trying. Sirach recognizes these hard facts when he writes with poetic flair:

> Wisdom walks with us [at first] as a stranger,
>   and she puts us to the test;
> Fear and dread she brings upon us
>   and tries us with her discipline;
> With her precepts she puts us to the proof,
>   until our heart is fully with her.

Sirach realizes that wisdom is not simply speculative ideas and a dictionary of facts. Wisdom blends and integrates, and most of all wisdom enables us to live and respond with one another as persons. We are not pushed around by facts and laws; we interact with patience and forebearance, with interest and enthusiasm, with responsibility and self-control. This kind of wisdom has to be grown into, slowly and carefully, so that it becomes totally ourselves. Sirach puts it this way:

> If we trust wisdom, we will possess her;
> our descendants too will inherit her.

Such wisdom is so thoroughly integrated into our character and person, that it is passed down within a family. At this point it might be likened to the wisdom that farmers transmit to their children, or even to the love and confidence that parents impart to infants by holding and caressing them.

This kind of wisdom is open and relaxed towards others. It enables us to live with love and consideration for our family, our neighbors, our co-workers. This wisdom is not stingy and fearful. Fearful persons cannot summon their full potential, whether for work or for joy.

As a very wise person, then, Jesus reprimanded his disciples for their jealousy and fear. They felt threatened, at least slighted by a man using the name of Jesus to expel demons. They said to Jesus—and we sense their satisfaction at such a decisive response:

> We tried to stop him, because he is not of our company.

Jesus' reply is just as decisive, and at the same time his words are strung together with strong wisdom. Jesus did not inquire about the doctrinal position of the other man but landed on solid, common sense ground.

> No one can perform a miracle in my name and at the same time speak ill of me. Anyone who is not against us is with us.

Words as simple as these are not easily learned; they are absorbed by long experience. Such a response, totally free of jealousy and fear, totally relaxed with nothing to lose, reflects a person at peace, peace in the biblical sense of a harmonious blending of all aspects of life, and therefore strong and secure.

While Jesus responded quickly, even picking up the final words of the disciple John, ''Do not try to stop him,''

nonetheless Jesus' reply came from a lifetime of walking the
path of wisdom, not as a stranger, with fear and dread, but
familiarly as a friend and with appreciation for its resources—as Sirach brings to our attention.

We are beginning to see the bridge between Sirach and
Mark's gospel. We will perceive the relationship even more
clearly by turning to the Epistle of James (Cycle II). Here
the central injunction advises us against arrogance, pretentious claims and selfish hoarding of resources. Such a life
can easily fall apart: ''You have no idea what kind of life
will be yours tomorrow.'' Truly wise persons can keep their
own counsel. They are rooted persons, not persons who
quickly make their profit and move off somewhere else.

If we walk life's path with wisdom, we become relaxed, generous and trustful. It is necessary to walk a long
time along that path with Jesus. In Mark's gospel we are already in chap. 9, and even one of Jesus' more intimate disciples, John, still doesn't manifest such wisdom.

Prayer:

Lord, my strength and trust are in you. Keep me faithful so that you can lead me to true wisdom. I cannot acquire
this gift by my own lowly endeavors. Through you there
will come that great peace which is bestowed upon everyone
who loves your law.

Thursday, 7th Week

Sir 5:1–8. Rely not on your wealth nor upon your strength;
    delay not your conversion to the Lord.
James 5:1–6. Those who heaped up treasures by injustice to

the poor will weep and wail over their final judgment. Your gold will devour your flesh like a fire.

Mark 9:41–50. A series of statements: reward for those who give a drink of water because of Christ; condemnation of those who give scandal; better to enter life with only one eye, hand or foot, than with both to be thrown into Gehenna.

Some of the statements of Jesus in today's gospel cannot be taken literally. In no way is Jesus demanding that we cut off hand or foot or gouge out an eye. Jesus' words might be understood in relation to his other remark brought to our attention last Friday (6th Week).

> Whoever would save their life will lose it, and whoever loses their life for my sake and the gospels' will save it (Mark 8:35).

As we place this latter statement alongside the one for today, Jesus is telling us: if we use both hands, both feet, both eyes and our other faculties exclusively for our selfish pleasure, we will lose everything. We will be thrown into Gehenna with both hands, both feet, both eyes and our other selfish possessions. They will be our downfall. But if we lose ourselves for Jesus' sake and for the sake of the gospel (that is, of spreading the good news of life, joy and trust), then we may seem to have only one foot, one hand and one eye for ourselves. We may seem to be entering into eternal life maimed. Actually we are preparing for the closest bonds possible with our brothers and sisters for all eternity. Together we will be sharing what others possess and forming one ''body'' with them.

In such a close, loving union, small acts of helpfulness take on a very special meaning:

> Anyone who gives you a drink of water because you belong to Christ will not, I assure you, go without their reward.

The Epistle of James (Cycle I) puts still more strength and bite into this position. Whatever we acquire unjustly as well as whatever we hold selfishly, to the harm of brother and sister, will turn against us:

> Your wealth has rotted, your fine wardrobe has grown moth-eaten, your gold and silver have corroded. [All these things] will devour your flesh like a fire.

James takes special note of "the just man [who] does not resist you." God does not forget the helpless person of whom we take advantage. Neither has God lost the memory of ourselves when we seem to be taken advantage of. These "shouts [of the poor and defenseless] have reached the ears of the Lord of hosts."

Offenses against charity and against silent and helpless persons have marred the lives of all of us. "All have sinned," Paul wrote very clearly (Rom 3:23). John put it in reverse:

> If we say, "We have never sinned," we make God a liar and his word finds no place in us (1 John 1:10).

Sirach, in Cycle I, is equally stern yet offers consoling advice. He makes it very clear: "Rely not on your wealth [nor upon] your strength.'' He even warns us: ''be not overconfident, adding sin upon sin.'' His final statement for today, however, is comforting, even if serious and absolute:

> Delay not your conversion to the Lord,
> put it not off from day to day.

God, this day, is offering the grace to save us from being cast into Gehenna with all of our healthy limbs, selfishly intact but with each one the center of regret and pain. Today—we cannot delay the conversion—God is giving us the *opportunity* to lose a hand, foot or eye in service of our neighbor. Or perhaps we can understand the statement better by saying: the opportunity to share hand, foot or eye; or better still, the opportunity to form a single body of love and loyalty as others walk with our feet, touch and work with our hands, see the beauty of life with our eyes. ''Today you have heard the voice of the Lord; harden not your heart'' (Ps 95:7–8).

Prayer:
Lord, happy shall I be if I hope in you. I have the promise of being like a tree, planted near running water whose fruit never ceases. Prevent me from being selfish, for then I will be blown away by the wind. Grant that I may know the happiness of the poor in spirit—poor by sharing hand, foot and eye; happy for never will I walk, touch or see alone.

Friday, 7th Week

Sir 6:5–7. Let your acquaintances be many, but one in a thousand your friend. A faithful friend is a sturdy shelter, a life-giving remedy found by those who fear God.

James 5:9–12. Take the prophets as your models in suffering hardship and in speaking the truth.

Mark 10:1–12. Jesus' condemnation of divorce and remarriage.

The gospel applies to marriage the ultimate conclusions to be reached from Sirach (Cycle I) and James (Cycle II) about friendship and truthfulness. If our acquaintances are to be many but only "one in a thousand" our confidant, then we might add, only one in ten thousand could be chosen as husband or wife. If we are to follow the example of Job and the prophets in our endeavor to suffer hardships, act patiently and speak truthfully—and this for the normal relationships of daily life—how much more long-suffering, patient and truthful we ought to be within the bond of marriage and family, of religious communities and church life.

A quality about friendship and marriage which sneaks up on us as we reread and meditate on today's scripture is the need to persevere over a long period of time. The selection from Sirach begins with the quick, passing salutation like "Good Morning!" Sirach opens his mini-essay on friendship by advising us:

A kind mouth multiplies friends,
and gracious lips prompt friendly greetings.

We begin with a smile; our first communication, imparted more intuitively than by direct statement, is one of interior joy and peace. We begin the day or the greeting in a good way—"Good Morning!" We show that we are at peace with ourselves and with God.

Sirach draws from long experience; this well tested wisdom is now being put to the service of the young people in his Jerusalem school (cf., Sir 51:23, "Come aside to me, you untutored, and take up lodging in the house of instruction"). Sirach is not only peaceful, he is also moderately cautious. His next pithy statement declares:

> When you gain a friend, first test that person,
> and be not too ready to trust that one.

Testing is done by observing if the friend remains "in time of distress." Does such a person take advantage of minor differences and tell "of the quarrel to your shame"?

This respected citizen of the holy city does not leave us in a suspicious frame of mind. Sirach gives the positive qualities of a true friend. Such a one turns out to be:

your other self	a treasure beyond price
a sturdy shelter	a life-saving remedy

Sirach sums up these qualities in a way typical of the sapiential movement in ancient Israel: "one who *fears God* behaves accordingly." Here, indeed, is a good insight, not only into the genuine friend but also into the fear of God. The true friend, as "a treasure . . . beyond price," turns out to be someone before whom we sometimes feel unworthy yet relaxed and happy, to whom we offer joy and fulfillment and yet seem to receive still greater joy and fulfillment in return. We sense a healthy fear of spoiling such a tender or delicate relationship. Such a fear resides in the depth of our greatest joy and is a God-given way of our remaining joyfully appreciative of the "treasure."

The transition from friendship to marriage is easy and spontaneous to recognize, yet long and serious to achieve. As friendship and marriage remain alive, the sturdiness of the relationship will necessarily be tested. When hardships

and misunderstandings will toss rocks and boulders in the
way, we are assisted by the blunt, even stern language of
James' Epistle (Cycle II):

> do not grumble against one another;
> look to the prophets ''as your models in
>   suffering hardships and in [practicing]
>   patience;''
> meditate upon the steadfastness of Job;
> you must not swear . . . Rather let your language
>   be ''yes'' if you mean yes and ''no'' if
>   you mean no.

Therefore, be dependable, honest, patient, quiet, steadfast.
These are the virtues that enable friendship and marriage to
journey over the mountain peaks, cold, windswept and
snowcapped, and so to reach the warm valley on the other
side. The Epistle of James, among the later New Testament
writings, touches on the later period of friendship and marriage, when trials and questions arise from within.

Friendship and marriage, to be genuine, are advised to
begin according to the careful, prudent advice of Sirach.
They need to overcome obstacles, catch their second wind,
and so reach the mountain top and begin the downward de-
scent of later life. What a pity to give up! In fact, what a be-
trayal of love it might be! In the stern language of Jesus such
a break must be called by the blunt, cutting and disastrous
word, ''adultery.'' Such a rending of love and trust was
never what God intended:

> At the beginning of creation God made them male
> and female; for this reason a person shall leave
> father and mother and the two shall become as
> one. They are no longer two but one flesh. There-

fore, let no human agency separate what God has joined.

Just as Sirach instructs us not to enter friendship—and by inference, marriage—lightly or quickly ("one in a thousand your confidant . . . first test that one . . . be not [even] ready to offer trust"), so also the final reading for today warns us just as seriously, do not disrupt and rend apart what God has united so carefully and so lovingly, so trustfully and so perseveringly.

Prayer:

Guide me, Lord, in the way of your instruction. My heart cries out for the love and help of friendship; my heart wants to give trust and delight in friendship. Share with me your kindness and mercy, your patience and forgiveness, so that my love and friendship be sustained by you and modeled upon you.

Saturday, 7th Week

Sir 17:1–15. God created us in the divine image, looks with favor upon our hearts, shows us his wonderful deeds that we may praise his holy name.

James 5:13–20. If in good health, sing a hymn of praise; but if sick, call in the elders, be anointed with oil and confess your sins. The prayers of a just person are powerful like Elijah's.

Mark 10:13–16. Jesus embraces and blesses the children who come to him; such is the kingdom of God.

The family or community is viewed from several angles or moments in its history. Sirach (Cycle I) seems to

stand above it all and allows his attention to make a grand
sweep from the beginning of time until the present, and to
include all the families and communities of earth. James'
epistle (Cycle II) concentrates on the adults and the sick
members of the family. Mark, on the contrary, looks to the
children. From reading the selection of Sirach we are left
with the conviction that families and communities cannot
survive without close bonds of loyalty, love and obedience.
James shows that we need the advice, prayers and anointing
of the elders. Mark is not too specific yet states clearly that
children model for us the correct attitude for belonging to
the Kingdom of God.

It is good to begin with Sirach where the dignity of human nature and of family relationships is stated with absolute certainty: "The Lord created humankind from the earth
and made us to the divine image." Even if the material substance is earthly, our shape, form and way of acting and
thinking image the divine. Sirach reaches into the details of
our bodily existence:

> He [God] forms the human tongues and eyes and
> ears and imparts to them an understanding heart.

Our tongues, eyes and ears are simply instruments by which
we communicate the desires and impressions of our heart. It
is in our ways of interacting with one another that the divine
way of life is most perfectly manifested.

God has no human body. Therefore, our imaging the
divine life must be in our actions with one another, our
bonds of love and loyalty, our creativity and fruitfulness,
our planting of wondrous mysteries at the heart of our actions. When God "looks with favor upon our hearts," the
divine image becomes apparent to others. "He shows his
glorious works."

Sirach sees the need of honesty and integrity; he recognizes the evil of sham and make-believe. Our "ways are ever known to him; they cannot be hidden from his eyes." Last of all, Sirach reaches outward to the world family of nations. He confesses the special election of Israel, who is "the Lord's own portion." That unique choice is available to all men and women through faith in Jesus. Here is the most complete blessing upon family and the most perfect of all divine images.

The Epistle of James concentrates upon the elderly and the sick members. Weakness and estrangement come upon every family, one way or another. Reconciliation reaches outward to include the spiritual or moral aspects—sin. It does not overlook the physical tensions that arise through sickness and offers prayers, anointing and the gathering of the elders around the sick person.

The healing is expected to be complete and integral, physical and spiritual. In answer to the question, "Is there anyone sick among you?" James recommends:

- ask for the elders of the church . . . to pray over the sick person, anointing that one with oil in the name of the Lord.
- declare your sins to one another, and pray for one another, that you may find healing.

And if someone should stray away, the other members of the community are not to ignore that brother or sister:

Remember this: the person who brings a sinner back from the [evil] way will save their own soul from death and cancel a multitude of sins.

At the heart, motivating this action we find kindliness and concern. At another place in Scripture we read:

> Above all, let your love for one another be constant, for love covers a multitude of sins (1 Pet 4:8).

Mark's gospel for today draws us to the children within the family. Here Jesus states a message inscribed deeply in the gospel and in our memory:

> It is to just such as these that the kingdom of God belongs.

From children the adults are asked to learn about the kingdom of peace and forgiveness, of life and hope, of trust and faith. We must never be too busy or too preoccupied to seek these virtues. The disciples considered Jesus' time and energy too precious for the Master to be distracted and bothered with the children whom "people were bringing . . . to have him touch them." At this Jesus became "indignant." Jesus, we are told, "embraced the children and blessed them, placing his hands on them." This human touch unites all three readings: Jesus embracing the children; the elders laying hands upon the sick and anointing them, God forming the tongues and eyes and ears of the human body. We must reach out and touch—of such is the Kingdom of God.

Prayer:

Lord, we know that we are dust, yet your touch of love and strength formed that dust into ourselves, made to your divine image and made to endure forever. As we reach out to touch others with love and help, may this lifting of our hands be like the evening sacrifice, like incense before you, a sweet smelling fragrance in which you take delight.

Monday, 8th Week

Sir 17:19–27. Repent from sin while you are still alive. The dead cannot praise God.
1 Pet 1:3–9. God is to be praised who brings us to a new birth which draws its life from the resurrection of Jesus Christ whom we love without seeing.
Mark 10:17–27. Go and sell what you possess and come follow me. Humanly it is impossible but with God all things are possible.

The book of Sirach, from which the readings in Year I are drawn represent one of the finest statements of Israelite religion up to the year 190 B.C. Sirach conducted a school (Sir 51:23) to train the sons of nobility in proper attitudes and behavior for all occasions *on earth*. A traditionalist in many ways, Sirach did not accept many new ideas in the air, like personal survival after death with reward and punishment. He took his theological stand close to the Sadducee priesthood who continued to deny the resurrection even in the days of Jesus and Paul (Matt 22:23; 1 Cor 15:12). In no way distracted by life after death, Sirach was able to concentrate upon a good and proper life on earth. He states very plainly in today's readings:

Who in the nether world can glorify the Most High
in place of the living who offer their praise?
No more can the dead give praise than those who have
never lived;
they glorify the Lord who are alive and well.

Sirach at the same time frequently slipped to the outer edge of earthly existence and seemed to intuit what he explicitly denied:

> Let us praise him [the Lord] the more, since we
>   cannot fathom him,
>   for greater is he than all his works. . . .
> For who can see him and describe him?
>   or who can praise him as he is?
> Beyond these, many things lie hid;
>   only a few of his works have we seen (Sir
>   43:29,33,34).

Sirach like ourselves turned out to be closer to the truth in what he affirmed about life than in what he denied! In his testimony to life, earthly existence and human language failed to communicate the sweep and vision of his heart, stirred enthusiastically by God's Spirit.

The Hebrew Scriptures themselves took the dare and leaped beyond this earth's horizons in Dan 12 and in 2 Macc 7; here we find a clear enough statement about life after death. Yet these same Scriptures did not develop all the consequences of faith in the resurrection. For this we turn to the New Testament.

The first Epistle of Peter, the readings for Year II, is one of the most optimistic documents in the New Testament; here the full glory of the Risen Jesus shines before us. In fact, this glory transforms us from within, for we have been reborn:

> a birth unto hope which draws its life
>   from the resurrection of Jesus Christ from the dead;
> a birth to an imperishable inheritance
>   incapable of fading or defilement . . .
>   to be revealed in the last days.

It is thought that many key lines in the First Epistle of Peter were drawn from a baptismal liturgy of the early church. Through baptism we begin a new life, the glorious life of Jesus, a source of extraordinary joy and strength now, a pledge of what is "to be revealed in the last days."

What may seem strange at first is also unmistakably true about this same epistle. We frequently read not only of Jesus' resurrection but also about "the distress of many trials." The author is not inferring—by the continuous reference to new life and its many joys—that we are exempt from suffering. Yet there is the clear affirmation that faith is being purified and "there is cause for rejoicing here." It seems that our greatest gifts and talents are not only the source of unbelievable bliss but also of our greatest tragedies and sorrows. Where we are most gifted, we tend to act passionately, impulsively, thoughtlessly, stubbornly, sinfully.

At this point we hear the words of Jesus in today's gospel:

My children! How hard it is to enter the kingdom of God! It is easier for a camel to pass through a needle's eye than for a rich person to enter the kingdom of God.

The riches and talents of life can destroy us unless they are surrendered completely in adoration of God and in the service of our family and neighbor. That paradoxical statement of Jesus comes back to us: only the person who loses his life will save it (Mark 8:35).

Our talents must be reduced to that very fragile root of existence where life begins and where life is sustained by God's Holy Spirit, where our finest intuitions occur, where our entire personality holds together, where we will survive beyond the time of all of our accomplishments. To this life in the mystery of ourselves, where we are being born anew, rising with Jesus from the tomb, drawn beyond the outer edge of our visible existence—this type of life is "humanly impossible. . . . With God all [such] things are possible," in fact absolutely necessary.

Prayer:

Lord, you give food to those who fear you. When we listen to your voice and sell all that we possess, we become afraid of our poverty and nothingness. Yet at that moment we receive the nourishing food of your grace; we are directed by the wonderful inspiration and intuitions of your Holy Spirit within us.

I will give thanks to the Lord with all my heart
in the company and assembly of the just.

Tuesday, 8th Week

Sir 35:1–12. This respected teacher of Jerusalem recommends temple sacrifices but warns that these must be accomplished with generosity towards the poor, obedience towards the Mosaic Law and freedom from bribes and extortion.

1 Pet 1:10–16. For our sake the prophets predicted the sufferings of Christ. Therefore, we are to be holy and receive the revelation preached to us by those sent through the Spirit. Into these matters angels desire to search.

Mark 10:28–31. We will receive a hundred times over and above whatever we have given up for Jesus.

The first readings for Years I and II seem to reflect very different movements within Israelite religion. When Sirach took part in the temple liturgy, joy brightened his countenance and delight put a mist over his eyes. In chapter 50 an exuberant, almost ecstatic blessedness sings in every line; here Sirach is extolling "the greatest among his associates, the glory of his people, . . . Simon the [high] priest."

The selection from 1 Peter directs our attention away from the liturgy to the prophets who frequently excoriated the temple priesthood for their laxity and self-serving ambition. The words of the prophet Hosea still flash with the fire in his eyes:

> With you is my grievances, O High Priest! . . .
> My people perish for want of knowledge!
>   Since you have rejected knowledge,
>   I will reject you from my priesthood. . . .
> They feed on the sin of my people,
>   and are greedy for their guilt (Hos 4:4–8).

The prophets passionately pleaded for social justice and kindly tolerance towards the poor. The words of the prophet Micah will always ring in our ears:

> You have been told what is good,
>   and what the Lord requires of you:
> Only to do the right and to love goodness,
>   and to walk humbly with your God (Mic 6:8).

Isaiah reduced the entire law to hearing the orphan's plea and defending the widow (Isa 1:16). Orphans and widows were the accepted symbols of defenseless people.

In a less fiery way, with more gentleness and poise than is evident with the prophets, Sirach expresses the same concern for the poor. In today's reading we see that "works of charity" are equivalent to offerings of fine flour upon the altar. "To refrain from evil . . . and to avoid injustice" turn out to be the best kind of "an atonement" sacrifice. Bribes and extortion must not even be spoken about, much less considered and acted upon.

Both Old Testament readings then reach towards the poor and the helpless. In this way the different writers "predicted the sufferings destined for Christ and the glories that would follow." The poor and the suffering require immediate attention so that the future will be much better. The future held the secret of God's concern; God cannot tolerate injustice for long. When Jesus appeared, he was one with the poor, he gravitated towards the poor and took action in their defense. The village of Bethany has such a prominent place in the gospels, not only because the word itself in the Hebrew language means "House [*beth*] of the poor ['*ani*]" but also because this city marked the spot where lepers came closest to Jerusalem, to overlook the holy city from the Mount of Olives.

To reach out and touch the leper separates us—as Jesus said would happen—from "brothers or sisters, mother or father, children or property." In one sense it renders us unclean, not fit to participate in temple ritual. Yet in another way it renders us "holy after the likeness of the holy One," Jesus who befriended lepers. "The last shall come first."

In the poor, we can see as did the prophets, a vision of Jesus, his sufferings and the glories that followed. Each person, ourselves included, particularly in moments of distress and pain, mental or physical, reveals the Lord Jesus, one with lepers, abandoned on the cross, shut away in the tomb, but also wondrously awaiting his resurrection.

Sirach then asks us never to forget the poor, even in the midst of elegant ritual with its pomp and circumstance. If we do not listen to the gentle voice of this scribe and teacher at Jerusalem, then the prophets will fling the gauntlet of their threats upon our conscience. At moments of prayer, when we are closest to God, we must be most mindful of the poor. All of us in our worry and suffering, and when we undergo persecution, as Jesus says in today's gospel, turn out to be God's poor ones.

Prayer:

Blessed are you, Lord of heaven and earth! You have revealed to little ones the mysteries of the kingdom. Keep us always your little ones, your poor ones, greatly in need of you. Enable us to see the pain and poverty in our neighbors. Then we will be one family where you are our God and our Savior. This family bond will put the right spirit into all of our prayer and worship.

Wednesday, 8th Week

Sir 36:1, 5–6, 10–17. By God's fidelity to the hopes and prophetic promises within Israel, he will make known his power and salvation to the ends of the earth.

1 Pet 1:18–25. We have been redeemed by the blood of Christ, purified through obedience to the truth, reborn by the everlasting word.

Mark 10:32–45. Jesus again announces his death and resurrection. His disciples argue over rank and privilege in his kingdom.

An attitude of fear introduces each of today's readings. The selection from Sirach for Year I begins with a prayer that God will "put all the nations in dread of you." The verse immediately before today's passage from 1 Peter warns the early Christians to "conduct yourselves reverently [or in the RSV, with fear] during your sojourn in a strange land." The gospel describes the disciples as filled with wonderment and fear, as they travel with Jesus on the road to Jerusalem.

A certain amount of fear is healthy, lest we foolishly gamble away the great possibilities of human life. Fear likewise takes the form of a delicate reverence before the privilege of life in close union with Jesus. Fear too will prevent us from being selfish or egotistical for it reminds us at once how much we need to cooperate with others and to share with others, if we are to receive God's gifts within the one large family of God.

The three readings for this Wednesday of the Eighth Week, Cycles I and II, guide us along the path of a healthy, strong fear lest we abuse or lose God's beautiful gifts. The Old Testament passage insists upon the respect which we must show towards God's gifts in others; the reading from 1 Peter directs our attention to reverence which ought to characterize worship and prayer before God. In Mark's Gospel, along with 1 Peter, we recognize the bond of family where true love reverences others and shares the best with them.

Sirach prays that "the nations" will be "in dread of" God and so respect God's gifts and blessings within Israel. Sirach is absorbed in what God can do for his chosen people. He lived and conducted his school during a time of peace, around 190 B.C.E., before the great persecution in Daniel and I and II Maccabees let loose its agony upon Israel. Yet he was not content with serenity and peace. From the earlier Scriptures he read of hopes still more stupendous, of promises and visions of peace across the universe. He begged God not to let his people be frustrated by their hopes nor to be dulled into complacency and compromise. Sirach quickly focused his gaze upon the holy city. Unlike other sapiential writers (as we see in Proverbs, Job and Ecclesiastes) Sirach delighted in the temple liturgy (*cf.*, ch 24 and 50). Magnificent liturgies provide a normal, healthy setting

for godly fear. Here wonder overwhelms us. This filial fear
unites us within the mystery of God's goodness and fidelity;
it never drives us away from God.

Sirach asks us to respect the talents and gifts of others.
Rather than be jealous and work against others, we ought to
pray to God and to encourage others. Our delight ought to
rest in their triumphs; our hopes, to be nourished by their
wholesome ambition. Liturgy ought to mirror these great
triumphs of God's grace in others. Thus God "will be
known to the end of the earth."

First Peter stresses still more the bond of union among
all God's people. Jew or Gentile, we were one and all redeemed by "Christ's blood beyond all price." The reference here recalls the blood ritual of Old Testament liturgy.
The blood was always drained from the sacrificial animal
(Lev 4:7) and was then sprinkled upon (or towards) the altar
and at times upon the people. In this way the liturgy proclaimed the one bond of life between God and his people.
Just as blood that flows outward from the heart unites all the
bodily members in one flow of life, so too are we united this
intimately with God through the precious blood of Jesus. It
is Jesus' blood that sanctifies and revitalizes each of us. The
wonder of the human body stirs fear and respectful care for
what God has created. With even deeper fear and wonder we
should ponder the mystery of our union with Jesus in one
body.

In the Gospel, although Jesus encountered opposition
from the disciples, he did not back down or go in a different
direction. He continued on his way to Jerusalem. Here, he
said, "the Son of Man will be handed over. His captors will
mock him and spit at him, flog him, and finally kill him. But
three days later he will rise." God's promises are so exalted
that before the event there is no way of understanding them.
Even though Jesus' enemies want to do away with him, lest

they lose their privileges and wealth, God will turn their political contriving against Jesus to world salvation. Even if the death of the sacrificial animal did not hold an important place in the Old Testament liturgy, still in Jesus' case the death of the sacrificial victim becomes a central act of redemption and church liturgy. ''This is my body to be given for you . . . my blood which will be shed for you'' (Luke 22:19–20). We are again in fear, not so much of death, but of life that has been sanctified and renewed by such a death as Jesus'.

By contrast with this exalted theology of hope and life, of martyrdom and self-giving respect for others, the action of Zebedee's sons, James and John, seems petty and even detestable. How can they intrigue for privileged places in the kingdom, seeking to outrank the other disciples, when Jesus has announced the giving of his life for everyone? Jesus' answer was very simple: ''Anyone among you who aspires to greatness must serve the rest.'' This is the mind of Jesus. This mind must be in us (Phil 2:5).

Prayer:

Lord, we feel so privileged by your goodness and your hopes in us, that we are afraid that others will spoil what you have given to us. Turn this false fear into a healthy fear by which we look to others for the help and the balance to sustain our own talents and possibilities. Enable us to share your pardon and compassion with others, and so to form one family of your elect people.

Thursday, 8th Week

Sir 42:18–25. God has strewn an infinite variety of life across the universe. Each part of it completes and complements the other. Even the future world is already alive in God's secret plan.

1 Pet 2:2–5, 9–12. We have been called out of darkness to taste how good the Lord is. God nourishes us as newborn babies with purest milk. Born through baptism into the church, we glimpse a wondrous theological panorama.

Mark 10:46–52. Jesus heals Bartimaeus of blindness because of his faith.

Today's readings think of us as a spiritual infant emerging from the dark womb into the light of day, and nourished with milk from the purest source of life. ''Be as eager for milk,'' 1 Peter advises us, ''as newborn babies— pure milk of the spirit to make you grow unto salvation'' and so to taste ''that the Lord is good'' (Ps 34:9). God is pictured here as a woman giving birth and nourishing her child. We are that child, especially at the moment of our baptism, but also at every moment of grace. Through faith and prayer, we cling to God as a child to the mother's breast. We absorb life, ''pure milk of the spirit.'' This milk is drawn instinctively and subconsciously from the source of life.

A child's reactions seem very simple. Yet we adults marvel at the complexity of a child's life and we wonder how any child survives. It does so, only through the vigilance and care of its parents. We meet here a paradoxical combination of utter simplicity and sophisticated interrelationships, of quick spontaneity and careful reflection.

1 Peter, for its part, changes its focus from newborn infant to the church. The intricacies of life within the child can be compared to the rich theology of the church. 1 Peter weaves into his narrative many involved ideas of Old Testament theology. The phrases are drawn from the Torah of Moses, the vision of the prophets, the liturgy of the temple. This easy interaction of the major lines of Jewish spiritual-

ity—which at times were even antagonistic to each other—
manifests long years of meditation, patience and a wholesome integrity before God. The author must have been a
type of person whose first reaction was respect, love and
wonder. To be this way, he had to respond initially with
spontaneous obedience, not with critical negativism. As a
result the author ended up strong and dependable. We see
the result of this sturdy character in the final lines:

> Though the pagans may slander you as trouble-
> makers, conduct yourselves blamelessly among
> them. By observing your good works they may
> give glory to God.

Like 1 Peter, the passage from Sirach also moves from
simple yet majestic wonders to intricate mysteries. His gaze
sweeps from the obvious beauty of the universe, where
everything develops with natural ease and grace, to the im-
penetrable depths of the human heart where emotions clash
and reasons collapse. He writes, for instance:

> He [God] plumbs the depths and penetrates the heart,
>   their innermost being he understands. . . .
> How beautiful are all his works!
>   even to the spark and the fleeting vision!
> The universe lives and abides forever;
>   to meet each need, each creature is preserved.

Our life of faith, then, must follow the quick spontaneity of the child that reaches towards its mother's breast for
"the pure milk of the spirit." We must be "blindly" obedient to these finest impulses of life and taste deeply the
goodness of the Lord. We must also read and study widely,

refine our theology, draw seriously from Scripture and Tradition. We must combine the impulsiveness of an infant with the studied carefulness of the adult. Then we will be at peace. We will be protected against evil desires.

Prayer:

Let us give thanks to the Lord and sing a new song. We have been made by the same word of the Lord which gathered the waters of the sea as in a flask. That same word calls us to life each moment of our existence, with wondrous possibilities. Let us enter his gates with thanksgiving, his courts with praise.

Friday, 8th Week

Sir 44:1,9–13. Israel's ancestors were blessed in themselves and in their descendants because of God's covenant with them and their fidelity to it.

1 Pet 4:7–13. Put your gifts at the service of one another. Serve with the strength provided by God. In times of trial rejoice that you share in Christ's sufferings.

Mark 11:11–28. Two episodes cast light upon each other: the cursing of the fig tree and the cleansing of the temple; yet at the center and conclusion of the gospel account is an insistence upon prayer.

Both the readings from 1 Peter (Cycle II) and the Gospel narrative of Jesus' driving out from the temple those engaged in buying and selling confront us with a fearful end of life. Technically it is called the eschatological moment. We read in 1 Peter: ''The consummation of all is close at hand.'' In the gospel the withering of the fig tree signals the end of the Jerusalem temple. Yet as we reread all three biblical passages for today, we see very clearly that life is not to stop and that our reaction is not to be passive submission.

Mark's gospel very clearly intends that we interpret the incident of Jesus' cleansing the temple within the context of his cursing the fig tree and its withering up. The story of the fig tree envelops the other incident, a style quite common in Mark's gospel. Jesus, therefore, was doing more than cleansing the temple. In fact, his climactic words, though drawn from the Old Testament, announce a new type of temple prayer and temple regulations:

> My house shall be called a house of prayer
>   for all people.

In Jesus' day, non-Jews were forbidden under pain of death to advance beyond the outer court of the gentiles; Roman authorities ratified this prescription. Jesus is drawing from an Old Testament passage, Isaiah, chap. 56. Yet, this text of Isaiah was generally disregarded up to this time. It came from a tradition which was not dominant in the life of Israel, yet the words turn out to be highly significant for understanding God's plans for the future of his people.

Even though the Old Testament in isolated places like Isa 56 announces a dramatic change, as Jesus also does in texts like today's gospel reading, nonetheless the total impact does not dull our initiative but advises us how to live more prayerfully and more generously towards others. We are meant to take control and to react positively. Already, an important message is being flashed to us. In times of drastic change and sudden crisis, we should not stop living. With strong faith and with prayerful awareness of God's presence, with kindly regard towards others and with a sense of a good future in our descendants, we carry on.

The reading from Sirach (Cycle I) advises us to look to our ancestors in order to do the proper thing for our posterity:

> Now will I praise those godly people,
>   our ancestors, each in their own time. . . .
> Through God's covenant with them their family
>   endures,
>   their posterity, for their sake.
> And for all time their progeny will endure.

Sirach bridges the past and the future and finds its firm connection in God's covenant. Fidelity to God and to God's bond with us will carry us over the deepest chasm and most dreadful rupture in our life. No matter what may have happened, death of one's spouse or children, great financial loss, serious disturbance of one's health—nothing can break the bond of God's covenant that unites ancestors with descendants. God will always respect our human relationship.

And as we read further through today's readings, we find one of the most helpful catechisms for daily living. First, the faith to move mountains. It is interesting how St. Paul will link this statement with the still greater necessity of charity:

> If I have faith great enough to move mountains,
> but have not love, I am nothing (1 Cor 13:2).

Jesus also asks for perseverance in prayer and forgiveness. In fact, it is the willingness to forgive that enables our prayers to find their way before God.

The practical advice continues in First Peter. Here we meet a text also from the Old Testament (Prov 10:12). The link with the ancestors is kept very firm. In cleansing the temple, Jesus also referred back to Isaiah. Peter advises us: "Be mutually hospitable without complaining . . . put your gifts at the service of one another, each in the measure that each has received." Even while doing one's best, this generously, we are "not [to] be surprised that a trial by fire is occurring in your midst . . . Rejoice instead, insofar as you share Christ's sufferings." Suffering, therefore, puts us in contact with the greatest of our ancestors, Jesus Christ, who continues to live through the bond of the new covenant.

We overcome every trial, we can take control and look to the future because of the bond of God's love for us in Christ Jesus. Therefore, no matter what happens, we need the practical instructions of today's biblical passages.

Prayer:

Lord, you come to judge the earth, but your judgment is one of mercy and generosity. Help us, especially in times of crucial judgment and critical decision, to continue living with mercy and generosity. Then our life's path will lead to festive dance as we exult in your glory in our midst.

Saturday, 8th Week

Sir 51:12–20. When I was young, wisdom came to me in her beauty, and until the end I will cultivate her.

Jude 17:20–25. Pray in the Holy Spirit, persevere in God's love, and welcome the mercy of Our Lord Jesus Christ which leads to life eternal.

Mark 11:27–33. Jesus agrees to explain the source of his authority if his questioners declare whether John the Baptist's baptism was of divine or human origin.

We are asked to be honest before others, open to correction and devoted to ancestral wisdom. Otherwise, like the questioners in today's gospel, we will fail to recognize the presence of Jesus our Savior; or we may fall into the trap of some early Christians, condemned in the Epistle of Jude (Cycle II). They followed a secret way of salvation which so emphasized the sanctification of the spirit that the body was left to all kinds of libertine, immoral actions. While Mark and Jude are tense with conflict and serious mistakes, Sirach (Cycle I) is calm and self-confident that fidelity over the years to ancestral wisdom has brought beauty, peace, a clean heart and a joyful feeling within one's entire self. In this way one opens the gate to the true secrets of life.

Clearly enough we must be honest with ourselves and with others. We must also allow God to set the agenda and state the question. God is never unreasonable, but as the prophet Hosea observed with agony, centuries ago: "I am God, no human being!" The context of Hosea presented the divine mercy as reaching far beyond human compassion. The full statement of Hosea reads:

> My heart is overwhelmed,
>   my pity is stirred.
> I will not give vent to my blazing anger. . . .
> I am God, no human being,
>   the Holy One present among you.
>   I will not let the flames consume you (Hos 11:8–9).

If God's mercy transcends ours, "as the heavens are above the earth" (Isa 55:9), so also does God's honesty. God does not play games. God works within reality, another name for honesty. Unless we recognize what is real God cannot interact with us. Very truly, dishonesty sets up a more formidable barrier to God's presence with us than many of our worst sins. These can be touched and forgiven by God's excelling mercy, but only if we are honest enough to admit that there are sins to be forgiven. The epistle of Jude is also conscious of honesty, as when he writes:

> Correct those who are confused; the others you must rescue, snatching them from the fire.

Jude seems to be combatting a situation, like Jesus in today's gospel, where religious leaders feel that their secret possession of truth and of holiness frees them from being honest and above board. To protect their secret truth they permit themselves to lie or to be devious. In the case of the early church, these same religious persons felt interiorly or spiritually sanctified to such an extent that they could ignore normal discipline and control over their lives, particularly in such physical acts as eating or physical expressions of love. These people were not honest to admit the integral unity between body and soul, the physical and the spiritual.

Jude attempts to point out the true, interior wisdom. He identifies its source in "the prophetic words of the apostles," "praying in the Holy Spirit," "persevering in God's love," and "welcoming the mercy of our Lord Jesus Christ." The wisdom of our ancestor in the prophetic words of the apostles and the wisdom of the Spirit in the secret moments of prayer, the wisdom imparted by mercy and compassion towards others, the wisdom from believing in our Lord Jesus Christ, divine and human, integrally at peace with human body and with divine spirit . . . this wisdom is open for everyone of good will to seek and obtain. Even if it is God's gift, and can never be obtained by human effort, still God gives it freely and lavishly. And as we walk this way towards true wisdom, we are gradually absorbed into a mystery beyond all comprehension, the mystery of the Holy Trinity. The three persons of the Holy Trinity are mentioned in Jude's words: "praying in the *Holy Spirit* . . . persevering in God [*the Father's*] love, welcoming the mercy of *our Lord Jesus Christ.*" Here we encounter the most genuine, most real dimension of life, God as Father, Son and Holy Spirit.

Sirach writes from Old Testament times before the revelation of the Holy Trinity. Yet the same approach to faith is found in both Testaments. From our reading of the Book of Sirach these past two weeks (Cycle I) we saw how practical and down to earth this teacher was. Yet ever so often flashes of profound mysticism cut across his lines, as in chap. 43:

> Let us praise God the more, since we cannot
>   fathom him,
>   for greater is he than all his works; . . .
> Extol him with renewed strength,
>   and weary not, though you cannot reach
>   the end (Sir 44:29,32).

In today's reading, we see Sirach, now an elderly, highly respected scholar and teacher, confessing: "until the end I will cultivate her," that is, true wisdom. He will be at the end of his search, and yet all along he possesses this secret:

> I became preoccupied with her,
>   never weary of extolling her,
> My hand opened her gate
>   and I came to know her secrets.

By an honest acceptance of reality Sirach was guided into this pursuit of wisdom. He was willing to be instructed and "from earliest youth" "my feet kept to the level path" of discipline and self-control.

If the Scriptures ask us to meditate today on honesty before God and before our neighbor, we are not only led along the path of reality, with our feet firmly on this earth, but we are also being guided into a heavenly mystery, a mystery of transcendent wonder, kindness and eternal life. If we are honest, we pursue this journey with Jesus who will then answer every one of our questions.

Prayer:

Lord, keep me always honest and open before you, so that your decrees will refresh my soul, enlighten my eyes and bring a sweetness greater than honey from the comb. As I thirst for you, Lord, in the mystery of your goodness, I find my thirst already sated with your refreshing presence.

Monday, 9th Week

Tob 1:1–2; 2:1–9. Tobit is living in exile away from the promised land yet faithful to the Law and compassionate towards the neighbor.

2 Pet 1:2–7. God has freely bestowed on us everything necessary for a life of genuine piety. We have become sharers of the divine nature.

Mark 12:1–12. The parable of the man who leased his vineyard to tenant farmers and went on a journey. The tenants kill even the man's son. They will be severely punished and the vineyard given to others.

The liturgy invites us to reflect upon two books, each written rather late for the collection of Old or New Testament scriptures: Tobit (cycle I) was one of the last to be added to the Old Testament, Second Peter (cycle II) to the

New Testament. They seem to have a common spirituality that links them as well with the gospel parable for today: how to live at a distance from the Lord; how to survive in a foreign land; how to react when religion or God has let us down. In both Tobit and Second Peter people have to face up to some false impressions left with them by their ancestors in the faith; in the gospel people cultivate the false impression that they can live recklessly or at least selfishly because of God's absence or seeming indifference.

The direction to our meditation fits in well with "Monday," the proverbial blue or tired day when we put aside the happy leisure of Sunday and settle down again to the work-a-day world. The glorious promises, offered to us in the Sunday liturgy, run up against the stolid block of the secular world: financial concerns, monotonous housework, the grind of punching the clock at one's employment or the discouraging worry of being out of work. The wonderful ideals of Sunday seem to collapse like a deck of cards or a paper house, once we start living again in our "foreign land," foreign because of God's apparent absence.

For these and many other reasons we need the book of Tobit, where religion and everyday life blend harmoniously, where ancient traditions come alive for support and perseverance, where God returns because of Tobit's persistent faith. This book is rightly called a religious novel. The crucial question is not: did it really happen? but rather, what is the religious message in the events? This religious message was a strong reality in the heart of the inspired author. This person used a story form, figures of speech, and the ancient setting of the Assyrian exile, lines from the prophets and especially from the Book of Proverbs, to insist that the tragic and baffling turns of our life are truly leading us to peace and joy for ourselves, for our family and for our congregation of believers.

Second Peter may have been one of the last books to be composed and added to the New Testament. The author takes up a question which St. Peter never had to face: will the glorious second coming of Jesus be delayed indefinitely? It seems that once the Romans destroyed Jerusalem in the year A.D. 70 and later unleashed the violent persecution of the Christians—yet Jesus did not return as victor and Messiah—some Christians felt betrayed by their new religion, others were lost in a quagmire of doubt. Peter had already been martyred in A.D. 67. The inspired author of this epistle, like the author of Tobit, placed his writing within a much older setting, drew upon the traditions of the earliest days of Christianity, even upon the lifetime of Jesus, now almost a century ago, in order to insist upon a firm continuity from the past into the future, from God's majestic presence then to God's supportive presence now.

The gospel anticipates just this kind of problem. The owner of the vineyard seems to have vanished, the tenant farmers can live recklessly, even killing the owner's son, in order to seize total control of their lives and the property. When Jesus first spoke this parable, he remained within the Old Testament meaning of the puzzling but familiar text:

> The stone rejected by the builders
>   has become the keystone of the structure.
> It was the Lord who did it
>   and we find it marvelous to behold.

Directly from Ps 118:22–23 but closely related to Isa 28:16, this passage states that God will always be faithful and to prove it, God will choose even the least likely person or the neglected or abandoned talent, and turn it or him or her into the keystone of the new life. Christians later reinterpreted this text to announce God's transfer of biblical religion to the gentile or foreign world after the fall of Jerusalem to the Romans in A.D. 66–70.

These ancient books tell our life story. We too feel abandoned, perhaps like someone led down a blind alley by the wonderful promises of religion, now with little or nothing to show. God, it appears, has gone to a strange country and left us to merciless tenants. We feel ridiculous, and like Tobit we suffer for our fidelity to God.

The story of Tobit, as charming and as intriguing as any novel can be, moves our heart the most. Who will not love and admire the person who risks whatever is left of security and peace, to give an honorable burial to a murdered and abandoned stranger? Second Peter will instruct us the most clearly, as it pedagogically links up the virtues of piety, self-control, perseverance, faith and care for one's brother and sister. The gospel holds the key which will eventually solve our dilemma. Upon the foundation of the least likely part of our character and family circle, God will build our peaceful home on earth and our eternal dwelling hereafter. Respect for the least part of ourselves enables us to welcome Jesus at the Second Coming.

Prayer:

Lord, in you I put my trust. You are all the more my refuge and my fortress when you seem far away. In my distress and loneliness I call upon you.

Tuesday, 9th Week

Tob 2:9–14. A typical family scene of tender goodness, of faithful perseverance, even of disagreement and quarreling!

2 Pet 3:12–15, 17–18. Our true security lies in our faith in
   God's justice, in our honest and wholesome way of life,
   and in the guidance of the Scriptures.
Mark 12:13–17. ''Give to Caesar what is Caesar's, but to
   God what is God's.''

   Even though the selection from Second Peter (cycle II)
begins with the awesome, tumultuous appearance of ''new
heavens and a new earth,'' the writer quickly settles down to
ordinary life and homespun virtues. The reading from Tobit
(cycle I) turns out to be one of the most charming episodes
of family life to be found in the Scriptures. It includes all
that can happen: accidents—truly ''accidental''—that inflict
severe hardship; the necessity of the other spouse working to
supplement the budget; a kind deed from a neighbor; a family quarrel, caused more by ignorance and zeal than by any
ill will. Finally, in the gospel, we are delighted, as we always are around the family table or during an evening conversation, by clever humor that hurts no one but still
manages to put the haughty person in his place.
   It is good for soul and body to find our daily family
scene reenacted in the Scriptures. If our lives are that clearly
reflected in the Bible, then God must certainly be present in
our homes, even in our quarrels and banter! The principal
virtue is perseverance, its principal quality is faithfulness,
the bond between perseverance and faithfulness is love.
Love and truth are genuine if they sparkle with humor. To
bridge and harmonize these qualities, one needs steady
shoulders and a well-balanced head. We are reminded of a
brilliant platitude from one of the most scintillating and
enigmatic writers in the Bible:

   Be not just to excess, and be not overwise, lest
   you be ruined. Be not wicked to excess, and be

not foolish. Why should you die before your time?
(Eccle 7:16–17)

The author, sometimes called Qoheleth (a word that means
the assembly or congregation, or more specifically their
leader), is asking religious people to keep their feet on the
ground. If we read the inspired statement correctly, it seems
to infer that a little wickedness is not all that bad—but don't
be a fool!

Tobit's wife feels that her husband's piety is a bit too
much! When he doubts her honesty over the gift of a young
goat, she can take it no longer:

"Where are your charitable deeds now? Where
are your virtuous acts? See! Your true character is
finally showing itself!"

It may seem strange that the Scripture passage for today
(cycle I) ends right there, with Tobit's wife exasperated and
the blind Tobit rendered speechless! How can we, the congregation, respond: "This is the word of the Lord"?

The gospel also ends with no answer, only a very
clever, profound but general remark: "Give to Caesar what
is Caesar's but to God what is God's." If only Jesus had explained exactly what belonged to Caesar in distinction to
what belonged to God! People, nonetheless, down to our
own day, listen with "amazement" that knows "no
bounds."

Jesus may not always silence our questions with clear
answers, but Jesus will always suffuse trust and honesty and
for those who are sincere, compassion and forgiveness.
After all, the Pharisees and Herodians who questioned Jesus
were not seeking an honest answer. As the gospel points
out, Jesus looked at them, "knowing their hypocrisy." His

first reply began with the question: ''Why are you trying to trip me up?''

Second Peter also seeks an attitude of prudence and trust while we await ''new heavens and a new earth where . . . the justice of God will reside.'' ''Justice,'' in the biblical sense, means the fulfillment of all God's promises so that reality conforms justly with promise and hope. Although this fulfillment is accomplished by God, we contribute our family virtues and attitudes of human vintage:

- ''Be found without stain or defilement.'' In other words, be honest and conscientious. Live actively according to the movement of the Spirit.
- Be ''at peace in his sight.'' At peace with yourself and with your family and neighbors. Do not act or speak so that you must hide and dissimulate. Such people are never at peace.
- ''Consider . . . our Lord's patience.'' What more necessary virtue in the family!
- ''Be on your guard lest you be led astray [and you] forfeit the security you enjoy.''

If then we follow the homey example of Tobit and the practical advice of Second Peter, if we are sincere and open with Jesus—if, indeed, we accomplish what is easily within our power—God will fulfill in us what is beyond even our dreams, ''new heavens and a new earth.''

Prayer:

In every age, O Lord, you have been our refuge. By trusting in you, we learn to believe in one another. As we delight in your holy will, what happiness will be ours! You will manifest already in us your heavenly kingdom. Your work and your glory will be seen by our children and children's children.

Wednesday, 9th Week

Tob 3:1–11, 16. In anguish both Tobit and Sarah pray to God for deliverance from their earthly sorrows and from ridicule; each asks God to let them die.

2 Tim 1:1–3, 6–12. "Stir into flame the gift of God." Paul is not ashamed to undergo hardship. Christ has robbed death of its power.

Mark 12:18–27. When people rise from the dead, they will be like angels, they neither marry nor are given in marriage. The Lord is the God of the living, not of the dead.

Jesus' remarks about marriage leave us baffled and unsure. Yet one fact is clear enough, our heavenly existence will belong to *us*. *We* are the ones who rise from the dead, in such continuity with our earthly existence that what we do on earth determines the joy of heaven or the punishment elsewhere. Yet, we will be radically different, and so will our entire earth be transformed. Yesterday's reading from Second Peter announced "new heavens and a new earth"; we are told in the Book of Revelation, "there shall be no more death or mourning, crying out or pain, for the former world has passed away" (Rev 21:4).

Even marriage and family will be different—transformed, yes! but not destroyed. If earthly existence affects our heavenly life, then our marriages and families will have a strong impact as well. In fact, love is the determining factor. Our final judgment will be decided on whether or not we fed the hungry, gave drink to the thirsty, clothed the naked, comforted the sick, visited prisoners. "As often as you did it for one of my least brothers and sisters, you did it for me" (Matt 25:40). If love for strangers and for the ministers of the gospel is so rewarded and so remembered for all eternity, how much more the love and self-sacrifice in marriage and family.

The close tie between marriage and eternity becomes more apparent from the first readings for today's liturgy. The selection from Tobit (cycle I) not only joins Tobit and the distant Sarah in prayer, but it also hints to the answer of each one's prayer: the marriage of Tobit's son to Sarah. This marriage came as a result of Tobit's blindness and the search for the son's security. The marriage itself brought a cure to Tobit's blindness, enabled him to see his grandchildren and to enter eternity with peace.

Another bonding of heaven and earth through marriage is seen in the Second Epistle to Timothy (cycle II). The pertinent lines are omitted in the liturgical passage for today, as it proceeds from v. 3 at once to v. 6. In between, we read a testimony to Timothy's family and to the close friendly relationship between Paul and that family:

> Recalling your tears when we parted, I yearn to see you again. That would make my happiness complete. I find myself thinking of your sincere faith—faith which first belonged to your grandmother Lois and to your mother Eunice, and which (I am confident) you also have (2 Tim 1:4–5).

When Paul was awaiting his death by execution and martyrdom, his mind was reaching back serenely and gratefully to the family ties of his disciple Timothy.

The first reading (cycles I and II) speaks of fidelity

within marriage, its sufferings and its hopes. In the gospel Jesus declares that suffering will find an abundant reward, its hopes will be fulfilled beyond one's dreams. Jesus, moreover, seriously defends the resurrection of the body, so that the instrument for giving and receiving love and affection, for feeding the hungry and clothing the naked, will itself be revived and transformed.

Like every other aspect of heaven, the way by which human love will be manifested remains God's mystery. It will not be frustrated, for ''he is the God of the living, not of the dead.'' God does not destroy but transforms. He loves all that he has created.

In fact, Jesus' style of reasoning with the Sadducees ''who hold there is no resurrection,'' would not convince them or anyone else unless there is faith in God's love and compassion. The passage from the Book of Exodus, ''I am the God of Abraham . . . Isaac . . . Jacob,'' was never interpreted of the resurrection during the long centuries between Moses and Jesus. Faith in God as sharing life and love, in God the source of intimacy and trust, in God as bountifully generous, makes the difference. God will not raise us to half-life nor to half-love. What the fullness of life and love will be remains God's secret, the supreme object of our trust and faith.

Prayer:

Lord, teach me your ways. I will tread your path that leads to ever more abundant life, never alone for you inspire persevering love and strong trust by your example and by my dear ones, your greatest gift to me. In sorrow or joy I always lift my eyes to you.

Thursday, 9th Week

Tob 6:11; 7:1, 9–14; 8:4–7. The marriage of Tobiah and
    Sarah.
2 Tim 2:8–15. Paul bears with his imprisonment ''for the
    sake of those whom God has chosen.'' God always re-
    mains faithful.
Mark 12:28–34. The first and second commandments: love
    of God and love of neighbor. Such love is worth more
    than any burnt offering or sacrifice.

Some of the Scripture's finest expressions on marriage
occur in today's reading from the Book of Tobit (cycle I).
The supreme law of love is given to us in the gospel. In the
selection from Second Timothy (cycle II) we are reminded
of God's fidelity and of our need to persevere faithfully,
''even to the point of being thrown in chains,'' that our love
be genuine. Today's reading from Second Timothy, in fact,
begins with a reference to Jesus' resurrection from the dead.
In other words, the bonds of love, presented beautifully in
Tobit and in Mark's gospel, must be tried by fire, not out of
suspicion or doubt, but out of the need to become even more
beautiful and pure. This final stage will be fully manifest in
the resurrection from the dead.

Words worthy of a marriage invitation are spoken by
Raguel, the father of the bride. He says to Tobiah, the bridegroom:

Sarah is yours according to the decree in the Book
of Moses. Your marriage to her has been decided
in heaven! . . . From now on you are her love,
and she is your beloved.

This sense of God's blessing continues in the lovely prayer of Tobiah and Sarah:

> Blessed are you, O Lord of our ancestors. . . .
> You made Adam and you give him his wife Eve. . . .
> You said, "It is not good for the man to be alone."
>   . . .
> I take this wife of mine
>   not because of lust,
>   but for a noble purpose.
> Call down your mercy on me and on her,
>   and allow us to live together to a
>   happy old age.

After blessing God and receiving God's blessing, we are told that they "went to bed for the night."

As we found on the preceding days of this week, what is presented as a lovely story in Tobit, is reexpressed in the other readings more theoretically. The gospel speaks of the "commandment" of love. We normally do not think of love as a law or commandment but as a spontaneous response of our whole being. Yet experience shows how easily we can love selfishly and less than the "noble purpose" which called Tobiah and Sarah together in marriage. God must reaffirm that genuine love is:

> with *all* your heart,
> with *all* your soul,
> with *all* your mind,
> and with *all* your strength.

Genuine love reaches out to others as though they were an extension of ourselves:

> you shall love your neighbor as yourself.

What neighbor is closer than one's spouse? Such love "is worth more than any burnt offering or sacrifice." Without such love every other action, no matter how sacred and holy, no matter how grand and heroic, loses its primary value. With such love "you are not far from the reign of God."

In Second Timothy, Paul speaks in greater detail about the difficulties to be mastered and overcome:

- even to the point of being thrown into chains.
- to die with the other, that we may live with them.
- to hold out to the end.
- always to remain faithful.
- stop disputing about mere words.
- make yourself worthy of God's approval.

The trials of love are not always meant to correct and purify what is wrong but in the case of the more noble forms of love, as that between the elderly couple, Tobit and Anna, God was seeking to make the good better, the pure brighter and more beautiful, the faithful all the more tenacious. The psalmist speaks thus of God's word, always good and pure:

The promises of the Lord are sure,
    like tried silver, freed from dross,
        sevenfold refined (Ps 12:7).

Silver ore was placed in a burning cauldron. With strong heat the slack was burnt off and the pure substance remained. Such is the way of true love. It requires a lifetime to become pure and strong, ready for eternal life.

For these reasons we badly need the help of one another. God generally divides the times of sorrow and purification, first this one suffers, later that one. We support one another, the strong looks after the weak. Sooner or later the table is turned and the strong one is now weak and turns to the partner for aid. Yet even if we fail one another, there is still hope.

> If we are unfaithful God will still remain faithful,
> for he cannot deny himself.

God will assure our reunion, our forgiveness, our hope.

Prayer:
　　Lord, may we love one another so that our love will grow and become ever more noble and pure. This is the path of greater love along which you call us to follow your way. Bless our marriages with faithfulness and perseverance, with children and fullness of life. All your paths are kindness and constancy. May we never lose our way; yet even if we do, let us hear your voice, calling us back.

Friday, 9th Week

Tob 11:5–15. Anna and Tobit are reunited with their son Tobiah who smears the ointment on the father's eyes. "I can see you, son, the light of my eyes."

2 Tim 3:10–17. Remain faithful to what you have learned and believed. From your infancy you have known the sacred Scriptures, inspired of God and useful for teaching.

Mark 12:35–37. Jesus silences his adversaries through a Scripture text which had many interpretations and by its mystery pointed beyond its words.

　　Scripture can be as clear and charming as the story of Tobit; it can also be as baffling as Ps 110 which Jesus quotes to silence the religious leaders at the temple. Texts like the religious novel of Tobit reinforce the normal, basic virtues of loyalty and kindliness, a way of life open to everyone at once. Other texts like Ps 110 gradually took on the character of announcing the messianic future, a way that is hidden in God and not open at once to everyone.

Anyone with a wholesome attitude and a compassion for others feels tears brimming in one's eyes in reading about the reunion of the young man Tobiah with his parents. The only training that one needs to interpret Tobit is a good heart, a common-sense experience and a kindly love for others. This type of formation comes first of all from the home and then from a person's circle of friends. Later it is strongly helped by church and religious communities.

Paul refers to this kind of background when writing to Timothy. Paul writes: ''From your infancy you have known the sacred Scriptures.'' Earlier in this same epistle he mentions his happiness when thinking of the sincere ''faith which belonged to your grandmother Lois and to your mother Eunice.'' A good home prepared Timothy best of all for his apostolic ministry.

Such a home setting ought to be reflected in our churches and synagogues. The Jerusalem temple was called the ''house of God.'' In the Hebrew this word ''house'' once referred to a nomad's tent that covered the entire family under one ''roof.'' Such a tent-dwelling presumed intimacy, trust and a common sharing of each one's sorrow or joys. The first dwelling for the ark of the covenant was such a tent. David was prohibited from building a house of cedar and mighty stones, because, as God says, ''from the day on which I led the Israelites out of Egypt to the present . . . I have been going about in a tent under cloth'' (2 Sam 7:6). The family home then determines the attitudes for church and temple. It also provides the setting or context for interpreting Scripture.

When we turn to the gospel, other kinds of tears come to our eyes, tears of sorrow and regret. Religion has been turned into a business or profession; temple as church has become a place for controversy. Such always seems to be the case when church people put more stress upon such esoteric questions as the timing of the end of the world and its accompanying phenomena, than upon the elementary virtues of love, patience, forgiveness, generosity, and prayer.

Jesus refuses to answer the question about the messianic age on the grounds of the questioners. We are reminded of that other time:

> Once being asked . . . *when* the reign of God would come, Jesus replied: "You cannot tell by careful watching *when* the reign of God will come. Neither is it a matter of reporting that it is *'here'* or *'there.'* The reign of God is already in your midst" (Luke 17:20–21).

Jesus will not identify the coming of the kingdom with "when" or "where" or "how." It is, on the contrary, "already in your midst."

To experience God's kingdom already in our midst, we must persevere a long time with hopes, rather than demand a clear answer for the future. Like Tobit, we wait with blindness yet with tender love. Like Anna, we take our stand "watching the road" on which God's son will return to us. God will reward such patient waiting with new eyesight. We will each be able to exclaim: "I can see you, the light of my eyes." As we praise God, our words will repeat Tobit's hymn:

Blessed be God! . . .
> Because it was he who scourged me,
> and it is he who has had mercy on me.

In the reading from Second Timothy (cycle II) Paul lists the
virtues that marked Sarah and Tobit's life as well as his own:

> my resolution, fidelity, patience, love, and endur-
> ance, through persecutions and sufferings.

The warm love, the strong dedication of sharing the faith,
the vicissitudes of work and trials, all these prepare a person
to interpret the scriptures. All these wholesome qualities
take on new life ''through faith in Jesus Christ,'' handed
down from tradition and one's ancestors.

In all these circumstances the Scriptures become useful:

> for teaching—for reproof, correction, and training
> in holiness, so that the godly person may be fully
> competent and equipped for every good work.

If religion and home overlap as one dwelling of God in families and communities, then we receive the true interpretation of the Word of God.

Prayer:

Lord, we praise you. You give food to the hungry,
sight to the blind, protection to strangers. As you enable us
to love one another, you lead us to new insights into your
holy word. As we love your word, grant us peace and
strength.

Saturday, 9th Week

Tob 12:1, 5–15, 20. For God's glory the archangel Raphael reveals his identity, explains that the happy conclusion is due to prayer, fasting and especially almsgiving and Tobit's concern to bury the dead.

2 Tim 4:1–8. Paul, having fought the good fight and finished the race, is about to be poured out in sacrificial martyrdom. Timothy is to continue the task, teaching and never losing patience.

Mark 12:38–44. Beware of people who recite long prayers for appearance' sake, accept places of honor, yet devour the savings of widows.

The Scriptures today warn us against two false expressions of religion and offer practical advice for growing in a true religious spirit, till we finish the race and receive the crown that awaits us. Once again both the reading from the Book of Tobit (cycle I) and the gospel reflect a real life situation, while the selection from Second Timothy (cycle II) tends to be more theoretical and didactic. The more practical form is necessary, not only to hold interest but also to keep ourselves grounded on planet earth; the more speculative or straight-forward statement also serves the important role of saying it exactly as it is. We do not miss the point and can never claim ignorance.

It has already been mentioned that the Book of Tobit is considered a religious novel. Yet, it is probably ten times more realistic than an objective, historical account. As a fictitious piece of writing, the author was free to draw from many sources, all real and objective, but spread across many years, perhaps centuries. The story-teller can so adapt the account that readers or listeners will be forced to think of themselves. The point of the story is always in the reader's life rather than in that of the author!

The Book of Tobit combines heavenly visitors like the archangel Raphael with family events and household details. Tobit, the overzealous husband, seemed a religious fanatic to his wife. She had little pity for him, at least at first, when he lost his eyesight. Their arguments are reflected in every home. So also are the incidents in another home. The worries about a good marriage for the children must preoccupy every parent, as was certainly the case with Sarah's mother and father. Mixed into this account—fictitious for it never happened just this way, realistic for it is happening over and over again—is the story of the archangel Raphael who leads Tobiah to the house of his bride and provides a cure for Tobit's blindness.

In other words, religion must not be so ethereal as to overlook the humdrum, day-by-day living of ordinary family life; nor should religion be so earthly and social minded that it forgets about miracles, angels and the power before God of our prayers, fasting, almsgiving and burying the dead.

Most of all, the Book of Tobit is the story of a journey, as is so much of the Bible. Tobit, in this sense, belongs to the exodus out of Egypt, to Israel's return from Babylonian exile, to Jesus' journey to Jerusalem, and to Paul's four apostolic travels, finally from Jerusalem to Rome. A journey has a destination. It loses its meaning if the goal is forgotten. In the Scriptures, especially in Tobit, we must believe that all the small turns and delays, the difficulties and trials of one's way through life, Tobit's burying the dead and his blindness, Sarah's prayers and fidelity, will eventually make very good sense to us. Religion cannot be properly gauged by a single day or even by length of years. We must persevere with faith *to the end*. Then with St. Paul, we will declare:

> I have finished the race, I have kept the faith. From now on a merited crown awaits me; on that day the Lord, just judge that he is, will award it to me.

This quotation from Second Timothy ends significantly with an expectation of the Lord Jesus. The reward of religion is not wealth, prestige or any other worldly thing. It lies in the *person* of Jesus. ''The merited crown,'' writes Paul, will be awarded:

> not only to me but to all who have looked for his appearing with eager longing.

Religion's supreme reward lies in the full personal satisfaction and joy that is ours in Jesus. The Book of Revelation calls it ''the wedding feast of the Lamb'' (Rev 19:9).

Religion is denied its essential meaning if it degenerates into long robes, front seat in synagogues and churches, places of honor at banquets, long prayers. To show how false is such a make-believe expression of religion, Jesus called attention to the elderly woman who put two small copper coins, worth about a cent, into the collection box.

> This poor widow contributed more than all the others. . . . They gave from their surplus wealth, but she gave from her want, all that she had to live on.

This is another way of arriving at the end of the journey and of finishing the race. The widow gave *herself totally* to the

Lord. Paul, awaiting execution, has nothing more to offer, only his person and his spent life. Each is called to the wedding feast of the Lamb, full union with the person of Jesus. The wedding of Tobiah and Sarah, like every marriage, typifies our heavenly life.

Prayer:

Lord, you scourge and then have mercy; you lead us to the end of our journey when finally we understand the mystery of our life in you. When our strength fails with old age or sickness, you do not forsake us. Then we can proclaim your wondrous deeds throughout our life.

PART TWO

Sundays of Ordinary Time
Weeks 1—9

Second Sunday, "A" Cycle

Is 49:3, 5–6. In this Second Song of the Suffering Servant the prophet is called to be a light to the nations.
1 Cor 1:1–3. Paul sends greetings "to you who have been consecrated in Christ Jesus and called to be a holy people."
John 1:29–34. John the Baptist points to Jesus as the one "who ranks ahead of me . . . who is to baptize with the Holy Spirit." John did not recognize Jesus at first.

We are at the beginning of the long trek of "Ordinary Time," the thirty-four weeks which extend from now till the end of November and the start of Advent. The Scriptures are calling us to be people of hope, particularly of hope in the next generation. This attitude may seem strange at first. If we are taking our first steps into the new year, it would seem appropriate to concentrate on the work entrusted to us now, rather than to direct attention to the distant future. Nonetheless, the abiding spirit, reaching from beginning to end of the Scriptures, advises us to reach beyond our grasp—to quote an old proverb—and yet never to be discouraged and lose heart if our grasp is beyond our reach!

This realization that another generation will build on our foundation and come closer to the ideal for which we reach out with energy and hope imparts an exhilarating joy. We belong to a family and community, to a project and undertaking, far greater than our individual ability and lifetime. What little we achieve will blossom into a community achievement, bonded with love and trust. This kind of trust in the future requires heroic humility. We let the next generation pick up where we left off and accomplish far more, at times in ways that we never anticipated. Nonetheless, we are not losing anything; the new is bonded to us in love and affection, in faith and tradition.

Different moments of this "letting go" come to our attention in the biblical readings. When the prophet wrote what is now chapter 49 he was towards the end of his career. In fact, he may have been rejected by his own community. In order to establish peace within his heart, he turned to many ancient traditions, but especially to the Book of Deuteronomy and the prophecy of Jeremiah. From Deuteronomy he learned that Moses himself never entered the promised land but died on the other side of the Jordan (Deut 34). Yet, he led the people to this moment when they could feast their eyes upon this lovely country flowing with milk and honey and realize that they and their children will come to possess it. Similarly, the prophet Jeremiah felt rejected; he saw his ideals crumbling in dust, so that "my grief is incurable, my heart within me is faint" (Jer 8:18). Yet, Moses became the supreme model for Israel's religion, as Deut 34:10 admitted, "no prophet has arisen in Israel like Moses," and of all later prophets Jeremiah turned out to be the most influential upon the piety of the people.

From these sources the prophet who composed chaps. 40–55 in the Book of Isaiah was able to draw strength and inspiration and compose his "Songs of the Suffering Servant." As he wrote in today's selection, his best efforts have been small and "little," simply "to raise up the survivors of Israel." By entrusting to God himself and his cause, his hopes and the values of his life, he will become "a light to the nations" so that God's salvation "may reach to the ends of the earth." For this reason, the prophet confesses, "I am made glorious in the sight of the Lord."

This wonderful anticipation of world salvation flowed from heroic humility and drew its own heavy cost of suffer-

ing. The prophet was asked to let loose so that the next generation could accomplish dreams beyond his own best
hopes. This would be the prophet's glory.

This same spirit weaves its golden thread of hope
through the gospel account of John the Baptist. He was not
afraid to tell his followers:

> After me is to come a man
> who ranks ahead of me,
> because he was before me.

Yet, Jesus could not have come and accomplished what he
did, without the preparation which John the Baptist provided through his electrifying preaching and extraordinary
summons to justice, honesty and most of all hope in the new
age.

The same open heart is shown in the introduction of
Paul's letter to the Corinthians. He sends greetings to the
Church of Corinth whom he describes as

> consecrated in Christ Jesus
> called to be a holy people.

This exceptional hope in his religious community does not
stop there. Paul adds: ''to all those who, wherever they may
be, call on the name of our Lord Jesus Christ, their Lord and
ours.''

Today's biblical readings call us: to heroic humility, so
that the new generation can build on our accomplishments
and achieve far more than ourselves; to strong confidence
that the new will be a continuation of ourselves and a true
blossoming of ourselves; to continuous hope and optimism
that the least effort on our part will yield good fruit beyond

our dreams. In this way we are building a family that will reach for many generations into the future. Its glory and joy will appear only within the eternal happiness of our heavenly home.

Prayer:

"Here I am, Lord; I come to do your will." This is my delight. At times you may seem to overlook me for those to come afterwards. Yet you manifest the same humble and strong hope, allowing us to continue your work and even to achieve your ideals. Let me always wait upon you.

Second Sunday, "B" Cycle

1 Sam 3:3–10, 19. God calls the boy Samuel, who replies after the third summons: "Speak, Lord, for your servant is listening."

1 Cor 6:13–15, 17–20. Joined to the Lord, we are one spirit with him. As such, our "body is a temple of the Holy Spirit."

John 1:35–42. Disciples of John the Baptist turn to become followers of Jesus, pointed out to them as the anointed one and the lamb of God. Jesus changes the name of one of them from Simon to Cephas or Peter.

This Sunday's Bible readings blend two important themes: that of *call* and the other of *temple*. The young man Samuel is residing in the temple or sanctuary at Shiloh, some twenty miles north of Jerusalem, where the ark of the covenant was enshrined. Within the Shiloh sanctuary Samuel will be called to a revolutionary ministry that will sweep far beyond the dreams of the priest Eli and change the entire history of the people. Samuel will anoint the first kings of Israel, Saul and then David. In today's selection from First Corinthians Paul speaks of our bodies as "a temple of the Holy Spirit" and summons the Corinthians to a renewed respect for its dignity: "Shun lewd conduct [by which someone] sins against his or her own body." Finally, in the gospel, Jesus is proclaimed the "Christ" or the "anointed one," the "lamb of God," "rabbi" or "teacher." "Anointed one" associates Jesus with Israel's long history of kings and high priests, the anointed ones among Jesus' Israelite ancestry; "lamb of God" brings to mind the temple sacrifices, which commemorated freedom and new life.

A few key words have released many biblical memories; here as always the entire Scriptures find their "yes" in Jesus through whom "whatever promises God has made have been fulfilled" (2 Cor 1:19–20). This strong affirming "yes" is given to particularly those texts which center on "call" and "temple." Our meditation will help us to affirm a new "yes" of dedication and affirmation for our own call and the sacredness of ourselves as the temple of God.

Today's readings extend or enlarge what we normally mean by sanctuary, temple or church. The Scripture means far more than a building; it refers primarily to ourselves, body and soul, in our relationships within family and community, in the direction of our call or vocation. This larger concept of "temple" agrees with the ancient biblical word for temple. In the earliest traditions the temple was called in Hebrew, *mishkan,* a word that literally means a "tent" in which the entire family lived during nomadic desert wandering. The people assembled for prayer and worship at "the meeting tent" (Lev 1:1).

Similarly, at a later time the word for temple turned out to be the simple one for "house," in Hebrew *bavit, beit* or *beth* (cf., Beth-lehem, "house of bread"). In its earliest meaning, *bavit* did not refer to a structure but rather to people, the family. Gradually, to build a family came to mean to build a house for the family to live in. Temple, therefore, has many biblical ties to marriage, family and people who are bonded in love and good ideals.

At the sanctuary or temple of Shiloh, Samuel is summoned by God to undertake his prophetic ministry. As we know from later history, Samuel was to anoint the first kings of Israel and so to transform the entire history of the people. Through the king the twelve tribes were to be ever more firmly united and centralized. The kings could even take this centralization too seriously and use it as a means of coercing the people into forced labor and unjust taxation (1 Kings 5:27; chap. 11). The biblical ideal for royalty, however, was not to be denied. Like temple, it was meant to unite people as a single family; all their actions were intended to become worship and praise, undertaken in obedience to God's ideals for justice and goodness.

Paul stresses this bond of union and the holiness that is expected of people whose bodies form the temple of the Lord:

> Shun lewd conduct. . . . You must know that
> your body is a temple of the Holy Spirit, who is
> within—the Spirit you have received from God.
> You are not your own.

Any sin that violates the holiness of the body is compared to a desecration of the temple, a violation of its holiness and a serious offense against the goodness of God.

While each of us constitutes a temple of the Lord, altogether we form one large temple or sanctuary. The bonds of union which unite us in life become an extension of the temple in which the Holy Spirit dwells. Paul moves quickly from the bond of union which unites people sexually in marriage to the bond of union which unites us in prayer and faith with the Holy Spirit. Just as husbands and wives are members of one body, Paul makes use of this image to speak of the church in which "your bodies are members of Christ."

Whatever be our call or vocation, to marriage, religious communities, priesthood or single state, nonetheless we reach out towards others with our bodies, to speak and console, to touch and heal, to walk and come to assistance, to think and plan for their happiness. In all these ways we are acting within the temple of the Holy Spirit and offering worship to God.

We are sometimes called to enter the inner sanctum of this temple, into the Holy of Holies. Jesus says to us as to the first disciples: "What are you looking for? . . . Come and see." And so we enter into prolonged prayer and conversation with Jesus. From the joy of such intimacy with Jesus, we rush out to our family and friends to exclaim, "We have found the Messiah!" We are God's instruments, speaking each one's name, as once God called out in the sanctuary of Shiloh, "Samuel! Samuel!"

Prayer:

Lord, open my ears that I may always hear your voice. At times I forget that you reside within the temple of my body and I am tempted to think or act in ways that might even profane your holy temple. Open my ears so that I hear your calling me to small acts of forgiveness and kindness. You do not always ask great sacrifices and magnificent holocausts, only the small but heroic response, "Here I am, Lord; I come to do your will."

Second Sunday, "C" Cycle

Isa 62:1–5. Jerusalem will no longer be desolate and forsaken but will be overflowing with life. The Lord will address her as "My Delight" and her land will be called "Espoused."

1 Cor 12:4–11. There are many gifts and ministries, but one and the same Spirit who accomplishes each good action in everyone.

John 2:1–12. The marriage feast of Cana where Jesus works the "first of his signs" and reveals his glory.

In John's gospel the marriage of a young couple is blessed by Jesus' presence and made joyful by turning water into the best of wine in plentiful good measure. Isaiah looks upon another kind of marriage, the bond of union between God and his people Israel. The prophet sees a marriage which had become desolate and discouraging return to its first love and excitement. The Lord will call Jerusalem "My Delight" and the land "Espoused." The second reading recognizes the diversity which comes together in marriage and in the church.

It is important to note how biblical symbols develop. The starting point is always with ourselves and our human ways of life. In John's gospel a marriage invitation is extended to Mary (presumably Joseph, her husband, is already deceased), as well as to Jesus and his first disciples. As a matter of fact, the entire village would be asked to come. From such a normal human occurrence as a marriage reception, the evangelist St. John develops an extraordinary symbol of Christ's love for the church and the intimacy with which Jesus is united with each of us through faith.

Once the human institution is blessed and transformed

into the symbol of God's love and goodness towards us, new demands and expectations are made upon the human institution which inspired the symbol—in this case upon marriage. The first and second readings begin to develop these new ideals from marriage and in turn consecrate the human institution of marriage all the more magnificently.

Paul speaks of the "different gifts," "different ministries" and "different works." The repetition of the word "different" may become tiresome. Yet at times in marriage and in other human associations these differences become worse than "tiring" or "boring." They provoke a rupture of love and friendship, cause anger, bitter words and resentment. For his part Paul draws upon these differences to make a statement about the intimate bond of union among the three persons of the Holy Trinity:

> There are different gifts but the same *Spirit;* there are different ministries but the same *Lord;* there are different works but the same *God* who accomplishes all of them in everyone.

Lord refers to Jesus; God to the first person of the Trinity; Spirit to the third person. No bond of union, not even the happiest of marriages, can compare with the intimacy and total sharing that exist between the three distinct persons in the Holy Trinity, God, Lord and Spirit. Together, however, they form only one deity, one God.

The gifts, ministries and works, which converge peacefully and joyously in the Holy Trinity, can become the source of serious division in marriages, neighborhoods, religious communities and friendships. Paul refers to the "gift of tongues" and the gift "of interpreting the tongues." Yet, at times friendships and even marriages break down because of too much talking or too much explanation. Others become *jealous* at the "miraculous powers" which they see in members of their own family or neighborhood.

Even if the situation becomes desolate and happy marriages or friendships break down into isolated "forsaken" persons, there is still hope. Such is the unhappy marriage seen by the prophet Isaiah in chapter 62. In the last chapters of the book of Isaiah, chapters 56 to 66, the prophet is addressing the desolate scene of Jerusalem. Many buildings are in ruin, the people are taking advantage of one another in their desperate scramble for food and housing. It is the discouraging situation described very well by prophets Haggai, Zechariah and Malachi. Yet the prophet of hope listens to God's voice:

> For Zion's sake I will not be silent,
>   for Jerusalem's sake I will not be quiet,
> Until her vindication shines forth like the dawn,
>   and her victory like a burning torch.

God will renew the marriage bond with his people:

> You shall be called "My Delight,"
>   and your land "Espoused."
> As a bridegroom and bride rejoice with one another,
>   so shall your God rejoice in you.

This expectation is difficult; it demands heroic forgiveness. Yet it holds out the magnificent hope of renewing the initial joys of each marriage. It tells each person, whether married or not, those in priesthood and religious life, those within the single state, that each one's first and finest hopes will be renewed and brought back to life. Eventually God fulfills every good hope, and leads us into the intimate bond of life within the Holy Trinity.

Prayer:

Lord, whether we are young or old, at the beginning of our life's vocation or towards the end of it, whether we can look ahead with pure hopes and youthful enthusiasm or whether we are looking back with many disappointments and mistakes, we can each sing a new song. You place the words of the Psalm upon everyone's lips this Sunday: Sing a new song to the Lord, sing to the Lord, all you lands. Tell his glory among the nations.

Third Sunday, "A" Cycle

Is 8:23—9:3. Darkness and gloom give way to light and joy. Great, victorious moments are renewed.

1 Cor 1:10—13, 17. Divisions should cease, even those in the name of Paul, Cephas, Apollos or Christ. We have all been baptized in the name of the one Lord and Savior, whose cross has become our gospel.

Matt 4:12–23. Jesus returns to Galilee to begin his public ministry. Here he calls his first disciples, two sets of brothers who immediately follow him. He proclaims the good news of the kingdom.

Matthew's long, elaborate, four-chapter introduction to his work is completed with today's gospel reading. The evangelist again not only summarizes ancestral hopes but also announces a glorious future. In a practical way he provides helpers in achieving this goal. The first reading for today gives the larger Old Testament setting for one of Matthew's citations. In the second reading Paul offers a salutary piece of advice about one of the principal dangers that keep good people and good movements from accomplishing their goals, that small but disastrous human problem of jealousy!

Jesus is back in Galilee, about to begin his public ministry. For Matthew this geographical data sets the stage for the first of five great discourses, the Sermon on the Mount in chapters 5–7.

> The Kingdom of heaven is at hand. . . . Jesus toured all of Galilee. He taught in their synagogues, proclaimed the good news of the kingdom, and cured the people of every disease and illness.

At the very end of chap. 4 we are told about "the great crowds that followed him. [They] came from Galilee, from the Ten Cities [which were pagan and Greek], from Jerusalem and Judea, and from across the Jordan." The universal sweep of the kingdom is already brought to our attention; it will be solemnized at the end of Matthew's gospel with the commission to "make disciples of all the nations" (Matt 28:19).

Matthew, as we already noted, cites the text of Isaiah. It is interesting how the Hebrew phrase of Isaiah, "district of the Gentiles" has been transformed into "heathen Galilee" by Matthew. It is subtle change. The phrase reads in the Hebrew: *gelil hagoyim,* literally "the circle" or "the district of the gentiles." Matthew reads the common word "circle" or "district" as a proper name, "Galilee," which derives from the Hebrew *gelil.*

This kind of updating and adaptation must always be done. As a matter of fact, Isaiah refers to "the day of Midian," an episode in the Book of Judges (Judg 6—8). Yet the prophet does not intend to repeat literally the details of that military adventure; for Isaiah the kingdom is come in a non-violent way through God's extraordinary intervention.

Another instance of adaptation is brought to our attention in the second reading. Paul refers to the necessity of preaching the cross of Jesus. In another place Paul insists that "those who belong to Christ Jesus have crucified their flesh with its passions and desires" (Gal 5:24). Or again, Paul confesses that "I have been crucified with Christ" (Gal 2:19). Paul does not intend physical crucifixion with nails through hands and feet, as happened cruelly to Jesus. Paul is looking upon the crucifixion as a symbol which can be reflected in many different ways in peoples' lives down through the ages.

In order that this adaptation be made and the preaching of Jesus be relived in each person, whatever be the changing circumstances of their lives and times, there must be preachers of the gospel. For this reason, on Sunday morning, we do not simply read the Scripture; we need someone to break the bread of God's word into morsels that can be chewed, reflected upon, absorbed within the system and thus become the source of life and vitality. In one of the final sections in Matthew's long introduction, Jesus summons his first disciples who up till then were self-employed, fishing on the Lake of Galilee. Jesus says to them:

> Come after me and I will make you now fish for men and women.

In calling disciples to repeat, adapt and apply his message for people not only of Galilee but of the pagan Ten Cities, Jesus himself adapts the image of fishing to a religious meaning.

Close disciples of Jesus have their own kind of sinfulness. We do not have to wait till the time of St. Paul and his epistle to the Corinthians to know about this failure. Already within the gospels we find the disciples jealous of one another. John the Baptist's disciples were jealous of those who began to follow Jesus (John 3:26). Jesus' own immediate disciples became indignant of Zebedee's sons in their effort to obtain first places in the kingdom (Matt 20:26). Jealousy is the vice which hits "good" people and spoils not only their goodness but also the attractiveness of the gospel.

In writing to the Corinthians, Paul will not tolerate such jealousy and quarreling that sets good people against good people. He asks: "Has Christ, then, been divided into parts?" With good reasons people in today's pagan "Ten Cities" expect the disciples of Jesus to be bonded in forgiveness, love and most of all in attachment to the person of Jesus. They are expected to announce in their lives as well as in their words the cross of Jesus. Obviously, disciples will suffer if they are to avoid jealousy, often put their pride in their pocket, forgive and truly admire the good qualities and accomplishments of their brothers and sisters.

Prayer:

Lord, you are my light and salvation, my life's refuge. As I hear your voice, enable me always to be obedient at once and follow you. I will hear your voice, calling me away from jealousy and small-mindedness. Enable me to rejoice in the good deeds of others. In them I shall see the bounty of the Lord in the land of the living.

Third Sunday, "B" Cycle

Jon 3:1–5, 10. Because the people of Nineveh repented at the preaching of Jonah and turned from their evil ways, God repented of the evil that he had threatened to do to them.

1 Cor 7:29–31. The time is short. The world as we know it is passing away. Make use of the world as though not using it.

Mark 1:14–20. Jesus preaches that the reign of God is at hand. Reform your lives and believe in the good news. Then he called his first disciples; they abandoned their former occupation and went off in his company.

Not frequently, but usually at times and in ways that we had not anticipated, abrupt changes shake up our lives: a sudden death in the family; or the unexpected news of a terminal illness; a new friend who knocks us off our feet and becomes a permanent part of our lives; loss of employment after many years of experience. Each one of us can fill in the details of a situation where a radical change is forced upon us. We never expected it to happen to us, and so we are totally unprepared. Yet the episode is so real that we must admit the hand of God in what happens. Otherwise, God is not real or at least God is not a part of our real life.

The Book of Jonah confronts us with several serious, unexpected, even radical changes. First, we would never expect a prophet to disobey God and go first in the wrong direction, as Jonah did; nor for the prophet to continue in bad behavior by being angry at God when the foreigners repent and turn to God with sincere hearts. Second, the most brutal people of ancient times, the Assyrians, whose armies enforced peace by calculated cruelty, lest any subject people should even think of revolting for independence, are suddenly converted to the Lord. In fact, they appear more pious than the holy prophet Jonah whom God sent to preach to them. It is almost impossible for us today to imagine the results if a brutal, oppressive government should be converted and turn to the Lord. World politicians would be set on their head. Third, another sudden change happens in the Book of

Jonah. We are told that God "repented of the evil that he had threatened to do to them; he did not carry it out." God changed his divine mind and decided not to fulfill one of his prophecies. There are many oracles of God's word against Assyria in the Bible (Isa 14:24–27; 31:8–9; Book of Nahum). Fourth, the gospel confronts us with the sudden decision by the sons of Zebedee whom Jesus "summoned on the spot. They abandoned their father Zebedee . . . and went off in [Jesus'] company." Both the sons and the father, each in his way, were faced with serious consequences for daily life.

As mentioned already, these moments do not come often, but come they certainly do, and most of the time we are caught by surprise. We have no ready-made emergency plan! Perhaps with these incidents in mind, Paul wrote to the Corinthians: "those who make use of the world [should do so] as though they were not using it, for the world as we know it is passing away." There are other times when Paul gave much different advice. To those who quit their jobs on the pretext that the end of the world was right around the corner and the Lord Jesus would suddenly appear, Paul wrote very sternly: "anyone who would not work should not eat." He then adds:

> We hear that some of you are unruly, not keeping busy but acting like busy-bodies. We enjoin all such, and we urge them strongly in the Lord Jesus Christ, to earn the food they eat by working quietly (2 Thess 3:11–12).

While in today's selection Paul advises "those with wives or husbands should live as though they had none," at another place in the first epistle to the Corinthians, he writes:

In the present time of stress it seems good to me
for a person to continue as he or she is. Are you
bound to a wife or husband? Then do not seek
your freedom (1 Cor 7:26–27).

"There is an appointed time for everything," writes
the sage Koheleth, author of the Book of Ecclesiastes. "A
time to be born, and a time to die . . . a time to embrace,
and a time to be far from embraces" (Eccles 3:1,2,5). Today we are asked to consider those rare but most important
moments when our world as we know it suddenly falls apart.

Most important of all, we must hear the voice of Jesus
in the event. "Come after me." No matter how sudden the
event and how unprepared we may be, no matter how painful and seemingly bad and evil, somehow or other the hand
of God is present. We are not alone, nor are we victimized
uselessly, nor are we destroyed by fate.

We are given an opportunity to grow in purity of heart
and sincere dedication to God. We are forced to question
many of our motives for our former way of living that has
now collapsed. Have we been leading good and honorable
lives, simply to appear good, to assure ourselves of a profitable reward, to have bargaining power with God? Or instead have we been loving "the Lord, your God, with all
your heart, and with all your soul, and with all your
strength" (Deut 6:5).

What may be a profound disappointment to us, in some
strange or unusual way may turn into an opportunity of
grace for ourselves and for many others. Jonah's frustration,
at seeing the conversion of his enemies, became a symbol of
world salvation, centuries before the time of Jesus.

Somehow or other, we need to learn how to be, at one
and the same time, realists and mystics, using this world and

not using it, energetic yet totally dependent upon God, loving others yet also loving God with *all* one's heart, mind and strength, able to hold on and to let go.

When all is said and done, there is no explanation. We are faced with profound mystery. We must identify the mystery as "the reign of God . . . at hand . . . and believe."

Prayer:

Teach me your ways, O Lord. I badly need your direction, particularly for those sudden, unexpected and unprepared moments of change. As you teach me humble surrender, I ask you to remember your compassion and your kindness of old. I would not dare to address you in this way if you had not taught me these very words among the inspired prayers of the psalmist.

Third Sunday, "C" Cycle

Neh 8:2–6, 8–10. Ezra reads and explains the Torah to all the people. While the people were weeping, he told them that "rejoicing in the Lord must be your strength!"

1 Cor 12:12–30. Just as the body is one, but has many members . . . so it is with Christ. Each member has need of the other, each with different gifts.

Luke 1:1–4; 4:14–21. Luke introduces his gospel and then concludes his solemn introduction with Jesus' initial preaching at Nazareth, a summary of his entire ministry.

We are reminded today how the Scriptures, like the human body, grows and develops, extends itself through many different members and parts, absorbs nourishment and new experiences. God's will is not to be confined to any absolute, written law; rather it is to be interpreted within the united body of believers and within the needs and possibilities of each "today."

Although Ezra appears in the late history of Israel, around 428 B.C., he performs almost as another Moses. He is responsible for the final redaction of the Torah or first five books of Moses. These had been growing through the centuries, always in the authentic spirit of Moses and under his mighty patronage, yet reaching out to problems and needs, like royalty or intricate city life, which he had never experienced himself nor clearly foreseen for the people. Yet, when Ezra presents this final edition of the Torah to the people, he does more than read it to them. He also "interpreted it so that all could understand what was read." According to Jewish tradition, this incident marks the beginning of oral interpretation of the law.

These new translations in the popular, Aramaic language absorbed new insights and interpretations and came to be called the *Targum*. The age of Ezra also marked the beginning of the *Haggadah,* a collection of edifying and inspiring stories, exemplifying the ancient Scriptures in a new age. There gradually began to appear as well the many new ways of applying the ancient law to new circumstances, so that each moment would be sanctified by the will of God; this combination of Aramaic and late Hebrew legal tradition came to be called the *Talmud*.

We sense a similar type of development from ancient tradition to new insights in the introductory lines of Luke's gospel:

> I have carefully traced the whole sequence of events from the beginning, and have decided to set it in writing for you . . . so that you . . . may see how reliable [is] the instruction.

Luke had already referred to "many [others who] have undertaken to compile a narrative of the events which have been fulfilled in our midst." In other words, the gospel, like the Torah of Moses, had been growing and developing with the preaching of later disciples. For this reason, we finally end up with four gospel accounts besides the very different "gospel"—at least quite different in form and emphasis—which "I [Paul] preach" (Rom 2:16).

In his first sermon at Nazareth, Jesus too stressed the need to adapt and apply the message. Jesus declared:

Today this Scripture passage is fulfilled in your hearing.

"Today!" brings its own set of circumstances, some of them not clearly understood and certainly not clearly anticipated ahead of time. It was by surprise that the Messiah should come out of Nazareth; no one expected that this inconspicuous city should beget the true and unique Son of God. Furthermore, in the continuation of the sermon, as recorded in chapter 4 of Luke's gospel, Jesus draws upon the ancient scriptures, again to surprise the people with a new, although authentic interpretation.

The final clarity in God's message does not come, simply by knowing the Hebrew or Greek text, nor by living in the neighborhood of Ezra or Jesus. In each case the Scriptures needed to be explained because the initial reaction of the people was not accurate. Ezra corrected them when they began to weep; Jesus asked the people to reach outward to gentiles. However, explanation was possible only with a strong sense of unity among the people—unity among themselves, unity with their religious leaders, unity of the leaders with the needs and conditions of the people, unity with all

that we call "today," when "this Scripture passage is fulfilled in your hearing."

Here is where the second reading comes forcefully to
our rescue:

> The body is one and has many members, but all
> the members, many though they are, are one
> body; and so it is with Christ.

The Greek text is even stronger in the final phrase: "and
thus is Christ." Each member must attend to the other.
Again Paul gives the radical reason:

> It was in one Spirit that all of us, whether Jew or
> Greek, slave or free, were baptized into one body.
> All of us have been given to drink of the one
> Spirit.

Paul later enumerates the many different gifts of the Spirit:
"apostles, prophets, teachers, miracle workers, healers, as-
sistants, administrators, those who speak in tongues, [those
with] the gift of interpretation of tongues."

Only through this bond of unity among the members of
the body of the Lord, a bond of unity that reaches outward
to the needs and hopes of each "today," can we grow strong
in the Spirit of God, sturdy in abiding by God's holy will,
and as Ezra advised, finding our strength by peacefully rejoicing in the Lord. In unity we learn the correct and helpful
application of Scripture to our own age and place.

Prayer:

Your words, Lord, are spirit and life. If they are alive,
then they belong to each day of my life, absorbing something of each day so as to guide me and strengthen me. Grant

me loyalty to your body, the Church; keep me close to your Spirit, the soul of the Church; and allow all of us together to grow in your likeness.

Fourth Sunday, "A" Cycle

Zeph 2:3; 3:12–13. God shall leave behind a people humble and lowly, the remnant of Israel.

1 Cor 1:26–31. God chose people absurd, weak and despised, so that no one could boast before God but rather find in God their wisdom, justice, sanctification and redemption.

Matt 5:1–12. By means of the beatitudes the disciples are instructed, that in weeping they can rejoice in God and that in single-heartedness they can see God.

The Beatitudes open the first of Jesus' five major sermons in the gospel of Matthew. Jesus had just called his first twelve disciples (Matt 4:18–22). Matthew, moreover, had just summarized the entire missionary program of Jesus: "He taught in their synagogues, proclaimed the good news of the kingdom, and cured the people of every disease" (Matt 4:23). After this we are told:

> When he saw the crowds he went up on the mountainside. After he had sat down his disciples gathered around him, and he began to teach them [by means of the Beatitudes].

We find ourselves then at a grand opening. A dramatic change has taken place in the history of Israel. The Gospel of Mark summarizes it all the more succinctly:

> This is the time of fulfillment. The reign of God is
> at hand! Reform your lives and believe in the gos-
> pel (Mark 1:15).

Luke, likewise, signals us to take note of the crucial, new
moment in salvation. In the synagogue of Nazareth, Jesus
began his first discourse, first reading from the prophecy of
Isaiah and then declaring solemnly and unequivocally:

> Today this Scripture passage is fulfilled in your
> hearing (Luke 4:21).

This same sense of an abrupt change or at least of serious reversal of what people expect can be spotted in the
other readings for this Sunday. In the selection from Zephaniah comes the final part of this prophetic book. Up till
now the prophecy is generally dark, gloomy, even totally
pessimistic. From this material the church derived the extraordinary song, *Dies Illa, Dies Irae,* once sung at all funeral Masses, ''That day, a day of wrath.'' These lines
within the prophecy sound like booming blast and roaring
thunder. Yet the prophet does not end in such a downbeat
way:

> I will leave as a remnant in your midst
> a people humble and lowly.

From this prophecy comes a Hebrew word, popularly used
among us, the *anawim,* ''you humble of the earth.'' Out of
loss and destruction there will emerge ''a people, humble
and lowly, who take refuge in the name of the Lord: the
remnant of Israel.'' Here is another prophetical word, al-

most a technical term for the messianic people, the "remnant," already put into common use by the prophets Amos (5:15) and Isaiah (10:19–22).

This new, humble messianic remnant "shall do no wrong and speak no lies." They will be direct and sincere, honest and open as the sky. They are "the single-hearted [people who] shall see God," according to the Beatitudes. With clear 20/20 vision they shall peer into the heavens and see God; with the same clarity they shall articulate that vision to others: "no wrong . . . no lies; nor . . . in their mouths a deceitful tongue," as we are told in the selection from Zephaniah.

Strangely enough, even in our poverty and disgrace, in the midst of our mistakes and humiliation, we can still pretend to be something different and better than we are. At least such was the problem with the Corinthians whom Paul addresses with blunt speech and stern correction:

> Consider your own situation. Not many of you are wise . . . [nor] influential [nor] well-born. God chose those whom the world considers absurd to shame the wise. . . .

And if we should read the entire First Letter to the Corinthians, we find that Paul is almost continually arguing with them, correcting them, at times with tears and at other times even sarcastically.

When anyone of us is silenced, humiliated, corrected for wrong doing, disgraced by our own or someone else's mistakes; when we are subjected to illness that can seem to deprive us of human dignity or at least of our adult independence; whenever we are faced with reversals which cause our limitations and weakness to be apparent to others;

whenever, in short, we can no longer be in full control of our actions, responses and destiny—we face what seems "that day, a day of wrath." We can also transform it, like Zephaniah, into a day of blessing. It can become the occasion of Jesus' messianic triumph in our family and community. We can find ourselves in the rank of that "people, humble and lowly, who take refuge in the name of the Lord: the remnant of Israel."

In the depths of our private person, in the roots of our family and community existence, we learn what we had known all along but never thought to be important. Yet now it imparts sanity and salvation: "It is God who has given you life in Christ Jesus." Jesus becomes "our wisdom and also our justice, our sanctification, and our redemption." Each of these words is heavy with biblical theology. As we unpack them a bit, we see their important message of salvation at a critical time of our lives:

> "our wisdom," in that Jesus reaches across
> our life and puts it all together in an entirely new
> way;

> "our justice," because no longer do we seek to
> fulfill petty desires, worldly ambitions, materialistic demands; our most noble desires are fully
> and justly fulfilled;

> "our sanctification," that cleanses us from unworthy motives and selfish concerns and unites us
> in a totally new and deeper way with God;

> "our redemption," because Jesus is totally one
> with us, for he endured the humiliation of the
> cross and shared in our death.

Therefore, when we are ''poor in spirit,'' ''sorrowing,'' and ''lowly,'' Jesus says to us: ''How blest!'' With a new singleheartedness, we ''shall see God.'' We can become peacemakers. We can ''be glad and rejoice, for your reward in heaven is great.''

Prayer:

Lord, you keep faith forever and secure justice for the oppressed. When we become blind, you give us new sight to view our lives and our world correctly. When we are homeless, we want to protect strangers. When we are humiliated, we know how to sustain our neighbors in their moment of shame. In this way, Lord, you come to reign in our lives.

Fourth Sunday, ''B'' Cycle

Deut 18: 15–20. God will raise up a prophet like Moses from your own kin and put his words on the lips of that prophet.

1 Cor 7:32–35. An unmarried person is totally concerned about the Lord's affairs and about pleasing the Lord, while a married person's interests are divided.

Mark 1:21–28. Jesus spoke as one with authority and the people were spellbound. With the same authority Jesus drove out evil spirits.

We are asked to consider how honest and how authentic we really are. Each of us carries our measure of dishonesty and bias, of partial blindness to the truth and favoritism towards our own insights and personal causes. We are being called to question in a healthy way our motives and interests. In other words, we are not being asked to search into our flagrant sins and faults, at what is obviously wrong and easily recognized as such; God is questioning us, whether or not we are doing the right thing *for the right reason.* Are we using religion and God for our personal benefit? In some ways we are faced with what was the most difficult moment in the vocation of the prophet: how to tell good people that they are not good enough or that they are good for the wrong reasons!

In the first reading God is saying to the people through his faithful servant Moses:

> A prophet like you will the Lord, your God, raise
> up for you from among your own kin.

Even such a sacred institution as prophecy was open to derailment and to misdirection; it must be reevaluated and judged by comparison with Moses: "a prophet *like you.*"

Old Testament prophecy certainly declined. In 1 Kings 22 prophets are pitted against prophets; the good prophet Micaiah even sees how "the Lord has put a lying spirit in the mouths of these prophets of yours" (1 Kgs 22:23). Amos, the first of the classical prophets with books to their name, even went on record to deny: "I am no prophet nor a member of a prophetic band" (Amos 7:14). Jeremiah's greatest antagonist came from a person whom the text calls, without qualification, "the prophet Hananiah" (Jer 28:1). The problem did not lie so much in false theology, nor necessarily in the open immorality of the "false prophet." Rather, their motivation was destroying their credibility.

Prophecy was to be judged by comparison with Moses. We read elsewhere in the Bible: "no prophet has arisen in Israel like Moses, whom the Lord knew face to face" (Deut 34:10). In the same chapter where this canonization of

Moses took place, we are told of the heroic obedience of Moses and his willingness to remain with the people Israel, even if it meant that the dream and goal of his lifetime were to be denied fulfillment. He was to die on the far side of the Jordan River and never enter the promised land. As he looked out upon the beautiful country, God said:

> This is the land which I swore to Abraham, Isaac and Jacob that I would give to their descendants. I have let you feast your eyes upon it, but you shall not cross over (Deut 34:4).

In this context Moses is declared "the servant of the Lord." For personal, selfish reasons he could have rushed ahead. It is overdramatizing the incident, and yet somehow it also brings out the tragic pathos, if we add: God would not permit his servant even to put his toe into the River Jordan. He must die on the other side with the people Israel.

From this background we begin to understand Paul's words in First Corinthians:

> the married person is busy with this world's demands and is occupied with ways to please the spouse. This means that such a one is divided. The virgin—indeed, any unmarried person—is concerned with the things of the Lord, in pursuit of holiness in body and spirit.

The question here strikes at the motivation and spirit that abide at the heart of the married and unmarried. Without any doubt the Bible blesses marriage. After creating humankind male and female in the divine image, "God blessed them, saying: 'Be fertile and multiply.' . . . God looked at everything he had made, and he found it very good'' (Gen 1:27,28,31). Again we read in Genesis:

> The Lord God said: ''It is not good for man or woman to be alone. I will make a suitable partner'' (Gen 2:18).

The editor then reflects upon the divine action:

> That is why a spouse leaves father and mother and clings to their married partner, and the two of them become one body (Gen 2:24).

Almost immediately in Genesis husband and wife turn selfishly against their partner and the first recorded sin in the Bible takes place.

By contrast in today's gospel Jesus does not act out of selfish motivation. Rather he speaks ''in a spirit of authority!'' He never uses his divinity for his own benefit. If he works miracles it is out of compassion for the unfortunate and the helpless. When challenged to display miraculous powers for his own sake—for instance, when he hung dying upon the cross—he remained silent and inactive:

> People going by kept insulting him, tossing their heads and saying, ''Ha, ha! So you were going to destroy the temple and rebuild it in three days! Save yourself now by coming down from that cross!''

We also notice the personal response of Jesus towards the man with an unclean spirit. We are told that ''Jesus rebuked him sharply: 'Be quiet! Come out of the man!' '' One of the manuscript readings even supports an angry reaction on Jesus' part. It is as though he was unable to restrain his sorrow and anger that a fellow human being should be afflicted this sorely and pitifully. Seeking the Father's will in all his human actions, Jesus gives the model for prophecy, for marriage, for the single state. Seeking the Lord alone, one can give herself or himself totally to the happiness of spouse, of neighbor, of religious community. Here then is the authentic credential enabling one to act with prophetic authority.

Prayer:

Lord, today when I hear your voice, soften the hardness of my jealous and selfish heart. You have placed much goodness within me; you have surrounded me with a family and community of exceptional goodness. May I worship you in all that I do, by remaining loyal to these obligations of love.

Fourth Sunday, "C" Cycle

Jer 1:4–5, 17–19. Jeremiah's call to prophecy; his strength against all opposition.

1 Cor 12:31–13:13 The hymn to charity.

Luke 4:21–30. Jesus' first discourse at Nazareth leads to rejection, even to a threat against his life.

At the heart of today's readings lies a serious warning which can also be the source of our peace and joy: unless we are willing to share our best gifts, we will lose what little we possess.

We begin with Jesus' first discourse at Nazareth which included a reading from the prophecy of Isaiah. It was read

in last week's gospel. The Spirit of the Lord, according to
the prophecy of Isaiah,

> has sent me to bring glad tidings to the poor,
>   to proclaim liberty to captives
> Recovery of sight to the blind
>   and release to prisoners (Is 61:1; Luke 4:18).

As Luke develops this opening sermon of Jesus, Israel is
asked to share these blessings of the jubilee year with foreigners. Jesus cites the example of Elijah who miraculously
supplied food for the "widow of Zarephath near Sidon."
The prophet Elisha healed the foreign commander "Naaman
the Syrian."

Miracles were never intended as a show of power and
grandeur, nor as a way of bolstering one's wealth and security. Again to quote from Isaiah 61, miracles are worked by
God "to bring glad tidings to the poor."

To share our best with others is always difficult; it also
brings our greatest joys and gifts. We have only to cite the
example of marriage. When parents share their greatest possession, their own sons and daughters, and give their con-
sent to the marriage of their children, they lose their prized
possession but they gain another son or daughter and the
blessing of grandchildren.

The difficulty of sharing with a wider family shows up
poignantly in the prophecy of Jeremiah. The short reading in
today's Eucharist evokes a memory of the prophet's trauma
and sorrow. We sense the opposition of his own family, who
turn against him in chaps. 11 & 12:

> Even your own brothers, the members of your
> parents' house, betray you. . . . Do not believe

them, even if they are friendly to you in their
words (Jer 12:6).

Fellow prophets turned against him, as we note in chap. 28,
when the prophet Hananiah humiliated Jeremiah before all
the people.

Jeremiah struggled through a lifetime of such trials. He
disputed with God, at times against God, in what are called
his "Confessions":

> You are just, O Lord,
>   but I must still argue my case against you!
> Why does the way of the godless prosper? (Jer 12:1)

Only at the end of his life did he have a clue or insight. The
"blame" is to be placed at God's doorstep. God had
planned it that way from the beginning, even before Jeremiah was born, much less in possession of his free will:

> Before I formed you in the womb I knew you,
>   before you were born I dedicated you,
>   a prophet to the nations I appointed you.

Jeremiah wrote these words as his life was coming to an
end, a life of seeming failure. Even in the last recorded
events of his life down in Egypt, where he was dragged
against his will (chaps. 42–44), he is found rejected by his
own people. The mystery of it all could be accepted peacefully in the recognition that such was the will of God.

Once Jeremiah could reach blindly, totally and lovingly towards God, then, and only then, a reason rushed to
his rescue: "a prophet to the nations I appointed you." Jeremiah's ministry was not to be restricted to the small circle

of his own people; his family was to embrace the world. By giving up what he prized most, he was given love and appreciation a thousand times overflowing.

The second reading for today, not only lies at the heart of today's liturgy, placed in between the selection from Jeremiah and that from Luke, but it also lies at the heart of our meditation: by losing we gain. By losing our selfishness we gain a world of love in return. Paul incorporates into his Epistle to the Corinthians an early hymn to charity. Love is

patient	not prone to anger
kind	does not brood over injuries
not jealous	limitless in forebearance
not snobbish	never fails

Yet, in giving away, we must not act with "a noisy gong, a clanging cymbal." Even if we work miracles and "have faith great enough to move mountains, but have not love, I am nothing." Even "if I give everything I have to feed the poor and hand over my body to be burned, but have not love, I gain nothing."

Charity such as this led Jesus to the cross. It expects the same of us. In his Epistle to the Galatians, Paul enumerates the fruits of the spirit, "love, joy, peace" etc. He then adds:

Those who belong to Christ Jesus have crucified their flesh with its passions and desires. Since we live by the spirit, let us follow the spirit's lead. Let us never be boastful, or challenging, or jealous toward one another (Gal 5:24–26).

The fruits of the spirit, the qualities of true love, are presented in the context of being "crucified" with Jesus. We are also promised the hope of the resurrection. We are gifted with new strength and integrity on earth. The last sentence in today's gospel reveals the strength by which we are led to a new life. It is also a symbol of Jesus' own resurrection from the dead:

> He went straight through their midst and walked away.

Like Jeremiah, he walked away, a prophet to the nations, to a family across the universe. We share that promise if we share our best.

Prayer:

Lord, we take refuge in you. What you ask at times is difficult; it even seems to take away our prized possessions. Yet, you are our hope, our trust from our youth. On you we have depended from our mother's womb. In following your will, we will see the victory of your justice and the fulfillment of your hopes in our lives and families.

Fifth Sunday, "A" Cycle

Is 58:7–10. Do not turn your back on your own; share your bread with the hungry. Then light shall rise for you in the darkness.

1 Cor 2:1–5. Paul came among you in weakness and fear but also with the convincing power of the Spirit. Your faith rests not on human wisdom but on the power of God.

Matt 5:13–16. You are the salt of the earth . . . the light of the world. Let your light shine before others so that they may give praise to your heavenly Father.

Light is a key word found explicitly in today's first and third readings; in the second reading Paul advises us that light does not come from "wise" argumentation and clever sophistry but from the cross of Jesus: "I would speak of nothing but Jesus Christ and him crucified." If we slip back again to the first reading, we are directed to those people among us who are "hungry," "afflicted" and "homeless" in order to be in the presence of "Jesus Christ and him crucified". It is helpful to retrace our steps.

"Light," we said, is the key word. Important statements are found in Isaiah and in the gospel:

> Do not turn your back on your own,
>   then *your light* shall break forth like the dawn.
> You are the *light* of the world.

Light, it is important to note at once, adds nothing to the place which it illumines. Chairs and tables are in a room whether there is light or not; flowers and vegetables are growing outside at night as well as in the daylight. Whether it is dark or lightsome in the place, everything remains the same. Well, almost!

Light adds nothing, but it makes all the difference whether we walk into a dark room and crash into chairs and tables, or whether we can see well enough to sit down comfortably and eat our delicious family dinner at the table. Outside, in the darkness of the night, we run the risk of walking on the flowers; with sunshine we enjoy their delicate beauty.

Not only does light enable us to enter into a comfortable and enjoyable relationship with our surroundings, but light does still more. It adds no new chairs, nor flowers, but it brings warmth. Warmth, in turn, draws new life out of the plants and vegetables. It adds a stronger dash of color to flowers. Light attracts.

Jesus said that "you are [not only] the light of the

world, [but also] the salt of the earth." Many of our remarks about light can be applied to salt. Salt adds no extra weight to a piece of meat, but it sharpens the flavor and makes the food more delicious.

If we are the light of the world and the salt of the earth, then our role towards one another is meant to attract the goodness in others and enable it to develop. As light we are to provide the illumination so that the talents and hopes of others can be seen and acted upon. As the light of our families and neighborhoods, of our parishes and religious communities, we speak and act in such a way that people do not crash into one another with anger and spiteful words, or as Isaiah wrote, with "false accusation and malicious speech." Again in the words of St. Paul, we encourage trust and confidence; we do not resort to "wise" argumentation and clever turns of speech. We are the instrument of peace, warmth and love, of respect, dignity and full life.

With this background we begin to appreciate how the prophet Isaiah combined light with care for the hungry and homeless. By sharing our bread, opening our homes and clothing the naked, then "you do not turn your back on your own." We have formed one large family. At this point the prophet adds:

Then your light shall break forth like the dawn,
and your wound will quickly be healed.

Caring for others by curing their sickness and removing their wants, enables ourselves to "be quickly healed." Through love and compassion a divine light shines about us and surrounds us with a warm, loving family. So true is this that Isaiah repeats the idea:

If you remove . . . oppression,
    false accusation and malicious speech;
if you bestow your bread on the hungry
    and satisfy the afflicted;
Then light shall rise for you in the darkness.

    This bonding of light with concern for people's suffering leads us very naturally to Paul's words in First Corinthians. Paul does not use the word light, but he does employ a synonym for light. He speaks of true and false *wisdom*. True wisdom, which seems foolishness to many human beings, is found in "Jesus and him crucified." This divine wisdom seems weak and ineffective. Yet if one sees the image of Jesus Crucified in the suffering people of today's world, then we acquire true wisdom and are surrounded with divine light. Our words and actions manifest "the convincing power of the Spirit."

    In this way, like light and salt, we enable the best in others to come forth; we enter into good, happy relationships. Jesus put it most beautifully:

Your light must shine before others so that they
may see goodness in your acts and give praise to
your heavenly Father.

Prayer:

    Lord, you are our light, shining into the darkness of our lives. You forgive our faults and attract the best within us, that like plants we may reach towards you, our sun. Enable each of us to reflect your light to one another so that we may be your instruments in forming family and community. Then we will live peacefully with one another and give glory to you.

Fifth Sunday, "B" Cycle

Job 7:1–4, 6–7. Job bemoans the drudgery of life and his
"assigned months of misery."

1 Cor 9:16–19, 22–23. Paul is under compulsion to preach
the gospel. He has made himself all things to all men and
women, to save at least some.

Mark 1:29–39. Jesus heals Simon's mother-in-law, cures
the sick in Capernaum, seeks solitude and prayer, returns
to preaching the good news.

A severe contrast is presented to us in today's biblical
readings. Job is tired of life; his nights drag on and, as he
complains, "I am filled with restlessness until the dawn."
Paul and Jesus, on the contrary, seem under a compulsion
(the very words of Paul), driven into intense activity. Yet
these two opposite moments of human existence are closely
associated. The very active person usually longs for extended moments of quiet and retreat; in the gospel Jesus
tried to slip away for solitude and prayer.

At times very active people have quiet and inactivity
thrust upon them by sudden sickness like a stroke, or by the
economic situation which leaves them unemployed, or by
retirement and old age. No matter how long anyone prepares
for any of these eventualities, when the sword cuts through
the pattern of one's existence, to leave a person in a new situation, it seems that no preparation has been made. Everyone must undergo the psychological process of acceptance
and adaptation.

Sometimes this process is called the stages of dying,
the different mental states that the dying go through as they
gradually depart from this earthly life: stages of anger,
depression, denial, acceptance and peace. The psalms for
suffering people, like the Book of Job, reflect these stages of

dying. It is not that the person is actually dying, only that sickness and other forms of inactivity have many parallels and comparisons with dying.

Like Paul and Jesus, Job too had had his stint of busyness and intense preoccupation. He had raised seven sons and three daughters. He was responsible for a large estate which included "seven thousand sheep, three thousand camels, five hundred yoke of oxen, five hundred she-asses, and a great number of work animals" (Job 1:3). Suddenly his livestock was stolen, his children were swept away by a storm, and he himself was stricken with skin disease. He could not easily nor quickly accept this total loss, this complete inactivity. For thirty-six long chapters he argues with his friends and comforters; he demands an audience with his Maker:

> I will carry my flesh between my teeth,
>   and take my life in my hand.
> Slay me though he might, I will wait for him;
>   I will defend my conduct to God's face (13:14–15).

Job helps us, not just by companionship in our misery but also by assuring us that these human reactions to sickness and inactivity are normal. They speak a message to us from God, even an elusive and silent God. These moments are from God and lead back to God, particularly in our dying moments but equally as well in other times of crisis.

There are other times, on the contrary, when God calls us to intense activity. These times also carry a special message from God and have their own momentum to lead us to an ever more intense union with God. Paul writes:

> I am under compulsion and have no choice.
> I am ruined if I do not preach.

We are reminded of Jeremiah's famous statement when he had decided to speak no longer in God's name.

> It becomes like fire burning in my heart,
>   imprisoned in my bones;
> I grow weary holding it in,
>   I cannot endure it.

Even in the excitement of preaching the gospel this incessantly, Paul felt his weakness and loneliness. We all share this helplessness when driven by demands upon our time from all sides. Even a reaction as negative as this turns to the effective preaching of the gospel.

> To the weak I became a weak person with a view to winning the weak. I have made myself all things to all men and women in order to save at least some of them.

In a context of weakness and its concomitant loneliness Paul makes his well known exclamation: ''I have made myself all things to all men and women.'' No human reaction was to remain outside of his experience, at least those reactions that come from excessive activity. At times such as these, we will occasionally act abruptly and sternly, we will show our bias and prejudice, our impatience and anger. All of these human imperfections show up in Paul's correspondence with the Corinthians. These represent the excessive side of his virtue, particularly the virtue of compulsive zeal to keep the Corinthians faithful to the gospel.

Still another reaction is seen in Jesus. After intense activity in Capernaum where ''the whole town was gathered outside the door'' of his home, Jesus rose ''early the next morning [and] went off to a lonely place in the desert; there he was absorbed in prayer.'' In the midst of activity we must take measures to seek space and time for private prayer. Yet, as will usually happen in a busy home or parish or community, even here ''Simon and his companions managed to track him down; and when they found him . . . he said to them, 'Let us move on to the neighboring villages so that I may proclaim the good news there also. That is what I have come to do.' '' Activity too, no matter how tiring and possibly distracting, was also a call from God.

Scripture calls us to spend ourselves for the gospel, out of charity for others. It also prepares us for the painful results of activity: physical tiredness, sickness, anger, impatience, weakness. It reminds us of the absolute necessity of seeking solitude and prayer, even if it does not leave us as long as we would wish in this quiet retreat.

Prayer:

Lord, your wisdom has no limits. We learn more of your wise governance of our world and our life, by each new incident of our experience. You are always gracious and good, sustaining the lowly, healing the brokenhearted, binding up our wounds. As you number the stars, so you call each of us by name and summon us to your work, within our family and community.

Fifth Sunday, ''C'' Cycle

Isa 6:1–8. The prophet's inaugural vision and call to ministry.

1 Cor 15:1–11. Paul transmits the creed preached in the early church about the resurrection of Jesus. ''I handed on to you what I myself received.''

Luke 5:1–11. A miraculous catch of fishes. Peter's protestations of unworthiness; Jesus' call of Peter, James and John to be fishers of men and women for the kingdom of God.

God calls us in many different ways to different vocations in life. While the circumstances vary a great deal, nonetheless, each one's call shares with that of others a dramatic decisiveness, perhaps the element of surprise, which abruptly changes one's life. In many different ways! For instance, just by chance a man or woman meets a future spouse who happened to be visiting at the home of a mutual friend. The new vocation may come when an automobile veers out of control, strikes a pedestrian and cripples that person for life. The injured man or woman is called to an entirely new way of life. The innocent driver will never forget! In surprising ways too a latent, sleeping vocation to religious life or priesthood, to lay ministry in the church or to a single career, is awakened and must be dealt with. A clear "yes" is demanded by the person's conscience.

The prophet Isaiah is summoned by God to a new ministry while at prayer in the temple; Simon Peter and the brothers, James and John, receive the call while fishing. In the second reading we are not told in any detail of Paul's call to be an apostle; that is found thrice in the Acts of the Apostles: Acts 9:1–19; 22:3–16; 26:2–18! Paul, however, in today's reading, refers to the central place of Jesus' death and resurrection in the preaching of the first disciples and in the faith of the earliest church. He refers as well to the appearance of the risen Jesus in his own life:

> I handed on to you first of all what I myself received, that Christ died for our sins in accord with the Scriptures; that he was buried and, in accord with the Scriptures, rose on the third day; that he

was seen by Cephas . . . the Twelve . . . five
hundred brothers and sisters, James, then by all
the apostles. Last of all he was seen by me.

Each vocation has the elements of death and resurrection. An older way of life is left behind as the person takes a
resolute turn in another direction.

This decision is reached, as already remarked, in many
different ways: in the midst of profound prayer or while
going about one's normal employment or work. Paul was
knocked off the horse and blinded by the Spirit while
fiercely persecuting the early Christians. We must be always
ready for God's call; no moment is too sacred or too secular
for God not to intervene and summon us in a new way, so
definitive in its break with the past, so compulsive and so
demanding, that to say anything else but ''yes'' would do
serious harm to our personality and to our future. Even when
we seem well prepared, by a habit of obeying God's inspirations, we will still be overwhelmed and surprised. The
prophecy of Isaiah contains an important text. Israel had
been more than adequately prepared by prophecies, and yet
the fulfillment took them by surprise:

Things of the past I foretold long ago,
they went forth from my mouth,
I let you hear of them;
then *suddenly* I took action and they came to be (Isa
48:3).

The Hebrew word for ''suddenly'' means ''by surprise,'' as
we see in another prophetic book:

Lo, I am sending my messenger
to prepare the way before me;

And *suddenly* there will come to the temple
    the Lord whom you seek. . . .
Who will endure the day of his coming? (Mal 1:1–2).

In calling us to something new God is not suggesting
that the previous way of life was bad or unworthy. Peter, we
would take for granted, was a good fisherman, even though
he admitted in today's gospel, ''Master, we have been hard
at it all night long and have caught nothing.'' Isaiah too
must have been a very effective politician at the royal court.
Also as prophet he speaks his message in a form that turns
out to be the golden age of Hebrew poetry.

God was calling each one to something new which
scared them. Isaiah declared: ''Woe is me, I am doomed!
For I am a man of unclean lips.'' Similarly, ''Simon Peter
fell at the knees of Jesus saying, 'Leave me, Lord. I am a
sinful man.' '' Neither person was all that sinful; only they
felt very incapable of the new vocation and the way that it
brought them into the immediate presence of the all-holy
God.

Their vocation called them beyond their realm of ability or desires. Rather than deny their talents and the dignity
of their way of life up till this moment, God sanctifies all of
their talents and enables the disciples to achieve far more
than they thought possible. What at first seemed a death to
an earlier, good way of life now becomes a resurrection.
This resurrection brings new life out of their same body and
same talents.

The resurrection is at the heart of the Christian message. Paul insists on this in today's selection from First Corinthians. Yet the resurrection means as much our
participation in Jesus' rising from the dead as it does our belief in Jesus' personal resurrection. Paul describes the quality of resurrection in his call to be an apostle:

I am the least of the apostles; in fact, because I persecuted the church of God, I do not even deserve the name. But by God's favor I am what I am. This favor of his to me has not proved fruitless.

Prayer:

Lord, enable me to believe in you and in your resurrection. I confess that you will complete in me what you have called me to do with my life. Your kindness pursues me; you will not forsake the work of your hand. In the sight of the angels I sing your praises.

Sixth Sunday, "A" Cycle

Sir 15:15–20. We are responsible for our actions. At the same time God is all-seeing and remains in control of the universe.

1 Cor 2:6–10. God's wisdom is mysterious, planned before all ages, for those who love him.

Matt 5:17–37. Fulfillment of the law and the prophets reaches beyond the letter of Scripture to new expectations of the Spirit.

In several ways Scripture invites us to consider some real, healthy but difficult tensions in our human existence. No clear answers are given to us. Yet by recognizing the different realities of our human situation, we will not allow ourselves to be drawn too far in any single way and so be incapacitated and lose our balance or equilibrium. At times we cannot find an intellectual solution to the tension and seeming contradiction. Yet by faith in God's goodness and in God's presence within the circle of our family and community, we settle at a most peaceful point in our soul. We thereby find the strength and intuitive wisdom to make our finest decisions.

The first reading from Sirach juxtaposes what the sapiential literature normally separates into distinct chapters: on the one hand personal responsibility for our individual human actions and on the other hand God's all embracing wisdom and power. Nothing takes God by surprise; nothing destroys the divine plan for the universe. Yet people are free to make their own judgments and must take the consequences of their actions:

> If you choose, you can keep the commandments. . . .
> There are set before you fire and water;
> > to whichever you choose, stretch forth your
> > > hand. . . .
> Immense is the wisdom of the Lord;
> > he is mighty in power, and all-seeing. . . .
> The eyes of God see all he has made;
> > he understands every human deed.

These lines of Sirach are drawing upon a repertoire of ancient biblical passages, from Deut 30:15,19; Jer 21:8; Ps 33:13–19. If we pursue any of these texts and read the fuller setting, we are far along the way of a healthy solution to life's mysteries. For instance, in Deut 30, God is speaking to the people Israel:

> Here then I have today set before you life and prosperity, death and doom. If you obey the commandments of the Lord, your God, which I enjoin on you today, loving him, and walking in his ways, and keeping his commandments . . . , you will live and grow numerous, and the Lord, your

God, will bless you in the land you are entering to
occupy.

Choose life . . . by loving the Lord, your
God, heeding his voice, and holding fast to him
(Deut 30:15–16, 19–20).

Love and trust break the impasse over law. Such an attitude of heart also cuts through the enigma of human freedom and divine control. By loving the Lord, your God, the
intimate bond between ourselves and God unites the best
that we can do with a humble trust that God will lead us still
further into the way of peace and happiness.

Deuteronomy was one of Jesus' favorite books. He
quotes from it at special moments, during the temptation
scene in the desert (Luke 4:1–13) and when questioned
about the greatest commandment (Matt 22:34–40). Somehow or other the spirit of Deuteronomy lies at the base of Jesus' sermon on the mount. Like Deuteronomy, Jesus has not
"come to abolish the law and the prophets. I have come not
to abolish them, but to fulfill them." When Jesus introduces
the commandments of the Torah with the statement, "You
have heard . . . ," Jesus is not substituting another set of
laws for the earlier one. Rather Jesus is drawing attention to
the spirit behind the law.

Very understandably, Jesus is insisting that the avoid-
ance of adultery is not the key to a good marriage. Rather
there must be such loving and constant trust between the
spouses, that neither looks at someone else with lust in the
heart. Such an interior response would be unthinkable. Neither is Jesus laying down a new law to gouge out one's eye
or to cut off one's hand if they scandalize. Rather Jesus is
seeking a healthy, dependable sense of right and wrong, so
that good judgment avoids what is scandalous and strong
convictions smother even the first movement of temptation.

In some way we are back again to a type of good intuitions or to what St. Thomas Aquinas called "knowledge by connaturality." We know the right answer by second nature. Because we live honestly, we have a good instinct for being honest and can quickly smoke out deceit. Because we have become accustomed to a wholesome family life, we recognize immediately what is dangerous and hazardous to it, without a long process of dialogues and anguished decision-making!

We are instinctively recognizing what Paul describes as God's "mysterious, hidden wisdom." This is a spirituality for the "mature." It is reached less by logic and reasoned discourse, but more by faith in a loving, compassionate God and by a consistent obedience to one's conscience, less by argumentation from others and more by their good example. This type of wisdom leads to joy and peace of mind far beyond human prudence and philosophical reasons. Paul writes of this wisdom:

> Eye has not seen, ear has not heard, nor has it so much as dawned on anyone what God has prepared for those who love him.

For a further meditation on the biblical ideal of law and obedience, we can turn to Ps 119. It is the longest psalm in the Bible, perhaps because we need time to grow into this divine wisdom. Ps 119 is also the response to the first reading this day.

Prayer:
Lord, I confess in the secret of my heart, how happy are those who follow your law. For this happiness I must seek you in each step that I take. In my desire for you I ac-

quire the true spirit of obedience. Give me discernment that I may keep your law with all my heart.

Sixth Sunday, ''B'' Cycle

Lev 13:1–2; 45–46. Lepers must dwell outside the camp after being declared unclean by the priests.

1 Cor 10:31—11:1. Do all for God's glory; give no offense; seek no personal advantage.

Mark 1:40–45. Jesus cures the leper and orders him to tell no one. The leper, however, makes the whole matter public!

Once again Jesus does the impossible—cures a leper—and then asks the impossible—tell no one! In this mysterious sequence it becomes evident that Jesus can work miracles but he has no intention of being known principally as a miracle worker. Jesus does not want us to think that miracles are at our beck and call!

Further, if Jesus can work miracles, yet only on occasion and in the right setting, then Jesus must recognize a purpose in suffering, sorrow and loneliness. As a matter of fact, Jesus seems to be prodding the minds of the people of Nazareth in this direction, when he declared to them:

> Recall, too, the many lepers in Israel in the time of Elisha the prophet; yet not one was cured except Naaman the Syrian (Luke 4:27).

This man was not demanding a miracle, nor expecting Jesus to do it automatically. The leper came with a request and knelt down in addressing Jesus. He appealed to Jesus' compassion and asked a personal decision in his regard: ''if you *will* to do so.'' Jesus does not work the miracle as a manifestation of power; rather, he was *moved with pity*. There is another phrase here which can be easily overlooked: *Jesus touched the leper*. At that very moment, Jesus became ceremonially unclean; he incapacitated himself for entering temple or synagogue. Jesus could not liturgically pray to his Father! But Jesus had bonded himself with the leper and the outcast; Jesus formed family and acted to bring personal joy to his new brother and sister.

In the second reading Paul seeks to extend the ways by which we reach out to others and widen our family circle. This series of ''one-liners'' converges upon a disinterested outgoing love:

- whether you eat or drink—whatever you do;
- to Jew or Greek or to the church of God;
- please all in any way I can;
- seeking not my own advantage but that of the many;
- imitate me as I imitate Christ.

Each phrase seeks to strengthen the bonds of love in family and community and also to invite an ever increasing number of people, whether ''Jew or Greek,'' that is, everyone, into this family. Ultimately Paul acts ''that they may be saved.'' Yet, the principal way of securing salvation lies in bonds of family and community.

Here in family no one acts for spectacular reasons. Most of the time we nurse the sick and bring them back to life or we care for those afflicted with contagious disease, in order to restore the joy and healthy peace of the family. Here the right hand should not know what the left hand is doing (Matt 6:3).

Within this context we can properly understand the stern law in the first reading, that lepers be separated from places of habitation and cry out, "Unclean, unclean!" The Bible wants to preserve the health and strength of the population against contagious disease; the people did not possess our knowledge of disease, medicine and prevention. Even today we have isolation wards in hospitals. We must underline the principal reason: the preservation of health in the wider family.

We are left with amazement at the spontaneous compassion of Jesus in *touching* the leper. We are also reminded of the way that Jesus gravitated to the village of Bethany, a few miles east of Jerusalem. The word itself means, "House (*Beth*) of the lowly (*anaw*)." Bethany was the closest point that lepers could come to Jerusalem. From its hilltop they could see the temple and the holy city. While in Jerusalem Jesus made his home at Bethany!

Prayer:

Lord, we turn to you always in our times of trouble. We believe that you will fill us with peace, joy and salvation. Peace when our sickness continues, joy when we are cured, salvation in any case. We ask you to cure us of everything that separates us from a loving, compassionate reunion in our family and community.

Sixth Sunday, "C" Cycle

Jer 17:5–8. Each person experiences desert dryness at times; only the one with faith and deep roots in God survives and even bears good fruit.

1 Cor 15:12, 16–20. If our hopes are limited to this life only, we are the most pitiable of all people. If Christ has been raised from the dead, he is the first fruits and we will follow.

Luke 6:17, 20–26. How blest you poor . . . you hungry. The reign of God is yours. Your reward shall be great in heaven.

What is entitled the ''Sermon on the Mount'' in Matthew's gospel has become the ''Sermon on the Plain'' in Luke's gospel! Matthew wants to see Jesus as another Moses, giving the new law to the people yet directing it primarily to church leaders; he gathers only his first disciples around him on the mount, whom he separates from the great crowds milling around him in the preceding verse of Matthew's account. The last verse of Chapter 4 in Matthew refers to ''the great crowds that followed him from Galilee, the Ten Cities, Jerusalem and Judea, and across the Jordan''; the very next verse, v. 1 in chapter five, states that Jesus ''went up on the mountainside [and] his disciples gathered around him.'' Luke, on the contrary, pictures Jesus' ''coming down the mountain [and stopping] at a level stretch where . . . a large crowd of people was with him.'' Luke reaches out immediately to all the followers of Jesus and addresses them in the personal way, ''Blest are *you* poor.'' Matthew portrays Jesus speaking in a more distant, third-person way, ''Blest are the poor in spirit.''

What the evangelists did, we also must do—adapt the words of Jesus to our own setting and to our special needs. Sometimes we should hear the gospel as addressed immediately to ourselves, ''Blest are *you* poor.'' At other times God calls us to mediate the gospel message to others and to present the word of God as a general call to holiness, ''Blest are the poor in Spirit.''

The Scriptures must be adapted as well to the changing circumstances of our life. It is not that truth changes. It is our life that changes, as Jeremiah points out, from a time of drought to a time of plenty; or again in the gospel, from a time of poverty and tears to a time of comfort and joy. Or we are living in a community where different people are in the midst of different circumstances, some with trial and suffering, others with achievement and peace. Not only the tone of our voice but also the choice of words from Scripture must be adapted.

The basic doctrine of our faith, the resurrection of Jesus, remains always at the root of our existence. Paul insists upon this facet of our belief:

> If our hopes in Christ are limited to this life only, we are the most pitiable of people. [If] Christ has been raised from the dead, [then, he becomes] the first fruit of those who have fallen asleep.

If Christ is the first fruit, we too will follow as second and third growth on the same healthy vine.

Jeremiah reminds us that our faith is not so much rooted in a doctrine as in the *person* of God. Jeremiah, of course, did not know Jesus as a distinct person of the Holy Trinity, but Jeremiah as someone seriously dedicated to prayer and frequently shown at prayer in his prophecy (12:1–5; 15:10–21) was drawn into profound, personal union with God. In today's reading, Jeremiah writes:

> Blessed is that one who trusts in the *Lord,*
> whose hope is the *Lord.*

The doctrine of the resurrection, therefore, should lead us to the person of the Lord Jesus, already risen from the dead, fully alive, the first fruits of those who have fallen asleep in death, the pledge that our own tears will be wiped away, our hunger filled with nourishing food, our bereavement with the presence of our loved ones, our unjust situation remedied with truth and new opportunity.

Because our faith is rooted in a person, not simply in a doctrine, and because the person is Jesus, already risen from the dead, then we are not waiting till the end of our lives for the fruits of the resurrection in our own lives. Luke writes, ''How blest are *you* poor, the reign of God *is* yours'' already at this moment.

The presence of the risen Jesus brings us peace and confidence; it already imparts dignity to our body, confidence within our hopes. The hands with which we reach out to touch and help others are the hands that will be ours for eternity. What we do now for others will enable us—if we dare paraphrase an incident in the risen life of Jesus—to say to others, ''Take your finger and examine my hands. Put your hand into my side.'' Already we are forming the body that will exist eternally.

We also realize that the resurrection is not only rooted in the person of Jesus, but it also reaches outward to form a family and a community of people most fully alive to one another, with respect and love, with gratitude and hope.

Prayer:

Lord, grant that I may always hope in you and not place my confidence in the counsel of the wicked or in the company of the insolent. Let me delight in your law and meditate on your word and so be drawn into the personal mystery of your goodness.

Seventh Sunday, ''A'' Cycle

Lev 19:1–2, 17–18. Love your neighbor as yourself.
1 Cor 3:16–23. You are the temple of God. Do not be wise

in a worldly way. All things are yours, you are Christ's, and Christ is God's.

Matt 5:38–48. You must be perfect as your heavenly Father is perfect. Love your enemies. Should anyone press you into service for one mile, go two miles with them.

The second reading declares the sacredness of our human life: ''you are the temple of God.'' Not only Paul in this declaration from First Corinthians, but the other two readings extend the boundaries of this temple which ''you are'' to include even our enemies, ''Love your enemies, pray for your persecutors.''

We are honored and even exhilarated to be reassured how sacred is our human body as the temple of God. Every human action without exception, therefore, can be compared to the construction of a church and even to the sacred actions within the completed church. Our homes and neighborhood, our places of employment and relaxation are all considered to be an extension of the church. In this comparison all of us become priests functioning within the sanctuary of our homes; our activity turns into a liturgy of worship.

We are exhilarated; we are also quieted by the serious realization that every offense against ourselves and our neighbor, and especially every sin committed against members of our family can be typed as a sacrilege, profaning the temple of God. As Paul writes for us in today's reading: ''The temple of God is holy, and you are that temple.'' Sacrilege is the sin against holiness and against God.

At times the ''sacrilegious'' sins against the temple of God seem to be restricted to the area of sexuality and to offenses against chastity. St. Paul himself speaks in this way later in the same epistle:

> Do you not see that your bodies are members of
> Christ? Would you have me take Christ's mem-
> bers and make them the members of a prostitute?
> . . . You must know that your body is a temple of
> the Holy Spirit (1 Cor 6:15, 19).

Paul also speaks of ourselves, the temple of God and the
member of the body of Christ, in a much wider context.
Within chapters twelve and thirteen of First Corinthians
Paul expands upon the idea of the Christian community's
forming the one body of Christ and therefore like Christ to
constitute the temple of the Holy Spirit. Paul then proceeds
to insist upon love that is "patient . . . kind . . . not jealous
. . . not putting on airs . . . not snobbish . . . not rude
. . ." Paul places much more emphasis upon the expectations of neighborly and family love, and its offenses, than
upon sins against chastity.

Likewise in the gospel Jesus insists upon the wide embrace of love, indeed upon a new kind of *heroic* love:

- offer no resistance to injury.
- go the extra mile.
- do not turn your back on the borrower.
- love your enemies, pray for your persecutors.

Jesus is conscious of asking something extra:

> You have heard . . . "An eye for an eye . . ." but
> what I say to you is . . .
> If you greet your brother and sister only . . . do not
> pagans do as much?

All these actions, pleasing to God, are undertaken within the
sanctuary of our bodies.

Yet, we have all heard just the opposite within our families and employment. Unfortunately, we ourselves have said to others: do not let that other person trample all over you! Strike first, lest the other party hit you first! Don't be naive! Make others sign on the dotted line. Such statements occur over and over again in Christian communities.

We must explain still further the Old Testament reference to "an eye for an eye, a tooth for a tooth" (Exod 21:24; Lev 24:20). First of all, the Hebrew Scriptures were softening the severe terms of ancient law codes, which sometimes required more than one eye for an eye; the Bible was also formulating laws against criminal behavior. Crimes were punished. Yet there is not a single instance in the Bible where they were punished with physical mutilation like gouging out the eye.

The first reading from Leviticus, a central book in Old Testament law, reaches beyond a code for criminal behavior. Chapter nineteen of Leviticus gives a series of strong recommendations—actually interpreted by the rabbis as laws—by which:

> You shall not bear hatred for your brother or sister
> in your heart. . . . You shall love your neighbor
> as yourself.

First of all, we notice the qualification, "in your heart." Not only were angry actions and words outlawed, but interior emotions were to be controlled. "You shall not bear hatred . . . in your heart." The actions within the temple of our bodies are to be inspired and directed interiorly "in your heart."

In today's reading from Leviticus, for the sake of brevity, verses three to sixteen are omitted. Here the farmer is told not to reap the harvest to the very edge of the field, "nor shall you glean the stray ears of grain . . . nor pick your vineyard bare, nor gather up the grapes that have fallen.'' The Torah offers this reason:

> These things you shall leave for the poor and the alien. I, the Lord, am your God.

Later, the Israelite was warned:

> You shall not curse the deaf, or put a stumbling block in front of the blind, but you shall fear your God. I am the Lord.

Each of these stipulations is concluded with ''I am the Lord,'' a refrain which brings us back to the thought of St. Paul. We are the temple of God. Wherever we find ourselves, at home, in the place of our employment, in our yard or farmland, we are living immediately in God's presence and our actions become acts of worship to the all holy God.

The entire universe becomes the temple of God. One of the ancient psalms declared such to be the case:

> The heavens declare the glory of God,
>   and the firmament proclaims his handiwork.
> Day pours out the word to day,
>   and night to night imparts knowledge (Ps 19:2–3).

Prayer:

Lord, you are kind and merciful, to consecrate my life in such an ennobling way. Enable me to imitate your kindness: pardoning iniquities, healing all wounds, not requiting others according to their sins but rather, like yourself, slow to anger and abounding in goodness.

Seventh Sunday, "B" Cycle

Is 43:18–19, 21–22, 24–25. See, I am doing something new. You burdened me with your sins, but it is I who wipe out your offenses.

2 Cor 1:18–22. Paul's word, like that of Jesus, is not alternately "yes" and "no." All God's promises receive their fulfillment in Jesus.

Mark 2:1–12. The healing of the paralytic and the forgiveness of his sins.

The second reading sets the seal of fidelity upon God's word and upon the preaching of the church. Paul links together these two announcements: "As God keeps his word, I declare that my word to you is not 'yes' one minute and 'no' the next." As we glance back at Isaiah's prophecy, we realize that fulfillment of God's word may reach beyond our limited understanding of it. God can take us by surprise. And that is exactly what happened in today's gospel. God surprised the sanctimonious person, scandalized that sins be forgiven this easily; God also took all human laws by surprise in healing the paralytic. As we look still further into these readings we see that the bond of consistency and God's "eternal" yes will be found in the compassion of God.

Typical of other places in his correspondence with the Corinthians, Paul loses his calm and shows more than a little streak of impatience, possibly of anger! He must have been accused of vacillation, first "yes" and then "no." Several times in today's short reading Paul insists that such was not the case, neither with himself nor with Silvanus and Timothy his co-workers at Corinth. This fidelity to his word, however, does not depend on Paul or on any human authority. It relies upon the fidelity of God: "As God keeps his word . . ."

Paul looks to Jesus in whom "whatever promises God has made have been fulfilled." He then adds:

> It is through him that we address our Amen to God when we worship together.

The bond of God's fidelity to his promises is the same bond that unites Christians in their faith and in their worship. Therefore, it is not simply a matter of God, by divine power, reaching out to complete what he has promised; rather God shows this fulfillment within the bonds of family and community. Paul's fidelity to the Corinthians as well as the fidelity of the Corinthians to one another becomes the pledge and assurance that God is in their midst and writing the final "yes" and "amen" to his promises.

This cohesive, unifying form of the Christian community does not depend upon externals, at least not as its principal basis. God is at work, breathing the Spirit into each believer. This Spirit is the deposit or down payment, of what will be received most fully in the eternal kingdom of God. Paul put it this way:

> God is the one who firmly establishes us along with you in Christ; it is he who anointed us and has sealed us; thereby depositing the first payment, the Spirit in our hearts.

What we have already received is essentially the same as what we will receive most fully in our eternal home. Such is the meaning of the Greek word, ''first payment,'' used here by Paul.

There is continuity, therefore, between our present age and the full reception of God's promises in heaven. Yet, it is an understatement to say that heaven will still take us by surprise! Once we surrender to the Spirit, God's holy spirit will accomplish far more than we can ever imagine. In the first reading, the prophet Isaiah theorizes about this element of surprise! The gospel, moreover, shows us surprise in action. Again, the unifying factor is to be found in something interior.

The author of Chaps. 40–55 in the Book of Isaiah was writing and preaching during the Babylonian exile. Perhaps through a keen political sense, which in turn was intensified by faith, the prophet was announcing the end of the exile. God's ancient promises would catch up with the present moment. This great event lies in close continuity with God's earlier fulfillment of prophetical words. The prophet rests his case on God's fidelity:

> See, earlier things have come to pass,
>   new ones I now foretell;
> Before they spring into being,
>   I announce them to you (Isa 42:9).

Almost contradicting himself in his consistent way of speaking of the future in the language and hopes of the past, the prophet now declares:

> Remember not the events of the past,
>   the things of long ago consider not,
> See I am doing something new!
>   Now it springs forth. . . !

In still another passage the prophet reenforces this startling nature of prophecy-fulfillment:

> Things of the past I foretold long ago . . .
> then *suddenly* I took action and they came to be
>   (48:3).

How can God act suddenly and surprisingly, if he has predicted and warned the people ahead of time? In answer the prophet assures us: fulfillment is always a "yes" to the past with more besides. God is not niggardly and he expects us to believe in his generosity.

His generosity is dependent upon his extraordinary compassion. Isaiah writes that while God did not weary us, we have wearied God by our crimes. We have made God our servant by the sins with which we burdened God. God's happiness is burdened by us and divine freedom is enslaved to us! These are extraordinary lines.

This same compassionate kindness to carry the burden of others and to forgive offenses appears clearly in the gospel. While healing the physical ailment, Jesus forgives sin. If Jesus reaches beyond the expectation of religious people at that time, he had every right to appeal to their faith in the ancient scriptures. Once again in Jesus they receive their "yes" through his loving way of going the extra mile in fulfillment.

Prayer:

Lord, no one of us can appeal to our integrity and goodness, but the Scriptures reassure us that we find our "yes" to every hope in your compassionate kindness. Lord, you have regard for the lowly even in their faults and failures.

Seventh Sunday, "C" Cycle

1 Sam 26. Selected verses tell the story how David could
   have had Saul executed and his persecutor removed, but
   David would not harm the Lord's anointed.
1 Cor 15:45–49. Although we are created after an earthly
   image, we are being transformed according to the heavenly person, Jesus Christ.
Luke 6:27–38. Love your enemies; do good to those who
   hate you. The measure you measure with will be measured back to you.

St. Luke continues Jesus' "sermon on the plain" (see
the Sixth Sunday, "C" Cycle). Jesus makes heroic demands of his followers. As we meditate upon all three readings, particularly Paul's statements in First Corinthians for
today, we realize that we have no other choice. We cannot
live simply a "natural" existence; "we bear the likeness of
a heavenly person," Jesus Christ. Either we will succeed
heroically or we will collapse miserably. Even a person who
has not known the gospel message is called to this heroic,
"supernatural" way of life. Such a one is described in the
first reading. There we see that David had no freedom except to respect his enemy and to spare Saul's life, even at the
risk of serious future dangers for himself.

It is important to take notice of the development of
thought in the second reading. "First, came the natural and
after that the spiritual," Paul writes very succinctly. The
first Adam came from the earth; the second Adam, Jesus
Christ, comes from heaven. We too begin our life, resem-
bling the earthly Adam, but we are already called to bear the
likeness of the heavenly Adam.

In other words, we are called to live a heavenly existence within our earthly body, to be conformed to Jesus, the

heavenly model, while we follow our earthly way of life. We are expected to live a super-human life within our human body.

To become still more specific, our charity is expected to reach beyond the love that good, earthly people manifest. Our forgiveness must extend even to our enemies, because "sinners love those who love them," Jesus declared. As children of God by reason of the spirit of Jesus which abides in us, we are called to live in a way modeled upon God's love, forgiveness and generosity.

> [Then] you will rightly be called children of the Most High, since God himself is good to the ungrateful and the wicked.

The key, given us by Jesus to unlock the secret of this way of life, has been filed and sharpened for us by St. Luke. Where Matthew writes: "Be perfect as your heavenly Father is perfect," Luke hears Jesus say: "Be compassionate, as your Father is compassionate." We do not seek perfection but perfect compassion!

To act in this way may seem to risk everything. For David, it meant risking his life yet again. Even though Saul repented this time, nonetheless Saul later took up arms against David and marched his troops into the wilderness of Judah to track down the fugitive. We also notice the spirit with which David treated Saul. David extended heroic compassionate and wholehearted forgiveness. The liturgical passage omits the touching, dramatic conversation between David and Saul, once David draws to Saul's attention how he could have slain the king. David, while shouting perforce from "an opposite slope . . . at a great distance" (1 Sam 23:13), nonetheless speaks affectionately:

Saul: "Is that your voice, my son David?"

David: "Yes, my Lord the king. . . . Please, now, let my Lord listen to the words of his servant."

Saul: "I have done wrong. Come back, my son David."

David: "As I valued your life highly today, so may the Lord value my life highly and deliver me from all difficulties."

Saul: "Blessed are you, my son David!"

Saul and certainly David at this moment were striving to "be compassionate as your Father is compassionate."

This biblical goal of modeling our daily actions upon those of God who "is good to the ungrateful and the wicked," can seem so demanding as to lead to frustration. Why try, since it is impossible!

As mentioned already, we have no choice. Our gift of life is modeled on the life of Jesus, whose spirit is given to us as a pledge. This spirit, according to 2 Cor 1:22, is already the down payment, the earnest, the initial installment of what will be completely ours in heaven for all eternity.

Our modeling upon Jesus is not to be done by measuring up to laws and external norms but by an interior creation within us, through the gift of the Spirit who blends one with our spirit. It is not only God, then, but our own nature and very self, divinely modeled upon the spiritual and the heavenly, that puts this requirement upon us. As we follow obediently the promptings of our spirit, then we will experience:

Good measure pressed down, shaken together, running over, will they pour into the fold of your garment. For the measure you measure with will be measured back to you.

"Then your recompense will be great. You will rightly be called children of the Most High."

Prayer:

Lord, you are kind and merciful; you have compassion upon us, your children. As we live, brothers and sisters of your one family, enable us to respond to one another with the kind of love and forgiveness that you always manifest. Then with all my being, I will bless your holy name.

Eighth Sunday, "A" Cycle

Isa 49:14–15. God, our mother, cannot forget us, the children formed in the womb of divine love.

1 Cor 4:1–5. We are servants of Christ and mediators of the mysteries of God. The Lord is our one judge, to bring to light what is hidden in darkness.

Matt 6:24–34. Do not worry about your livelihood. Is not life more than food, the body more valuable than clothes? Your heavenly Father knows all that you need.

If we combine a major theme in the first and third reading, from Isaiah and Matthew, we see that God combines the love of both parents, mother and father. However, the Scripture is not stereotyping parental roles. True, only the mother forms the child in a womb. Yet, when it comes to other activities usually restricted only to men or only to women, these are indiscriminately attributed to God. The care of clothing and food, which most social groups claim is the exclusive role of *women,* is undertaken by God in Matthew's gospel. God clothes the grass of the field in splendor. Your heavenly Father, Jesus says, knows that you must eat, drink and be clothed. God also has an interest in the *man's* work—that is, what society says is to be performed almost exclusively by men—sowing, reaping and gathering into barns.

The Scriptures do not neutralize the distinction between man and woman, but they see each of the sexes *equally* reflected in God. God is neither male nor female; God is certainly no more male than female. According to the account of creation in Genesis, everything in some ways reflects the image and likeness of God (Gen 1:1–2:4).

These reflections may seem peripheral to today's readings. Yet, they may be justified by Paul's remarks in the selection from First Corinthians. We are not to pass judgment; that prerogative belongs only to the Lord. We are not to judge one sex superior to the other, one sex inferior to the other. We are not to attribute temptation more to one than the other; we are not to honor one above the other. The familiar statement of Paul to the Galatians sums it up succinctly:

There does not exist among you Jew or Greek,
slave or free person, male or female. All are one
in Christ Jesus (Gal 3:28).

In order to put Jesus' sermon on the mount in proper perspective, we need to remember how truly and completely God is father and mother to us. At first, our reactions may consider Jesus' recommendations to be beautiful poetry but practically impossible—when we are told: ''do not worry about your livelihood, what you are to eat or drink or use for clothing.'' Even Jesus' reason, put to us in the form of a question, seems less than convincing: ''Is not life more than food? Is not the body more valuable than clothes?'' Most parents would respond: without food there is no life; without clothes the body freezes.

Jesus is not unrealistic. Otherwise, he would never have fed the people in the wilderness. At that time he was solicitous: "If I send them home hungry, they will collapse on the way" (Mark 8:3).

Jesus was speaking, during the sermon on the mount, in a way to challenge and to stir up thought and conversation. Semitic people, moreover, delight in exaggeration and sweeping contrast, as when Jesus declared: "If anyone comes to me without turning one's back [literally in the Greek, without hating] father and mother, wife and children, brothers and sisters, indeed his very self, that one cannot be my follower" (Luke 14:26).

Within the sweeping and disturbing rhetoric in today's gospel, a solid core of truth, a gold piece of great price, lies hidden. Jesus is declaring: we are to love God first and foremost as we would love a parent. God is not simply a donor or benefactor; God is father and mother. Once we have found ourselves within this relationship of love and trust, then we can turn once again to Paul's letter to the Corinthians, read in today's mass.

Paul presents himself as servant and administrator. Words such as these presume prudential care for material goods, studious preparation for preaching the gospel, right handling of the Word of God. A good administrator acts with strength and conviction. Such is the character of Paul who defies anyone to judge his conduct: "the Lord is the one to judge me." Besides strength, an administrator should possess a spirit of humility by which we seek our "praise from God" and are willing to act in hidden or inconspicuous ways. A good administrator, moreover, can be trusted. Paul is not afraid of Christ the just judge who "will bring to light what is hidden in darkness and manifest the intentions of hearts."

While the first and third reading seem to reside within

the home, the second reading turns our attention to the business world. The first and second reading form the environment and establish the basic spirit of faith and love in God our father and our mother, by which we proceed to undertake our other public duties.

Prayer:

Only in you, O Lord, is my soul at rest. You are my safety and my glory, my rock of strength, my refuge. Resting in you and secure in your love, I shall not be disturbed. With this inner strength, Lord, you will direct me along the path of my other obligations.

Eighth Sunday, "B" Cycle

Hos 2:16, 21–22. God, the spouse of Israel, speaks to the people's heart and renews the first moment of their espousal.

2 Cor 3:1–6. The Corinthians are a letter, written by the Spirit. Theirs is a new covenant from the Spirit that gives life.

Mark 2:18–22. Wedding guests cannot fast if the bride and bridegroom are still with them. Other sayings here insist upon the new creation which we have become.

The first and third readings are obviously united through the theme of espousals. Hosea speaks of a wedding between God and the people Israel; Jesus of himself as the bridegroom of the new Israel. The reading from Second Corinthians modulates the theme from love and marriage covenant to that of spirit and new covenant. There are many points of contact by which the readings enlighten and enrich each other.

At first, it seems that Hosea and Jesus are referring to a wedding feast and the first days of marriage. Yet, once we carefully read the larger context of Hosea's prophecy and that of Jesus' preaching, we find that the marriage or covenant may be new, but they are also a return in a new way to what is old—in fact, not just old but also sinful.

Hosea compares the people Israel to an adulterous spouse. They are guilty of "false swearing, lying, murder, stealing and adultery" (Hos 4:2). If they pray, their words and piety are "like a morning cloud, like the dew that early passes away" (Hos 6:4). They are "arrogant," "silly and senseless" (Hos 7:10,11).

Jesus' entire ministry was summarized in a text of Mark's gospel which occurs immediately before the opening verse for today:

> "People who are healthy do not need a doctor;
> sick people do. I have come to call sinners, not the
> self-righteous" (Mark 2:17).

Therefore, both Hosea and Jesus were calling a people back to the happiest moment of their wedding day, long before they had spoiled their happiness by sinful compromises and outright injustices, long before their piety and love had become empty words and routine actions, quickly passing away "like a morning cloud." The people are being reminded by these two extraordinary religious leaders that God can do the impossible in their lives. What is generally impossible from a human side, actually happens with God. They are back again to the first moment of their espousal, to the innocence of their baptismal day, to the pure joy of their wedding day.

When Jesus declares in today's gospel, not to sew a patch of unshrunken cloth on an old cloak, not to pour new wine into old wineskins, Jesus is begging us to forget our sins and mistakes. In renewing the covenant of love with us, God is not patching up what has been torn and rent; neither is God attempting to put the sweetness of new life into a casing of bitter memories.

The freshness of new life, according to the prophet Hosea, extends across the universe for those in love. Such is always the case! In a verse that is omitted in today's reading, we are told:

> I will make a [new] covenant for them on that day,
>   with the beasts of the field,
> With the birds of the air,
>   and with the things that crawl on the ground. . . .
> I will let them take their rest in security.

Again in the verse that follows the end of today's selection, we sense more of the same excitement that reverberates across the universe by those in love:

> On that day I will respond, says the Lord;
>   I will respond to the heavens,
>   and they shall respond to the earth;
> The earth shall respond to the grain, and wine, and
>   oil.

The entire world is made new, and this newness is not a desert sweep of sand but a home fully furnished for the newly espoused couple.

This joy is conditioned upon the right spirit within the heart and upon the willingness to reach outward with love, compassion and fidelity. Hosea's famous statement occurs in today's reading:

I espouse you to me forever:
 I espouse you in right and in justice,
 in love and in mercy;
I will espouse you in fidelity,
 and you shall know the Lord.

All of Hosea's words bring centuries of tradition with them: *right* means that everything harmonizes; *justice* states that it can be proven at court; *love* according to the Hebrew word signifies a bond of blood; *mercy* comes from a Hebrew word that signifies the womb where life is formed; *fidelity* insists upon the integrity and genuineness of the love; finally *to know* expresses a most intimate experience between partners. Such is the ideal which Jesus offers *now* to all followers.

Paul expresses the same idea in a different way. This new covenant of love is "a letter written not with ink but by the Spirit of the living God, not on tablets of stone but on tablets of flesh in the heart." This love does not depend upon the stern, cold demands of "the written law" but upon "the Spirit [that] gives life." There is certainly a place in human society for written law codes. Jesus too repeated the ten commandments to the young man who asked: "Good Teacher, what must I do to share in everlasting life?" (Mark 10:17). Yet, all will agree that no marriage can survive on the stern law that condemns adultery.

Paul is promising the new covenant, written on the heart by the Spirit, and he is promising it for this very moment, now, today. No matter what may have been the failures of the past, we look to God's love:

It is not that we are entitled of ourselves to take credit. . . . Our sole credit is from God.

"The Spirit gives life" at this very moment. Life consists in the new espousals when joy resounds among the wedding guests and across the entire world.

Prayer:

Lord, you do not deal with us according to our sins; you do not requite us according to our crimes. You are kind and merciful, having compassion on us like parents having compassion on their children. You crown our lives with the innocent joy of our happiest moments. You pour the wine of your goodness into the new wineskins of our heart.

Eighth Sunday, "C" Cycle

Sir 27:4–7. The fruit of a tree shows the care it has had; likewise, a person's speech discloses the bent of his mind.

1 Cor 15:54–58. Death is swallowed up in victory. Your toil is not in vain when it is done in the Lord.

Luke 6:39–45. Jesus used images when speaking to the disciples. Among others, he stated that a tree is known by its yield. Each person speaks from his heart's abundance.

The Scriptures remind us of our responsibility as parents and teachers, as persons in various types of leadership; today's readings focus particularly upon our way of speaking and communicating. Although Jesus is addressing his own disciples, he sees them in their future apostolate as teachers and preachers of the word. The Book of Sirach comes from a veteran teacher who formed a "house of instruction" (*beth midrash* or "house of interpretation" in the Hebrew—Sir 51:23) for training future leaders especially in the area of politics.

Parents and teachers normally do not see at once the good (or bad) results of their efforts in rearing and instructing young people. They need the encouragement of Sirach and Luke's gospel: wait and give the tree time to bear fruit which ripens and matures. While writing to the Corinthians, Paul adds that we must wait till eternity for the full manifestation of the good fruit. Perseverance, then, and responsibility are the two main themes in this Sunday's biblical selections.

These two virtues of perseverance and responsibility form the backbone of character, while the other virtues of love and compassion fashion the heart. We meditate on the latter two virtues on another occasion (see the Fourth Sunday, "C" Cycle).

Jesus' examples refer more directly to parents and teachers than to any other group:

> Can a blind person act as a guide to another blind person?
> Why look at the speck in another's eye and miss the plank in your own eye?
> A good tree does not produce decayed fruit any more than a decayed tree produces good fruit.

Before socialized medicine had come to the state of Israel, it was not at all unusual to see the blind leading the blind. These outcasts of society grouped together for protection and assistance. Eye diseases were rampant from infancy on up. Almost everyone suffered from some kind of eye ailment. Fig trees, grape vines and thornbushes are everywhere throughout the land. Jesus drew his examples from everyday life. They reflect his own keen eye and compassionate heart. Jesus saw what was obvious, yet overlooked by many who claimed there was no poverty in the promised land! Jesus was challenging those people whose good eyes were blind to all the blind people in Israel. Jesus' instruction of parents and teachers presumes a heart attentive to the needy and suffering neighbor.

Jesus asks for honesty and authenticity. He despises the hypocrites who correct others for faults which they themselves make no effort to remove from their own lives!

Sirach enables us to perceive more implications in Jesus' instruction for parents and teachers. There is a growing momentum as we move from the gospel to the first reading, that parenting and teaching are serious occupations. People cannot undertake these tasks lightly nor continue in them in a slovenly or frivolous way without suffering the consequences. The results show up most of all in the lives of the young. Sirach refers to the potter and to the farmer; the results of each person's work will show up:

> The test of what the potter molds is in the furnace.
> The fruit of a tree shows the care it has had.

More serious attention is paid to oral communication. Sirach is proposing the example of the potter and the farmer in order to draw conclusions about speaking. The focus is once again, therefore, upon the teacher and parent:

> a person's faults [appear] when they speak.
> Conversation is the test of a person.
> A person's speech discloses the bent of the mind.

As adults we are asked to measure our words, particularly if we are judging, condemning or threatening. We should cross-examine whether our style of wit can be interpreted as sarcastic, cynical or pessimistic. Does it ridicule others in authority? Or maybe we are speaking in an imprudent way that is relaxed banter among older, more experienced people but heard as serious doubt or bitter sarcasm by the young.

At various times the Bible comes down hard upon people in religious leadership. We read in the prophecy of Hosea:

> With you is my grievance, O priest!
> My people perish for want of knowledge!
>   Because you have rejected knowledge,
>   I will reject you from my priesthood. . . .
> It shall be: like priest, like people (Hos 4:4,6,9).

These words were addressed to the priests, but they are applicable to anyone in positions of responsibility, like parents and teachers.

At the same time we cannot judge by what appears immediately on the surface. The potter must leave the fashioned clay in the furnace for the full length of time; a new olive tree does not bear fruit for at least seven years. Sometimes we must wait till death and beyond for the good fruit to appear. Paul writes:

> Be steadfast and persevering, my beloved brothers
> and sisters, fully engaged in the work of the Lord.
> You know that your toil is not in vain when it is
> done in the Lord.

So insistent is Paul upon this fact that he quotes from the earlier, prophetical book of Hosea, but reverses the meaning. The prophet had declared that God's "eyes are closed to compassion'' and therefore the Lord will no longer ''redeem them from death'' (Hos 13:14). Hosea summons death's plagues and sting: ''Where are you?'' Paul declares that the sting of death has been removed and its victory has been relinquished to a new ''victory through our Lord Jesus Christ.''

Prayer:

Lord, it is good to give you thanks. As I persevere in life, I see already the good fruit born with the passage of time. Because of your kindness and fidelity—virtues which I beg of you to grant to me—the just person will flourish like the palm tree.

Ninth Sunday, "A" Cycle

Deut 11:18, 26–28. Bind these words of God at your wrist and on your forehead. There is a blessing for obeying them, a curse for disobeying them.

Rom 3:21–25, 28. The justice of God works through faith in Jesus Christ for all who believe.

Matt 7:21–27. Those who do the will of my Father in heaven enter the Kingdom of God. The one who hears my words and puts them into practice is the wise person who built a house on rock.

We sense at once the tension between faith and good works. Here we are at the eye of the theological hurricane at the time of the Protestant reformation. The format of today's liturgy, however, brings us to the calm spirit, necessary for prayer and godly living. The first and third readings, which form the outer casing, insist upon good works, that which is a visible manifestation of faith; the second reading, at the center of the liturgical texts, emphasizes faith and the mysterious presence of the Spirit, the invisible source of good works.

Neither faith nor good works can survive without the other. In the world of botany, vegetables and trees quickly wither and die if cut off from their roots in mother earth; the roots will also die and disintegrate unless the leaves absorb dew, rain and sunshine from the air.

This blend of faith and good works appears in all three readings, even though each one has its own emphasis. Deuteronomy insists upon the role of the home and family. Many practical aids are provided for instilling a religious spirit in the children and for sustaining a godly attitude in the entire family. This importance of religious instruction in the home becomes all the more apparent if we read the entire section of chapter 11; the liturgy has omitted verses 19–25 for brevity's sake. Not only is the word of God to be taken into your heart and soul, the opening recommendation in today's reading, but it is to be:

> bound at the wrist as a sign,
> hung as a pendant on your forehead,
> taught to your children, at home and abroad,
>   whether you are busy or at rest,
> written on the doorposts of your houses and on your
>   gates.

Every moment of the family's life is to be surrounded by the word of God. This word is not a stern law nor an impersonal statement. It is a generous gift from a loving God. Chapter eleven begins and then follows through with the reminder:

Love the Lord, your God. . . . With your own eyes you have seen all these great deeds that the Lord has done (Deut 11:1,7).

Earlier in chapter six, when the same instructions were given about binding the words of God on wrist and over the forehead, a similar introduction is given:

Hear, O Israel! The Lord is our God, the Lord alone! Therefore, you shall love the Lord, your God, with all your heart, and with all your soul, and with all your strength. Take to heart these words which I enjoin on you today (Deut 6:4–6).

Israel is to receive the law in the same way that discipline and good order are established in the family—in a setting of love and trust, of gratitude and fidelity. Love and faith consequently are at the heart of all good works. Nothing, however, that we do for others in the family can adequately repay for their love which overflows into our heart and spreads throughout our existence. In the family we do not use the language of merit and reward, at least not in our finest moments of marriage and family; we always feel unworthy of our spouse and children, of our parents, brothers and sisters.

St. Paul associates this attitude of undeserved love with our redemption by Jesus Christ. No matter how conscientiously we follow the law and the prophets, what we receive from Jesus far outreaches even our imagination and extends beyond our visible works. As a matter of fact, we can no more produce redemption by our works than we can create our body. Physical life is a pure gift from God through our parents. From this example we can reread today's selection from Paul's letter to the Romans.

Also at stake in Paul's remarks is the biblical concept of justice. The Bible understands justice, not so much as reward and punishment carefully meted out for good or evil actions. Justice, instead, means the harmonious way by which a person lives up to the promises invested in him by God's gift of life, talents and social opportunities. When applied to God it refers to the way that God lives up to the divine promises of compassion and forgiveness. Thus God explained his name (or his very person) in a revelation to Moses on Mount Sinai (Exod 34).

God's justice then reaches with eternal promises into the heart of our lives. With this understanding we admit at once "that each person is justified by faith." Paul adds that justification comes "apart from the observance of the law." Nothing that we do, in obedience to the law, can by itself give us divine promises and achieve our union with Jesus.

With faith such as this, we build the home of our existence upon rock. Despite the violence of the winter rains, our home remains intact. If our faith remains strong and our dependence upon God continuous, then whatever we do will be sustained and spirited by Jesus. The law will then direct us, as we bring the remembrance of God's goodness into every facet of our lives—upon our wrist, over our forehead, at our doorposts.

Prayer:

Lord, be my rock of salvation. By faith I acknowledge that in you I live and move and possess my whole being. Let your face shine upon your servant and save me in your kindness. Then all of my actions will reflect the wisdom and goodness which you bring into my life.

Ninth Sunday, "B" Cycle

Deut 5:12–15. Keep holy the sabbath day. Remember that
    you were once slaves in Egypt, and the Lord, your God,
    brought you from there with his strong hand and out-
    stretched arm.
2 Cor 4:6–11. Continually we carry about in our bodies the
    dying of Jesus so that in our bodies the life of Jesus may
    also be revealed.
Mark 2:23–3:6. Jesus defends the disciples who pulled off
    grain to eat on the sabbath. He also cured a man whose
    hand was seriously impaired.

Today's biblical readings center upon the sabbath and
its implications for the death of Jesus. The controversy in
Mark's gospel over the observance of the sabbath reflects
the two different renditions of the ten commandments in the
Torah. The first, in Exodus, chapter twenty, is generally attributed to the "Priestly Tradition" that was preserved in the
Jerusalem temple. It tends to be more severe and also more
insistent upon the holiness of God. Here Israel was told:

> Remember to keep holy the sabbath day [for the
> reason that] on the seventh day he [the Lord]
> rested [from the work of creation].

Today's reading comes from the Book of Deuteronomy,
generally more compassionate in spirit, more hortatory in
style. The motivation is quite different for the sabbath observance:

> Take care to keep holy the sabbath day. [Even]
> your male and female slaves should rest as you do.
> Remember that you too were once slaves in

Egypt, and the Lord, your God, brought you from there with his strong hand and outstretched arm.

These two renditions of the Ten Commandments raise many critical problems, for God could not have written both simultaneously on stone tablets. Each, therefore, probably represents not only the revelation given to Moses but also a long tradition of preaching and application. Deuteronomy stresses compassion. Israel is not to work, neither should any slaves be required to labor, because you yourselves were once slaves. Your bones, God seems to say, ought still to feel the ache and pain, the tiredness and exhaustion, of those former days. Therefore, be compassionate now.

Jesus, in many ways, shows the influence of Deuteronomy in his preaching. He strenuously defends the spontaneous action of the disciples, pulling some grain off the stalks in the field (an action permitted by Deuteronomy, 23:25, to hungry travelers). When controversy erupts, Jesus does not slip away to allow the whole messy situation to be forgotten. Jesus deliberately pushes the issue before the entire assembly in the synagogue. Again he argues from the viewpoint of Deuteronomy:

Is it permitted to do a good deed on the sabbath—
or an evil one? To preserve life or to destroy it?

In forcing the issue, Jesus was alienating powerful groups within the religious system at Jerusalem. He was making enemies who would seek his death. It can be said that Jesus healed the man with an impaired or disabled arm, at the cost of having his own arm disabled by nails on the cross and rendered powerless in death.

Compassion, somehow or other, has a way of bringing us close to Jesus upon the cross. We cannot help the sick, it seems, without suffering their sickness. Yet, in this way, by taking upon himself the disability of the crippled man, Jesus saved the world's cripples.

Paul meditates upon this mystery of life by which shared suffering and compassion unite us very closely.

- suffering makes us realize that we possess the treasure of our life and faith "in earthen vessels" to make it clear that its surpassing power comes from God and not from us.
- therefore, we are afflicted but not crushed; full of doubts yet never in despair, persecuted but never abandoned, struck down but not destroyed.

As a result "we carry about in our bodies continually the dying of Jesus so that in our bodies the life of Jesus may also be revealed." Compassion that frees us from a rigid interpretation of law makes us submit to the most rigid of all laws, suffering and death. Yet we are thereby freed from selfishness and narrowness and are open to the full life of Jesus among the saints. "The life of Jesus may be revealed in our mortal flesh."

Prayer:
Lord, in every distress you hear my call for help. All you ask of me in return is that I hear the call of distress in my brother and sister. In following the example of your only child Jesus, I share not only in the glory of his resurrection but also in the joy of his world family.

Ninth Sunday, "C" Cycle

1 Kings 8:41–43. Solomon prays that the Lord honor and fulfill the prayers of foreigners offered in the Jerusalem temple.

Gal 1:1–2, 6–10. If anyone preaches a gospel other than the one you received, let a curse be upon that one.

Luke 7:1–10. The Roman centurion requests of Jesus the cure of his servant. He declares that he is not worthy for Jesus to enter his home. "Just give the order and my servant will be cured."

The major problem which faced Paul and the early church has become academic and pointless for us. It can be stated this way: must a gentile first become a Jew and submit to the full Mosaic law before becoming a Christian? Are gentile Christians as well as converts from Judaism required by the Mosaic law? Why should gentiles be exempt from the prescriptions which Jesus accepted and obeyed?

This question is academic, except that we have swung a full 180 degrees; we no longer permit Jews to remain with the Mosaic law and customs if they accept Jesus as Lord and Messiah. The *real* question for us can be stated this way: how tolerant are we towards the outsider, towards the person of another race or nationality? Will we accept them within our family and church? Do we allow them to preserve their customs and culture if they are called like ourselves to be disciples of Jesus?

Solomon welcomes into the Jerusalem temple "the foreigner who is not of your people Israel but comes from a distant land to honor you." This generous prayer enables Israel to make another similar prayer to God, this other time for themselves, exiled in a foreign land:

> When your people sin against you . . . and in your
> anger against them you deliver them to the enemy,
> so that their captors deport them to a hostile land
> . . . may they repent in the land of their captivity
> and be converted. . . . Forgive your people their
> sins and all the offenses they have committed
> against you, and grant them mercy (1 Kings 8:46–
> 50).

All of us at one time or another are foreigners and exiles,
sinners under the anger of God. We dare not exclude any
foreigners, lest we too become outcasts.

The prayer of Solomon flashes that extraordinary, important insight: we are all equal before God. We dare not put
barriers between us.

The gospel takes the lesson one step further. Here the
foreigner seems to have a stronger, more humble faith than
many believers. Jesus had to admit, spontaneously and ever
so honestly:

> I tell you, I have never found so much faith among
> the Israelites.

The foreigner, therefore, can instruct the insider how to
be a true disciple of Jesus. Many beautiful qualities are seen
in the Roman centurion: *generosity* towards the conquered
people, in building a synagogue for them at Capernaum;
compassion in asking a cure for his slave (the morality of
slavery was a moot question) at the risk of a refusal; *humility,* for "I am not worthy to have you enter my house"; *honesty,* for "I too am a man who knows the meaning of an
order, having soldiers under my command."

Even though the centurion had not gone through the ritual of becoming a Jew (circumcision) nor formally accepted

the religion of Moses, still he is seen as a person of faith. With such faith, Jesus seems to say, what keeps such a person from being a disciple?

With such faith, a person is ready for baptism according to Paul. To deny baptism, according to Paul, is to deny the gospel.

Paul's action—like generous, open love in any age or place towards the outsider—led to persecution even within the church. Paul responds with conviction and clarity:

> Whom would you say that I am trying to please at this point—human beings or God? . . . If I were trying to win human approval, I would surely not be serving Christ.

Difficult as it may be, we too may have no other choice when faced with bias and prejudice against our neighbor.

Prayer:

Lord, help us to manifest your kindness to all whom we meet, so that they are drawn to praise you, the Lord of life, who inspires the sharing of life. Remind us over and over again that we cannot maintain a true faith in you if we do not extend your kindness to others.

Trinity Sunday, "A" Cycle

Exod 34:4–6, 8–9. Moses ascends Mount Sinai with the two tablets of the law. There the Lord appears in a cloud and speaks the divine name: "The Lord! The Lord! A merciful and gracious God!" Moses pleads with the Lord to pardon wickedness.

2 Cor 13:11–13. Encourage one another. Greet one another:

the grace of the Lord Jesus Christ, the love of God, and
the fellowship of the Holy Spirit be with you all.
John 3:16–18. God so loved the world as to send his only
son, that whoever believes in him may have eternal life.

The feast of the Holy Trinity was introduced quite late
into the liturgical calendar. The prayers and particularly the
preface to the central eucharistic portion display a serious
concern for correct theology. Many centuries of controversy
led up to this final formulation of Christian belief in three
persons within the single godhead. The biblical readings
represent a much earlier stage when the doctrine of the Holy
Trinity was less explicitly formulated; it was imbedded
within the larger setting of fervent Christian life.

If John's gospel distinguishes Father and Son, the primary concern does not center upon the doctrine of the Trinity but rather upon the generous love of God the Father:
"Yes, God so loved the world that he gave his only Son."
A person, moreover, denies the mystery of the Trinity, not
by any direct confrontation, but rather by doubting God's
compassion and forgiveness towards us:

> God did not send the Son into the world
> to condemn the world,
> but that the world might be saved through him.
> Whoever believes in him avoids condemnation,
> but whoever does not believe is already condemned.

Not to accept God's willingness to forgive us through the
ministry of Jesus leaves us in our sins. We remain condemned. We fail to appreciate the mystery of God's intimate
life as Father, Son and Spirit.

God's love is so generous, that he takes the risk of our
rejecting his love and doubting his willingness to forgive.

Perhaps what a loving and lovable person fears the most is to be doubted and then rejected by another. After several such experiences, sometimes after a single such incident, people refuse to love any more, at least to manifest their love towards others. After repeated rejections, God still loves us. No matter what we have done and how often, God never sends his Son into our lives to judge and condemn us but that we might be saved—yet again.

In the second reading Paul presents the mystery of the Holy Trinity, again in a pastoral context of Christians' loving one another, forgiving one another, and ever ready to greet one another. In fact, the formula of greeting by which Christians reach out with patience and understanding reads like the mission of Jesus, sent by God the Father through the bond of the Spirit, to assure our salvation:

> All the holy ones send greetings to you: the grace
> of the Lord Jesus Christ, and the love of God, and
> the fellowship of the Holy Spirit be with you all!

In this way we comply with Paul's recommendation to the early church:

> mend your ways
> encourage one another
> live in harmony and peace.

By reflecting in our communities this conversion and forgiveness and by living in harmony and peace, we manifest the mystery of the Holy Trinity: the mission of the Son, sent by the Father, through the love of the Spirit.

Even though the mystery of the Holy Trinity had not yet been revealed in Old Testament times, nonetheless there are flashes of insight in this direction, momentary intuitions when the clouds parted. Today's selection from the Book of Exodus provides one such quick glance into the mystery of the godhead.

Moses climbed Mount Sinai where God met him "in a cloud." The mystery remains. As Moses stands majestically on Mount Sinai, holding in his arms the two stone tablets of the law, God passes by and proclaims:

> The Lord, the Lord, a merciful and gracious God,
> slow to anger, and rich in kindness and fidelity,
> continuing kindness for a thousand generations,
> and forgiving wickedness and crime and sin.

The sacred word of the law is to be interpreted with loving kindness and strong fidelity. What will later be seen as separate persons is here present within the cloud of divine mystery: the Word, the Almighty Lawgiver, the Spirit of loving obedience.

God is not giving Moses some theoretical knowledge about divinity. Moses at once begs God "to pardon our wickedness and sins, and receive us as your own." How humbly Moses identifies himself with all Israel: "*our* wickedness and sins." Moses is not seeking any personal preferment; instead, he asks, "receive *us* as your own." In a sense, the authenticity of the doctrine is found in the way that people speak a word of forgiveness to one another and so are united in the bond of love. Faith in the Holy Trinity is shown symbolically by our kindness and compassion.

Prayer:

Lord, you are blessed, Father, Son and Spirit. You manifest the interior mystery of your being by lavishing the *word* of forgiveness in a *spirit* of compassion. Enable me to reveal this mystery to others by my own compassionate love.

Trinity Sunday, "B" Cycle

Deut 4:32–34, 39–40. You must fix in your heart that the Lord is God in the heavens above and on earth below, and there is no other.

Rom 8:14–17. Led by the Spirit of God, we cry out with Christ, "Abba-Father."

Matt 28:16–20. Make disciples of all nations and baptize them in the name of the Father, and of the Son, and of the Holy Spirit.

The Book of Deuteronomy interprets Hebrew law and the Mosaic covenant as expressions of God's intimate and special love for the chosen people Israel. In one key passage we read:

> It was not because you are the largest of all nations that the Lord set his heart on you and chose you, for you are really the smallest of all nations. It was because the Lord loved you and because of his fidelity to the oath he had sworn to your ancestors that he brought you out with his strong hand from the place of slavery, and ransomed you from the hand of Pharaoh, king of Egypt (Deut 7:7–8).

A reading from Deuteronomy, therefore, is very appropriate on this feast of the Holy Trinity, not that the Hebrew Scriptures ever arrived at a clear revelation of three Persons in one God but that this book of the Hebrew Scriptures in particular reached into the depths of God's interior responses of love and compassion. Not only does Deuteronomy lead us profoundly into the mystery of the Godhead, but it also keeps us aware of God's expansive love, as the very late Book of Wisdom expresses it:

> . . . reaches from end to end mightily
> and governs all things well (Wis 8:1).

The old Latin translation still rings in the memory of many of us: God's wisdom, the practical plan of exercising love in our regard, functions *fortiter et suaviter*—"bravely and sweetly."

In today's selection from Deuteronomy, God is willing to take his case publicly to the world. Ask anywhere, God declares, and at any moment of time!

> Was it ever heard of?
> Did any god venture to take a nation as its very own
>   with strong hand and outstretched arm?
> Ask from one end of the sky to the other!

The conclusion is very obvious:

> You must now know, and *fix in your heart,* that the Lord is God in the heavens above and on earth below, and that there is no other. You must keep his statutes . . . that you may have long life on the land which the Lord, your God, is giving you forever.

Adapting this passage to the Christian mystery of the Holy Trinity, we see an image of the three Persons: God the Father's leaving a remembrance of his spirit of love in the word of Scripture, enabling Israel to respond with loving obedience—Father, Spirit and Word.

This passage from Deuteronomy also teaches us to transfer the most exalted and elusive mystery of the Holy Trinity into practical language. We find the traces of God's presence across the cosmos and within the sacred word; we are rightly expected to respond with our own obedience and with the loyalty implanted in the hearts of our children.

The interior mystery of the Trinity becomes the mystery of our own personal life in St. Paul's epistle to the Romans, eighth chapter. This chapter is sometimes called the "Gospel of the Spirit"; it has much in common with the early chapters of the Acts of the Apostles. Led by the Spirit of God, we are truly children of God. Therefore we cry out "Abba—Father!" This bond of adoption does not result from signing a legal document. We truly are God's children: "the Spirit gives witness with our spirit." Compared with Jesus, we are adopted children; compared with adoption in our contemporary law court, we are legitimately begotten children of God. God's life-giving Spirit reaches into the fiber of our existence to form us into the person that we are. This formation is similar to Christ's, and therefore we are called to "suffer with him so as to be glorified with him."

Once again the mystery of the Holy Trinity affects our day-by-day activity; it is not confined to theological manuals. This same outward sweep is present in one of the most explicit statements in the New Testament of three Persons in one God. At the end of Matthew's gospel the disciples are instructed:

> Go, and make disciples of all the nations,
> baptize them in the name of the Father,
> and of the Son, and of the Holy Spirit.

Teach them to carry out everything I have
    commanded you.
I am with you always.

This conclusion and final instruction in Matthew's gospel, despite its surface simplicity, is heavy with theological allusions and literary parallels. It is modeled upon the conclusion of the entire Hebrew Bible, which ends with the Second Book of Chronicles. See 2 Chron 36:23. We are also reminded of the awesome vision of the Son of Man in Dan 7:13–14. Jesus' assurance, ''I am with you always,'' echoes the opening chapter of Matthew's gospel:

They shall call him Immanuel,
a name which means ''God is with us.''

While the gospel is ending, the disciples are only beginning their world mission in the name of the three persons of the Holy Trinity. The world which was created as a reflection of Father, Word and Spirit, is to return to its origins through the preaching of the gospel. As we, individually and as family and community, are drawn into this mysterious and exhilarating homecoming, we are strengthened and consoled by Jesus' words, ''I am with you always.''

Prayer:
    Happy are we, O Lord, whom you have chosen as your own. We are created by the divine word, spoken by God the creator; that word conforms us into the image of God the Word Incarnate, your beloved One, whose Spirit enables us to cry out, ''Abba—Father!''

Trinity, "C" Cycle

Prov 8:22–31. Wisdom was poured forth, begotten by God
at the first before the earth, and as God's co-worker wisdom directed creation and found delight in the human
family.

Rom 5:1–5. We are at peace with God the Father through
the gifts given us by Jesus through the Holy Spirit, so that
we may continue with faith and hope in the midst of affliction.

John 16:12–15. All that the Father has belongs to the Son;
through the Spirit of truth these gifts are poured out on us.

Anyone who is well acquainted with the Book of Proverbs will be surprised that the liturgy chooses a reading from
it for this, the most profoundly theological of all feasts, that
of the Holy Trinity. With few exceptions the Book of Proverbs is the most earth-bound of all parts of the Bible. For instance: "A child who fills the granaries in the summer is a
credit; a child who slumbers during harvest, a disgrace"
(Prov 10:5). This child is not judged by the rightness or
wrongness of the action—whether or not laziness is a sin—
but by the credit or shame which redounds upon the parents.
The same problem of a lazy child is sized up with unforgettable wit: "The door turns on its hinges, the sluggard, on the
bed" (Prov 27:14).

Within this collection of quick, pragmatic sayings—
what someone has described as "the wisdom of many and
the wit of one"—there is a mystical reflection in chapter 8;
a selection from this latter poem is incorporated into today's
eucharistic celebration. Yet even in its reaches of exalted
poetic imagery, many contacts remain with the earthly concerns of the remainder of the book. While wisdom is seen to
emanate from God's mysterious abode, still it is most visible

to us, "established in the sky," across "the sea [and] its
limit," over "the surface of God's earth." This same wisdom which scientists and experienced farmers or gardeners
can determine in individual cases again slips beyond everyone's grasp when *all* of its facets converge like the rays of
the sun in blinding splendor.

Whether we speak of integral wholeness, consistency,
harmony, blending of colors or sound, it is most important
that we can put it all together. A technician who knows each
string of the piano or guitar repairs and tunes these instruments, and yet can remain incapable of putting the sounds
together in the melody of a song. Likewise, it is most important that we know more than individual items of clothing.
Generally we need to have a good sense for color, for the
temperature of home or outside, for the occasion that may be
a funeral or a birthday party, in order to wear clothes properly.

Proverbs insist that the merger of all details of life is
God's secret mystery. It is all around us and yet we cannot
perceive its harmony and strength without faith in God's
goodness, obedience to God's will, watchfulness in prayer.
In fact, the selection for today's Mass concludes with five
verses omitted from the lectionary:

> So, now, children, listen to me;
>   instruction and wisdom do not reject!
> Happy the one who obeys me. . .
> . . .watching daily at my gates. . .
> The one who finds me finds life,
>   and wins favor from the Lord (Prov 8:32–35).

The second reading from Paul's Letter to the Romans
puts it together in a still more compact way, like the links of
a chain:

Affliction makes for endurance, and endurance
for tested virtue, and tested virtue for hope. And
this hope will not leave us disappointed, because
the love of God has been poured out in our hearts
through the Holy Spirit who has been given to us.

Again the mystery of the Holy Trinity slips away from theological formulation and becomes an active ingredient in
daily life. Like Jacob's ladder, heavenly beings move back
and forth between heaven and earth, direct the ways of human life and offer generous blessing (Gen 28:10–15).

As God's Spirit directs our lives, to model them upon
the actions and words of Jesus, we walk upon earth but walk
towards a goal beyond this earth. Always there are hopes
which break the bounds and reach farther than its limits.
How necessary is the attitude of hope and optimism; how
much we prize the happy smile when the day is gloomy. No
matter the sickness or disability, we long to hear the encouraging word that we can do something constructive and
happy.

Jesus speaks in this way about secrets beyond our ability to understand or to put them into action by ourselves
alone. Yet, secrets are wonderful, for they guarantee surprises, joys and fulfillment beyond anyone's expectation.
Jesus said to his disciples:

I have much more to tell you,
but you cannot bear it now.
When that special one comes, however,
being the Spirit of truth,
you will be guided to all truth.
You will hear the announcement of things to come.
In all this glory will be given to me.
All that the Father has belongs to me.

Meditating upon these words, we see how each line reflects a separate facet of God's secret life; through prayer we become ever more at home with this mystery. We are drawn into the wonders of the Word which God speaks and of the bond of Love between Father and Word. Within the details of daily life, we are being guided to the fulness of this mystery of the Holy Trinity.

Prayer:

Lord, how wonderful is your name in all the earth. What I see very clearly draws me beyond the reach of my eyes. I find myself crowned with glory and honor. You introduce me into the secret of your personal life as Father, Son and Spirit.

Corpus Christi, "A" Cycle

Deut 8:2–3, 14–16. The Lord fed you with manna to show you that not by bread alone does anyone live but by every word that comes forth from the mouth of the Lord.

1 Cor 10:16–17. Sharing in the body and blood of Christ, we, many though we are, are one body, for we all partake of the one loaf.

John 6:51–58. The one who feeds on me will have life. This is the bread come down from heaven.

The Eucharist is food for the journey, nourishing us through the wilderness, where no one can survive alone. The Eucharist enables us to move forward as a community who support one another. The journey, according to the gospel reading, leads us to eternal life.

The book of Deuteronomy, from which we read on today's festival honoring the eucharistic body and blood of Jesus, clearly recognizes the difficulties of life's journey. After leaving a place of slavery, we are told that:

> The Lord, your God, . . . guided you through the vast and terrible desert with its saraph serpents and scorpions, its parched and waterless ground.

Yet, even these difficulties serve a good purpose in God's plans. We also read from today's selection in Deuteronomy:

> The Lord, your God, has directed all your journeying in the desert, so as to test you by affliction and find out whether or not it was your intention to keep his commandments.

Life's difficulties cannot be easily explained. God is not a sadist but a realist. Neither is God taken by surprise by life's events; they are deliberately within his plans. We are not able to harmonize them, a task which the long Book of Job found impossible. Human experience provides some hints. For instance, we value least what we obtain most easily and we prize, protect and tenderly love that for which—and often enough, we should add, for *whom*—we suffer the most. Yet, the most convincing reason for what breaks the harmony with our lives comes from the fact that Jesus was afflicted in every way as ourselves, even to be tempted. The Epistle to the Hebrews expressed it this way:

> We do not have a high priest who is unable to sympathize with our weakness, but one who was tempted in every way that we are, yet never sinned (Heb 4:15).

Scripture, moreover, links the Eucharist explicitly with our sins and the Lord's suffering:

> This is my body to be given for you. . . . This cup is the new covenant in my blood, which will be shed for you (Luke 22:19–20).

Matthew adds that "the blood [will] be poured out in behalf of many for the forgiveness of sins" (Matt 26:28). Paul states:

> Every time, then, you eat this bread and drink this cup, you proclaim the death of the Lord until he comes (1 Cor 11:26).

When Jesus, therefore, provides us with bread in the wilderness, he is truly present, sharing our sorrows and difficulties, even our temptations and death. Yet, even death becomes a way leading to an ever more intimate union with Jesus in life eternal.

The Eucharist is not any ordinary bread and wine. Deuteronomy refers to "manna, a food unknown to you and your ancestors." It must be received with faith, acknowledging it to be "living bread, come down from heaven," according to Jesus' words in today's gospel.

According to Paul's reasoning in the Epistle to the Corinthians, we must look with faith not only upon the living and life-giving bread but also with faith upon our brothers and sisters as forming "one body" with us. Unless we recognize Christ in our neighbor, we are not able to know accurately whom we are receiving in the Eucharist. Paul's words are very explicit:

Because the loaf of bread is one, we, many though we are, are one body for we all partake of the one loaf.

In First Corinthians Paul returns repeatedly to the doctrine of the one body of Christ, consisting of many members. Because there is only *one* Lord, Jesus Christ, therefore our one act of faith reaches to the members of Christ who form the church and to "the bread we break, a sharing in the body of Christ." Charity towards our neighbor, therefore, is the most essential way to prepare for worthy communion with Jesus in the Eucharist.

As mentioned already, if Christ shares our suffering as we trek through the wilderness, "the vast and terrible desert," then it also follows that we are to participate in the difficulties and trials of one another. In the Eucharist the suffering church proclaims the death of the Lord until he comes in glory.

Prayer:

Lord, we praise you for the living and life-giving bread, your gift of yourself to us in the Holy Eucharist. May we receive you worthily by the love which we manifest towards our neighbors and church.

Corpus Christi, "B" Cycle

Exod 24:3–8. At Mount Sinai Moses offered blood, symbolizing the covenant which the Lord made with Israel.

Heb 9:11–15. How much more will the blood of Christ, who through the eternal spirit offered himself up unblemished to God, cleanse our conscience from dead works to wor-

ship the living God. Jesus is the mediator of a new covenant.

Mark 14:12–16, 22–26. During the last supper Jesus took
    bread . . . and said, ''This is my body,'' and the cup,
    saying, ''This is my blood of the covenant, to be poured
    out on behalf of many.''

Today's readings on this feast of Corpus Christi, the
Body of Christ, direct our attention to the symbolism of
blood. Primarily it signifies life and the way that it unites the
various members of the body in one life. Only secondarily
does it take on the added symbolism of suffering and death.

The key text, explaining the import and purpose of
blood, occurs in the most important document dedicated to
Israel's liturgy:

> Since the life of a living body is in its blood, I
> have made you put it on the altar, so that at-one-
> ment may thereby be made for your own lives, be-
> cause it is blood, *as the seat of life,* that makes at-
> one-ment (Lev 17:11).

Because nothing sickly or dead was ever permitted within
the sanctuary and certainly not upon the temple altar, blood
and animals offered in sacrifice were not looked upon as
''dead'' but as symbols of the people of Israel who are offering themselves *completely* in all of their activity to the
God of life.

Blood unites and makes at-one-ment. Moses, according to the first reading, ''took half of the blood and splashed
it on the altar; the other half he took and sprinkled on the
people.'' This rite was accompanied with the formula:
''This is the blood of the covenant which the Lord has made
with you.'' In this ritual action of sprinkling blood on the al-

tar and on the people, all people could see the invisible reality of their union with God. They shared the same life.
Israel, therefore, was to be called:

> my special possession, dearer to me than all other
> people . . . a kingdom of priests, a holy nation
> (Exod 19:5–6).

The prophet Hosea carries the idea still further. "Israel
[is] a child I love . . . my son and daughter." God then
speaks with tender pathos and feminine imagery:

> I drew them with human cords,
>   with bands of love;
> I fostered them like one
>   who raises an infant to the cheeks;
> Yet though I stopped to feed my child,
>   they did not know that I was their healer
>   (Hos 11:3b–4).

Israel's ritual of the covenant, like the Eucharist for
Christians, expresses liturgically and symbolically what was
the inner reality of their community life. They lived from the
life of God, one God so that they formed one body, one people. In the ancient church, as a matter of fact, church was
called in the language of St. Paul, "the body of the Lord,"
while the Eucharist was considered the mystical body, that
is, a symbolical expression of the church.

If Jesus really dwelt within the church, then Jesus is
just as truly present in the Eucharist. The Eucharist becomes
a unique and special presence of Jesus, because it concentrates upon this aspect of the church as the body of the Lord.

Blood unites in a single life the various members of the
one body. It also purifies the body as it courses through the

arteries and veins. At the same moment, it is nourishing the members of the body. The reading from Hebrews for to-day's mass draws upon this new symbolism of blood as it directs our attention to the Jewish ceremony of Yom Kippur, the Day of at-one-ment. Serious, wilful sins have already been forgiven but there needs to be a public manifestation of this reunion of a once sinful people with the all-holy God. Blood in this case is sprinkled within the Holy of Holies—somewhat the way that Moses splashed blood upon the altar at Mount Sinai—to show that Israel is once again united with God with the full vigor of life.

Jesus is our new and everlasting high priest who is said to bring his own precious blood into the heavenly sanctuary. Again, we repeat that sins have already been forgiven; Jesus did not cleanse heaven of our sins! The blood ritual again symbolizes full reunion of life; it brings out the healthy expression of life:

> The blood of Christ, who through the eternal spirit offered himself up unblemished to God, [will] cleanse our consciences of dead works to worship the living God.

Yet, as mentioned already in this meditation, blood can also include a sense of suffering and death. More and more the Eucharist began to include the sign of Jesus' death and resurrection. It is implicitly present in today's gospel:

> This is my blood, the blood of the covenant, to be poured out on behalf of man.

In First Corinthians, Paul makes the contact of blood with the death of Jesus still more explicit:

> Every time you eat this bread and drink this cup,
> you proclaim the death of the Lord until he comes
> (1 Cor 11:26).

Again, however, it is death that leads to eternal life with Jesus in heaven. This is the idea behind the otherwise enigmatic statement of Jesus at the conclusion of today's gospel:

> I will never again drink of the fruit of the vine until the day when I drink it new in the reign of God.

We are told that after singing a hymn Jesus and the disciples "walked out to the Mount of Olives" where his "sweat became like drops of blood" (Luke 22:44).

Prayer:

Lord, we take up the cup of our salvation and call upon your holy name. In the holy eucharist we offer a sacrifice of thanksgiving and realize how precious in your eyes is the death of your faithful ones, first of Jesus and then of ourselves in union with Jesus.

Corpus Christi, "C" Cycle

Gen 14:18–20. Melchizedek brought out bread and wine, and being a priest of God Most High, he blessed Abram.

1 Cor 11:23–26. Paul hands down a tradition in which Jesus says over the bread, "This is my body" and over the cup, "the new covenant in my blood." In this way the community proclaims the death of the Lord.

Luke 9:11–17. Taking the five loaves and the two fishes, Jesus raised his eyes to heaven, pronounced a blessing over them, broke them, and gave them to his disciples for distribution to the crowd.

Today's readings for the feast of Corpus Christi or of the Body of Christ begin with one of the rare biblical allusions to Melchizedek. In the Hebrew Scriptures this mysterious person enters the text only here in Genesis, chapter 14, and in an equally difficult text, Psalm 110. In the New Testament Melchizedek is mentioned ten times, but the references are entirely within chapters 5 to 6 of the Epistle to the Hebrews, nowhere else! Melchizedek, moreover, is mentioned in the Dead Sea Scrolls found at Qumran. Here he ushers in the final age of the world, the fulfillment of all promises, the victory of God's people.

On this feast of Corpus Christi, we find that Melchizedek signals something extraordinary and unique, the victory of God's people, the beginning of the kingdom of God. The rabbis even discuss the unknown parentage of Melchizedek; the names of his father and mother are not given. According to a rabbinical maxim, whatever cannot be found in the Torah (the first five books of Moses) cannot be said to exist. They, therefore, conclude to Melchizedek's mysterious, even heavenly origin. The Epistle to the Hebrews will apply this idea to Jesus our High Priest:

> Without father, mother or ancestry, without beginning of days or end of life, like the Son of God he remains a priest forever (Heb 7:3).

The first reading compounds the problem still more! Melchizedek, though not a Hebrew nor a member of the Levitical tribe, much less of the high priestly family of Aaron and Zadok, nonetheless offers sacrifice to God Most High and blesses Abram. (The name has not yet been changed to Abraham—chap. 17.) A pagan priest blesses Abram and recognizes God's redemptive action in Abram's favor.

This long, somewhat difficult background to the Eucharist shows us a priesthood, different from Israel's and reaching out to the world. Abram worshipped "the creator of heaven and earth." The Hebrew Scripture was leading the people Israel to a moment when Melchizedek would reappear and reunite Israel with the world, as happened momentarily with Abram. The Eucharist too should provide the nourishment and strength for ourselves to reach outward to every brother and sister and still further to strangers. The charity of the Eucharist should have no limits in what it inspires within us.

The Eucharist, moreover, will prepare us for surprising turns in our life. Suddenly we will be expected to receive outsiders into our family, people who bring a new sense of "the heaven and the earth," their beauty and their challenge.

While the first reading from Genesis urges us to reach outward and to face up to differences, the second reading from Paul's First Letter to the Corinthians reminds us of the cost in suffering:

> Every time, then, you eat this bread and drink this cup, you proclaim the death of the Lord until he comes.

Just as Jesus' attempt to unite the poor and the outcasts with the secure and well established led to friction, opposition and finally his death, our own endeavors to reach outward and to recognize goodness in strangers will not be easy at all. The Eucharist provides the nourishment for this heroic outreach of charity; the Eucharist also symbolizes the unity and its cost in suffering. The Body and Blood of Jesus in the Eucharist is the Body broken on the cross and the Blood shed from the wounds of the crucified Jesus.

We have a long journey to go before we reach the ideal of unity in the Eucharist—before Melchizedek appears again to usher us into the messianic kingdom. We understandably become tired, even in danger of collapsing along the way. Here we find ourselves among the crowd which followed Jesus into an out-of-the-way place. Even though we, like the crowd, have already been healed of ailments, according to the opening words of today's gospel, still we find it very difficult to continue.

When Mark records Jesus' action of multiplying the five loaves and the two fishes, the evangelist uses the language of the Eucharist, repeated today in each celebration of mass. Jesus, we are told:

took the bread	broke the loaves
raised his eyes to heaven	gave them to his disciples
pronounced a blessing	for distribution

We can raise the question: does the statement that the leftover fragments filled twelve baskets in some way allude to the presence of Jesus within the church, the new twelve tribes of the people of God, or even to the preservation of the Eucharist in our tabernacles for the sick and for those unable to attend the regular eucharistic ceremony?

The principal symbolism, however, is that of a journey. The Eucharist is intended to nourish and strengthen us for continuing faithfully in our way of life. It provides charity and renewed faith to move onward as a single community; individuals cannot survive in the wilderness. It enables us to be ready when Melchizedek ushers us into the messianic kingdom.

Prayer:

Lord Jesus, you are a priest forever in the line of Melchizedek. As you come mysteriously into our lives, give us the faith to recognize you, the strength to suffer with you, the perseverance to continue faithfully by your side.

PART THREE

Feasts and Solemnities
of Ordinary Time

February 2, Feast of the Presentation of the Lord

Mal 3:1–4. My messenger prepares the way. Suddenly the Lord whom you seek comes to the temple, to refine and purify so that a pleasing sacrifice may be offered.

Heb 2:14–18. Jesus had to become like his brothers and sisters in every way, tested through suffering, to help those who are tempted.

Luke 2:22–40. In obedience to the law of Moses, Jesus was presented in the temple. He is greeted prophetically by Simeon and Anna. Afterwards, at Nazareth Jesus grew in size and strength, in wisdom and grace.

Today's feast is typified by light, at once a delicate, mysterious element as well as an overpowering and blinding force. Candles are blessed today. When lighted, their wick can be easily snuffed out. Yet these candles symbolize Jesus, our eternal light, our sun that illumines the path of our existence, the inspiration that the gospel is to be a light to the nations. The flickering flame of a candle can touch off a forest fire—fire that destroys, purifies and prepares for rebirth.

The biblical readings not only develop this double symbolism of the fragile and the mighty presence of God in light, but they also act as a "presentation of the Lord" in our own hearts and lives. Malachi, the last book of all the Old Testament prophets, leaves us uncertain whether the messenger, sent "to prepare the way before me," is to be understood as an awesome manifestation *of* God or as a messenger or instrument *from* God. If the light is God, it can seem overwhelming; if it is a messenger, the light can be humanly bearable. The Epistle to the Hebrews clearly identifies the manifestation of God in the "Son, the reflection of the Father's glory, the exact representation of the Father's being,

. . . superior to the angels" (Heb 1:3–4), yet like ourselves with "a full share" "of blood and flesh . . . like his brothers and sisters in every way [even to the point of being] tested." Finally in the gospel Jesus as an infant so corresponds to our human frailty, that Jesus must be carried to the temple and consecrated to the Lord, yet at that very moment Jesus is proclaimed:

a revealing light to the Gentiles,
the glory of your people Israel . . .
a sign . . . [so] that the thoughts of many hearts may
be laid bare.

Today's feast, consequently, offers that most special grace: to expend ourselves heroically for God (the symbolism of overpowering might in the light of the sun and in the light of purifying fire), and all the while to do this with delicate charity and the hidden light of persevering faith (the symbolism of the candle, easily snuffed out and bending to the least breeze around about it).

Malachi advises us clearly about "the refiner's fire" and "the fuller's lye." Each of these two substances possesses a fierce might, "fire" to refine and purify gold and silver, or "lye" to bleach cloth or fiber and produce an immaculately white piece. God is seeking to transform us into our very best self, so that our entire life "will please the Lord" in imitation of the great saints "in the days of old." God is paying us the highest compliment. God is saying to us: you can be as much a person of faith as Abraham and Sarah, as loving a wife as Rebekah, as loyal and wholesome as Joseph, as pleasing to God as this magnificent "cloud of witnesses" (Heb 12:1). As we read further in Malachi, this moment of purification and presentation to the Lord is called "the great and terrible Day" (Mal 3:23–24). As Malachi himself inquired, "Who will endure the day of his coming?"

The Epistle to the Hebrews makes the day endurable! The opening statement could not be more accurately on target. To appreciate its full force, we attend to the lovely nuancing of words. In reference to ourselves as God's children, we are told that Jesus "is not ashamed to call them brothers and sisters." The reading for today opens on a note still more encouraging and unifying:

> Since the children are people of blood and flesh,
> Jesus likewise had a full share in these. . . .
> Surely he did not come to help angels, but rather
> the children of Abraham and Sarah.

We remind ourselves that according to Paul's Letter to the Galatians, "if you belong to Christ, you are the descendants of Abraham and Sarah" (Gal 3:29).

Christ is "my messenger [sent] to prepare the way before me," according to God's word in Malachi. This messenger appears as fragile as an infant, and the light of this candle bears all the tenderness, the fear and the possibility of our "blood and flesh."

The fulfillment of Malachi's words comes, as already noted, when Jesus was presented in the temple. Mary and Joseph acted "in accord with the dictate in the law of the Lord," as given to Moses. According to Lev 12:8 their gift for the altar is even called a "sin offering." It is not that Mary or Jesus sinned, but rather that even good acts like begetting and giving birth to a child are intimately part of a human situation marred by selfishness and lack of responsibility. Jesus allows himself at the tenderest age to be integrally absorbed into our human scene.

We begin to see, moreover, how the infant Jesus is not only a tiny, flickering flame of a candle. Jesus also shows up at this moment as,

> A revealing light to the Gentiles,
> the glory of your people Israel.

Simeon is here quoting from the dramatic Songs of the Suffering Servant in the prophecy of Isaiah. This servant first speaks in this way about himself:

> I thought I had toiled in vain,
> and for nothing, uselessly, spent my strength (Isa 49:4).

God then speaks these consoling and strengthening words:

> It is too little for you to be my servant,
> [simply] to raise up the tribes of Jacob, . . .
> I will make you a light to the nations,
> that my salvation may reach to the ends
> of the earth (Isa 49:6).

The flame of this candle will spread over the earth, purifying, refining, transforming, yet in secret, very personal ways. Simeon, in blessing Joseph and Mary, said to the mother:

> This child is destined to be the downfall and the rise of many in Israel, a sign that will be opposed—and you yourself shall be pierced with a sword—so that thoughts of many hearts may be laid bare.

The prophetess Anna, an aged woman of eighty-four years with abundant wisdom and insight, also appeared on the scene "and talked about the child to all who looked forward to the deliverance of Jerusalem."

This sign of our deliverance, this candle which is the Lord, is taken today into our homes and communities. These places are the new Nazareth where the child, our flame of faith, will grow "in size and strength," be "filled with wisdom and the grace of God." This feast at one and the same time is consoling for us, strengthening, hopeful, fearful, demanding, like the flame of a candle.

Prayer:

Lord, we lift up the lintels and throw open the door of our heart that you may enter and be our light. You are our king of glory in the fragile wrappings of an infant as well as in the armor of a warrior, mighty in battle. Come, Lord, and be our consolation, our strength and our victory.

March 19, Solemnity of St. Joseph, Husband of Mary

2 Sam 7:4–5, 12–14, 16. The prophet Nathan promises an eternal dynasty to David.

Rom 4:13, 16–18, 22. Abraham and Sarah become the parents of many nations because of their faith. They hoped against hope.

Matt 1:16, 18–21, 24. Joseph, an upright man, accepts Mary as his wife, and her child, miraculously conceived, as heir to his own birthright within the royal family of David.

Today's feast, honoring St. Joseph as the husband of Mary, reaches into the most intimate fiber of our human existence and simultaneously leaves us awestruck with superhuman mystery. Joseph and Mary, even if they accepted God's unique call for virginity within their marriage, loved one another as husband and wife and showed by their eyes and bodily response that special kind of love observable only among married couples. They were not single people, even within the extraordinary circumstances of their marriage, and so in some genuine but mysterious way they are a model for every married couple.

The same is true about Jesus. As savior, Jesus is a model for everyone. He will declare himself to be "the way, the truth and the life." Jesus, nonetheless, is completely different from us in his divine life as second person of the Holy Trinity, preexisting from all eternity. It will never be said of us, as of Jesus, "In the beginning was the Word; the Word was in God's presence, and the Word was God" (John 1:1).

Today's feast combines normal, earthly existence with exceptional supernatural expectations. This combination is to be found in every human life. It will come differently for us than it did for the holy family of Joseph, Mary and Jesus. In fact, the blend of natural and supernatural shows up with special variations in the life of each individual as well as in each marriage or religious community. At that point where each of us is distinctly and uniquely different, our own very selves and no one else, God touches us with divine life. As our personality reaches outward into every segment of our human existence, into every relationship as husband or wife, as parent or child, as priest, religious or layperson, as married or as called to a single vocation in the world, at the heart of these all-important and basic points of our interaction with others, really at the deepest point of who we are as individual persons, here God touches us and shares with us the divine life of Jesus, the eternal Word and the only-begotten, fully divine Son of God.

Where we are *most human,* there we are expected to act *divinely* at key moments of our existence. Where we mysteriously locate our personality, God unites us with the second person of the Holy Trinity so that we form one body with Christ (1 Cor 12:27).

The biblical readings for this solemnity honoring St. Joseph, Husband of Mary (we should note that this feast has the highest liturgical ranking as a solemnity), show how God cuts across our human existence at key moments. Miracles of a spiritual and a physical nature happen. Even the interpretation or fulfillment of prophecy takes us by surprise. With all respect to the original, inspired authors of the Bible, they too are stunned by what God later makes of their words!

As an example of this "plus" factor in the New Testament fulfillment of Old Testament prophecy we site the first reading for today. The prophet Nathan announces to David an everlasting dynasty:

> Your house and your kingdom shall endure for ever before me; your throne shall stand firm for ever.

Both Nathan and David understood this prophecy to mean that an offspring of the Davidic family, expressed very graphically in the Hebrew text, "your seed sprung from your loins," will always rule the Israelite people from the capital city of Jerusalem.

Joseph, of the family of David, inherits this promise. Already for well over five hundred years, no Davidic king ruled from Jerusalem; this failure provoked serious problems of faith for the author of Ps 89:

> How long, O Lord? Will you hide yourself for
> ever? . . .
> Where are your ancient favors, O Lord,
>   which you pledged to David by your faithfulness?
>   (Ps 89:47, 50).

Joseph is now being asked to accept the fulfillment of the prophecy in a child, conceived by Mary without his intervention as the father. "He decided to divorce her quietly," we are told in today's gospel from Matthew. God intervenes again, informing Joseph of the miraculous conception of the child within Mary, advising him to "have no fear about taking Mary as your wife." The adoptive child of Joseph will inherit the promises and be "king" of Israel in a way that no king has ever functioned.

The same crisscrossing of the human and the divine shows up in the second reading. When Abraham and Sarah, now very aged, considered their bodies "as good as dead" for begetting children, they continue "hoping against hope," "believed, and so became the parents of many nations."

The alternate gospel for today's feast from Luke 2:41–51 has other surprises. "The parents [finding their boy in the temple] were astonished." And even upon hearing Jesus' reply, they did not grasp what he said to them about having "to be in my Father's house."

Each one of us, in our particular circumstances of daily lives, is going to experience the thrust of divine expectations. This divine presence will take us by surprise. Although it happens to everyone, none of us can fully prepare ourselves for it. It happens where each of us is uniquely different from every other person. Not even Mary could explain it to Joseph, only the angel from heaven. Each of us will have to respond: like Abraham and Sarah with faith and hope that is hoping against all hope, like Joseph with tender concern, responsibility and ultimate obedience, like Mary with loving surrender, and like all these saints with profound and continued prayer.

Prayer:

Lord, we draw upon Psalm 89, to sing your everlasting favors and your absolute faithfulness. With the psalmist we cry out, "How long?" when the best of our hopes seem frustrated. With Joseph, the husband of Mary, we will be obedient to your holy will.

March 25, The Solemnity of Mary's Annunciation

Isa 7:10–14. The Lord gives a sign to Ahaz that the king should have trusted in the Lord: life will come in the most unexpected way.

Heb 10:4–10. On coming into the world, Jesus said, "As written of me in the book, 'I come to do your will.' " By this will we have been sanctified.

Luke 1:26–38. The angel Gabriel announces to Mary that "you shall conceive and bear a son and give him the name Jesus." Mary replies, "I am the maidservant of the Lord. Let it be done to me as you say."

This solemnity honoring the miraculous, virginal conception of Jesus within the body of Mary as well as her free acceptance of this role as mother of God, is a marvelous tribute to the one person, chosen from millions of human beings to be the mother of God's only begotten Son. Alone of all men and women, Mary was to parent a child who was eternal and divine. During this solemnity in honor of Mary we marvel in such a wonder at the heart of our faith. We rejoice with Mary and we congratulate her. When the feast is over, however, we begin to ask what it means for ourselves. Mary is absolutely unique. This same feeling came to us on the feast several days ago in honor of St. Joseph, the husband of Mary. His role as husband turned out entirely different from that of every other husband (see March 19).

The biblical readings show how this feast of Mary's Annunciation to become the virginal mother of God reaches into our lives with a practical lesson, no matter who we are, "Jew or Greek, slave or free, male or female," and we may add, "married or single" (Gal 3:28).

The setting for the famous "Immanuel prophecy" of Isa 7:14 is not only political but is also caught up in an immoral compromise of political integrity. King Ahaz panicked over a threat to the throne. We are told:

> The heart of the king and the heart of the people
> trembled, as the trees of the forest tremble in the
> wind (Isa 7:2)

In the midst of feverish activity to defend the city, Isaiah says to the king:

> You did not look to the city's Maker,
> nor did you consider him who built it long ago (Isa
> 22:11).

Instead, the king declares himself and the kingdom of Judah a vassal of Assyria. Ahaz was willing to sell the independ-

ence of the people and reduce them to the demoralizing situation of subservience, the first time in over seven hundred
years, to save his own skin and to protect the throne.

Faced with such an immoral compromise, Isaiah's constant preaching was "faith." There are limits to politics;
there are responsibilities of every office beyond personal
ambition. These restrictions come from the common good
of the larger family or nation as well as from the promises
and expectations of God. Isaiah expressed it in a crisp saying, especially unforgettable in the Hebrew:

> Unless your faith is firm, you shall not be firm.
> *'im lo' ta'aminu, ki lo' te'amenu*

Not often, thanks be to God, but yet in key moments of life,
each of us will be in the position of King Ahaz. Every human solution in sight will be immoral. To act in any way
may involve us at once in serious, immoral compromise. As
Isaiah advises us on another occasion:

> By waiting and by calm you shall be saved,
> in quiet and in trust your strength lies (Isa 30:15).

God will be true to his word. The dynasty of David will
continue, in spite of the disastrous actions of Ahaz. Ahaz'
new wife will conceive, bear a son and shall call this child
symbolically "Immanuel." Truly we will know that "God-
is-with-us," the literal translation of the Hebrew word. This
statement becomes a prophecy to be fulfilled in a still more
marvelous way, when Mary, the virgin, conceives miraculously the son of God, all the more truly "God-with-us."
While the son of Ahaz was begotten in a normally human
way, still, the fact that this child succeeds to the throne of
David will be due to none of the political compromises of

Ahaz, his father, but rather to God's extraordinary intervention in favor of Jerusalem, as announced in still another text of the prophet (Isa 17:12–14).

The Epistle to the Hebrews, from which the second reading comes, summarizes Isaiah's obedient and confident faith by means of another Old Testament text:

As written of me in the [inspired] book,
I have come to do your will, O God.

This passage comes from earlier Old Testament places like Ps 40:7–8 and 1 Sam 15:22. Deeply entrenched in the Hebrew Bible is the strong realization that nothing can take the place of our own clear, decisive moral judgment. Not even sacrifices and offerings are desirable if they are being used to cover over our cowardice or infidelity. Yet, our decision-making at times reaches beyond our unaided intelligence and moral strength.

Like Mary in today's gospel, we may have many difficulties. So did King Ahaz in the time of Isaiah. In each case these were genuine problems. Both the prophet Isaiah and the archangel Gabriel were willing to deal with the questions. Yet the bottom line eventually is faith and obedience; here we must land if we are to be on steady ground:

If your faith is not firm, you shall not be firm.

We too should seek advice in our difficulties. It is wise to look for various alternate solutions. It is also expected that we think and act unselfishly for the good of our family and community; Ahaz was not to compromise the independence of the nation for the sake of his throne. There is also a closure on options, if these do not lead to any moral solution. With Ahaz we may be expected to find strength ''in quiet and in trust," or with Mary we may be strengthened by God to speak our *fiat*, "Let it be done to me as you say."

Prayer:

Lord, enable me to say, especially at crucial and difficult moments: "Here I am; I come to do your will." Let this statement of faith be inscribed within my heart and over the story of my life. Then your faithfulness and kindness will shine forth in my life.

Biblical Index

(Asterisk indicates a more extended reference)

Topical Index

ALSO BY CARROLL STUHLMUELLER:

Biblical Meditations for Lent
Biblical Meditations for the Easter Season
Biblical Meditations for
    Advent and the Christmas Season
Biblical Meditations for Ordinary Time
    (Weeks 10-22)
Biblical Meditations for Ordinary Time
    (Weeks 23-34)